Introduction to Agile Methods

Introduction to Agile Methods

Sondra Ashmore, Ph.D.
Kristin Runyan

Addison-Wesley

Upper Saddle River, NJ • Boston • Indianapolis • San Francisco
New York • Toronto • Montreal • London • Munich • Paris • Madrid
Capetown • Sydney • Tokyo • Singapore • Mexico City

For information about buying this title in bulk quantities, or for special sales opportunities (which may include electronic versions; custom cover designs; and content particular to your business, training goals, marketing focus, or branding interests), please contact our corporate sales department at corpsales@pearsoned.com or (800) 382-3419.

For government sales inquiries, please contact governmentsales@pearsoned.com.

For questions about sales outside the United States, please contact international@pearsoned.com.

Visit us on the Web: informit.com/aw

Library of Congress Cataloging-in-Publication Data
Ashmore, Sondra.
Introduction to agile methods / Sondra Ashmore, Ph.D., Kristin Runyan.
pages cm
Includes index.
ISBN 978-0-321-92956-3 (pbk. : alk. paper)
1. Agile software development. 2. Open source software. I. Runyan, Kristin. II. Title.
QA76.76.D47A83 2014
005.3—dc23

2014014568

ISBN-13: 978-0-321-92956-3
ISBN-10: 0-321-92956-X

Text printed in the United States on recycled paper at RR Donnelley in Crawfordsville, Indiana.
First printing, July 2014

For my sons, Drake and Dane, who encourage me to follow my dreams, and for my husband, Brian, who helps make them all possible.

—Sondra Ashmore

For my family and friends, from whom I am continuously learning.

—Kristin Runyan

Contents

Preface

What is Agile software development, and what does it mean when someone says, "Our team used Agile to develop to software"? In our experiences, we have encountered many people who can tell you about some of the Agile tools they have heard about or experienced, such as Scrum meetings or paired programming, but few touch on the fact that it is a fundamentally different approach to creating software.

Over the last several years, we were both teaching entry-level Agile software development courses—Sondra was teaching graduate students at Iowa State University, and Kristin was training her staff at her company—and we struggled to find a basic book on Agile software development that we could use in a classroom setting. When we met while doing volunteer work for a local technology nonprofit organization, we discovered that we were facing very similar challenges in finding the right book. It was that conversation that sparked the idea of writing our own book on Agile methods.

Our introductions to Agile were similar: We both were managing software development teams that were accustomed to using the more traditional method of software development called "Waterfall," and we took on the challenge of implementing some of the Agile software development tools into our projects, with the ultimate goal of becoming Agile software development organizations. Although we both jumped in and learned all we could about Agile software development, we quickly realized that Agile is a lot more than training people on new tools and methodologies. It did not take long to understand that our organizations had to make a cultural shift to become Agile, which introduced many more challenges than we had anticipated. The transition to Agile was not a destination, as our executive teams had predicted, but rather a journey that is constantly evolving based on the lessons we have learned, or *retrospectives* in Agile terminology.

We firmly believe that Agile methods offer very real benefits for the world of software engineering. Our goal is not to provide you with a comprehensive collection of everything there is to know about Agile software development, but rather to provide you with the basics you need to know to get started. Alistair Cockburn, who is featured in Chapter 3, applies the Aikido term "Shu-HaRi," meaning "to learn a skill or technique," to the process of learning Agile methods. First you are in the "Shu" phase, when you must mimic your teacher precisely to master the basics. Next is "Ha," where you start to learn from other teachers that help you build on your skills, and you begin to gain knowledge about the history and theoretical basis for the technique. Finally, you reach the "Ri" phase, where you become the teacher and make new contributions to the technique. It is our hope that after reading this book, you are well on your way to the "Ha" stage.

We start by introducing you to the history of Agile software development, then build on the tools and techniques that are common in most Agile organizations. We end by discussing how the process comes together to launch new and exciting products to the marketplace. We have included interviews with practitioners to give you a sense of what happens in organizations that have adopted Agile methods. Each chapter concludes with a summary, suggestions for additional reading, and review questions.

The following is a brief introduction to the information you will find in each chapter:

- **Chapter 1—The History and Value of Agile Software Development**
  This chapter provides the background of the Agile movement and compares Agile to the more traditional Waterfall methodology. We explore the use cases for both Waterfall and Agile and explain the pros and cons of each. The chapter introduces the Agile Manifesto, its values, and its authors. We review the 12 key principles of Agile and introduce a fictitious company, Cayman Design, that is used for example purposes throughout the book. We include an interview with Robert (Uncle Bob) Martin.
- **Chapter 2—Organizational Culture Considerations with Agile**
  Moving from Waterfall to Agile requires a cultural transformation, and this chapter delves into the impacts, benefits, and pitfalls. We explore the Agile transformation from the viewpoint of a team member, manager, and executive to help readers understand how roles and decision-making processes will change. Our interview with Scott Ambler brings the concepts together.
- **Chapter 3—Understanding the Different Types of Agile**
  This chapter describes the different Agile methodologies: Scrum, Kanban, Extreme Programming (XP), Crystal, feature-driven development (FDD), Lean software development, and the Dynamic Systems Development Method (DSDM). We provide descriptions and examples of when each methodology will work best. We outline the available certifications for

each methodology. An insightful interview with Alistair Cockburn is also included.

- **Chapter 4—Describing the Different Roles**
  This chapter provides roles and responsibilities for the various titles prominent in the different Agile methodologies. We start with a deep dive into Scrum and explore the nuances of roles such as product owner, Scrum master, and Scrum team. We then compare and contrast those roles with each of the methodologies described in Chapter 3 and specifically reference the commonalities. In addition to the standard descriptions, we explore how the different roles are deployed within organizations. This chapter includes compelling interviews from Roman Pichler and Lyssa Adkins.
- **Chapter 5—The New Way to Collect and Document Requirements**
  This chapter focuses on the front end of the Agile process, where customer and market feedback is incorporated into meaningful requirements. It addresses terms and ideas such as user stories, epics, acceptance criteria, understanding and measuring business value, prioritization, roadmaps, and burn-up charts. We also show how requirements can be enhanced with elements such as personas and usability. We dive into communication strategies and, finally, explore how Lean software development and the Lean start-up movement affect requirements. Our interview with Ellen Gottesdiener and Mary Gorman includes great insights.
- **Chapter 6—Grooming and Planning**
  As the development process progresses, requirements/user stories are "groomed" into usable input for the development teams. The requirements are prioritized, and we present several strategies for prioritization. The size of the user stories is estimated using a variety of techniques, including story points. Once the estimating is complete, the Sprint planning or XP planning game begins, incorporating the velocity of the team, current business conditions, and the amount of things such as technical debt and bugs. We explore the theory of triple constraints (scope vs. time vs. resources) and how the management of these can affect the development progress. Our interview with Mike Cohn showcases his breadth of experience in the practical application of Scrum.
- **Chapter 7—Testing, Quality, and Integration**
  This chapter explains how quality can be maintained and even enhanced using Agile tools. One of the key tenets of Agile is "frequent verification and validation" of working software, so we devote this chapter to different testing approaches, such as test-driven development, acceptance test-driven development, integrated testing, regression testing, and unit testing.

We provide a complete example of test-driven development, including code references. Our interview with Tim Ottinger rounds out all of the testing information.

- **Chapter 8—Tracking and Reporting**
  This chapter emphasizes the importance of tracking and reporting progress in the Agile process. To understand the tracking process, we define the necessary meetings such as the daily stand-up, Sprint review/demo, and Sprint retrospectives. We also dive into Kanban, because the tracking of a Kanban project is quite different. We demonstrate tools such as burn-up and burn-down charts and parking lots used in feature-driven development. We discuss how to measure success within Agile, including the ever-important metric of customer satisfaction. We conclude with an interview with Agile coach Kent McDonald.
- **Chapter 9—Agile beyond IT**
  This chapter explains how the implementation of Agile affects far more than the IT organization; the entire launch process for new products or enhanced features is now different and applying the four Agile values enhances the ability to deliver to the marketplace. We also showcase how the Agile principles can be applied to other organizations outside IT. Some in Marketing have adopted Agile quite thoroughly, even creating the Agile Marketing Manifesto. Our interview with Travis Arnold, one of the creators of the Agile Marketing Manifesto, completes the chapter.
- **Appendix—John Deere Case Study**
  The appendix presents an interview we conducted with three leaders at John Deere's Intelligent Solutions Group, who have helped lead their journey to become a more Agile organization.

We sincerely hope you enjoy exploring the world of Agile software development. We welcome your feedback and encourage you to visit our web site or follow us on Twitter for more information on Agile.

Sondra Ashmore, Ph.D., PMI-PMP/ACP
@Sondra1130

Kristin Runyan, PMI-PMP, CSPO, CSM
http://www.runyanconsulting.com
@KristinRunyan

Acknowledgments

We would like to extend our sincere appreciation to the following people who have given generously of their time and talents to make important contributions to this book.

- **Interviewees**—Robert (Uncle Bob) Martin, Scott Ambler, Alistair Cockburn, Roman Pichler, Lyssa Adkins, Ellen Gottesdiener, Mary Gorman, Mike Cohn, Tim Ottinger, Kent McDonald, and Travis Arnold
- John Deere, for their interviews and photos
- **Reviewers**—Brad Rasmussen, Brandon Carlson, Hastia Sartika, Steve Sieverding, and Robert Gilbert
- **Subjects in photos**—Anna Runyan, Kristin Runyan, Jacob Patton, Scott Clarke, Brian Ashmore, and Sondra Ashmore
- **Photographer**—Tim Runyan
- **Blackjack code author**—Brian Ashmore

About the Authors

Sondra Ashmore, Ph.D., is an IT leader who specializes in Fortune 500 corporations. Her areas of expertise include product management, project management, and new product development for IT offerings. She received her graduate education at Rensselaer Polytechnic Institute in technical communication and management, and at Iowa State in human–computer interaction. Her research focuses on the software development process, both Waterfall and Agile, and explores strategies to optimize the user experience. In 2012, she was recognized as a "Forty under 40" business leader by the *Business Record* and won the Women of Innovation award from the Technology Association of Iowa for business innovation and leadership for her work at IBM. Sondra is certified as a Project Management Professional (PMP), Project Management Institute Agile Certified Professional (PMI-ACP), and Stanford Certified Project Manager (SCPM).

Photo reprinted with permission from the Des Moines Business Record.

Kristin Runyan is a product delivery expert in Des Moines, Iowa, specializing in product management, Agile coaching and training, and leadership. She is certified as a Scrum Master (CSM), Scrum Product Owner (CSPO), Pragmatic Marketing Product Manager, and Project Management Professional (PMP). She is also a 2011 winner of the Women of Innovation award from the Technology Association of Iowa. Kristin got her undergraduate degree at Texas Christian University and her MBA at Saint Louis University. She is an avid blogger at www.runyanconsulting.com, and her Twitter handle is @KristinRunyan. Kristin enjoys living in the Midwest with her husband, two daughters, and black lab.

Photo courtesy of Businessolver.

Chapter 1

The History and Value of Agile Software Development

Learning Objectives

- Understand the history of software methodologies
- Compare and contrast Waterfall and Agile development approaches
- Learn how the Agile Manifesto was created and continues to influence Agile practices
- Read an interview with an Agile Manifesto author

This chapter provides the background of the Agile movement and compares and contrasts Agile to the more traditional Waterfall methodology. It describes the Agile Manifesto in detail and explores the key tenets of Agile, such as the following:

- Close collaboration between the programming team and business experts
- Face-to-face communication
- Frequent delivery of new, deployable business value
- Tight, self-organizing teams
- Reduced impact of changes in requirements

The 12 additional supporting principles of the Agile Manifesto are also introduced.

The Beginnings of Software Development as Methodology

Software development, also known as software engineering, is defined by the Software Engineering Body of Knowledge (Abran, Moore, et al. 2004) as a "systematic, disciplined, quantifiable approach to the development, operation, and maintenance of software, and the study of these approaches; that is, the application of engineering to software" (p. 23). The field of software development emerged in the 1950s with operating systems and became increasingly popular in the 1960s and 1970s as software became a focus in computing.

The first, and still the most popular, software development process is referred to as the **Waterfall** model. The Waterfall model advocates sequential phases of development in which each stage is completed before the next begins, with a focus on structure. For example, all software designs are completed before the coding phase begins. This methodology was introduced in the 1950s at a conference on software development methodology for SAGE, and it has continued to be the predominant software development methodology (Benington 1956; Larman and Basili 2003). Despite the popularity of Waterfall development, it has continued to be criticized in the field for being process heavy and unresponsive to the inevitable changes that arise during software development projects (McConnell 2004).

The Rise of Agile Software Development

At the turn of the century, the world of technology became increasingly inundated with requests for new features. This was particularly true for web sites because society was becoming more dependent on Internet conveniences such as electronic mail, e-commerce, and real-time news updates. Product development teams needed a new way to respond quickly to these demands to stay competitive in the changing market. The solution came in the form of Agile development, validating assertions by Whiteside and Bennett that software development needs to become more of an iterative process (Whiteside, Bennett, et al. 1988).

What is Agile development? What comprises Agile development methodology, and why is it getting the reputation as the superior approach to the Waterfall methodology? **Agile** is an overarching term that includes iterative approaches to software development that embrace the values of the Manifesto for Agile Software Development, which is discussed in more detail later in this chapter. Agile development methodologies are designed to flex and support the needs of the project and organization. Agile does not describe a specific approach, but instead offers a collection of tools and best practices that help development organizations focus on efficiency, collaboration, quality, and the creation of customer value. Agile development includes methodologies such as Extreme Programming, Scrum, and the Crystal Family; all of these versions of Agile development have their own nuances, but they share the goal of avoiding "a single pass sequential, document-driven, gated-step approach" (Larman and Basili 2003, p. 47). Table 1.1 compares Waterfall and Agile software development approaches.

Including usability specifications (the study of end user behavior and how these users will interact with the software) into iterative development processes was introduced in 2002, when iterative development was starting to gain popularity (Carroll and Rosson 2002). Carroll and Rosson (2002) state that usability designs should not be a static recommendation or design, but rather should evolve and be refined throughout the development process. Larman and Basili (2003) claim that although iterative development has been the new buzz in the IT industry in recent years, it is not a new concept. Researchers at IBM's TJ Watson Research Center published the first research document describing a process that had the most similarities to today's Agile or iterative development process (Zurcher and Randell 1968). This process was recommended to IBM executives in 1969 as "A model becomes the system" (Lehman and Belady 1985), but IBM did not start adopting the contemporary model of Agile development until the turn of the present century.

Review 1 At this point, the reader should be able to answer Review Questions 1–3.

Table 1.1 *Comparing Software Development Approaches*

Software Development Approaches	
Waterfall	**Agile**
Prescriptive	Abstract
Extensive documentation	Minimal documentation
Sequential	Continuous
Formal	Informal
Process focus	Communication focus
Gradual change	Rapid change

Manifesto for Agile Software Development

We are uncovering better ways of developing
software by doing it and helping others do it.
Through this work we have come to value:

Individuals and interactions over processes and tools
Working software over comprehensive documentation
Customer collaboration over contract negotiation
Responding to change over following a plan

That is, while there is value in the items on
the right, we value the items on the left more.

Kent Beck
Mike Beedle
Arie van Bennekum
Alistair Cockburn
Ward Cunningham
Martin Fowler
James Grenning
Jim Highsmith
Andrew Hunt
Ron Jeffries
Jon Kern
Brian Marick
Robert C. Martin
Steve Mellor
Ken Schwaber
Jeff Sutherland
Dave Thomas

Figure 1.1 *Manifesto for Agile Software Development*
Source: © 2001 www.agilemanifesto.org

The Agile Manifesto

The Manifesto for Agile Software Development (see Figure 1.1) was created in 2001 from a meeting of 17 practitioners who were interested in coming together in Snowbird, Utah, to discuss lightweight development methodologies. Most of the participants came to discuss the various approaches they had either developed or used extensively. The group formed the initial Agile Alliance group, whose mission was to promote a move to lighter development approaches and away from the heavy process of Waterfall development. They were not interested in merging their lighter approaches, but instead worked to find an overarching term that accurately described all of the available lightweight approaches.

After much debate, the term "Agile" gained consensus from the group, and they proceeded to create the "Manifesto for Agile Software Development." According to Williams and Cockburn (2003) and the practitioners who authored the *Manifesto for Agile Software Development*, Agile is a process for developing software that values

> individuals and interactions over processes and tools, working software over comprehensive documentation, customer collaboration over contract negotiation, responding to change over following a plan. (p. 39)

The practitioners were careful to use the term "over" in an effort to be less prescriptive and instead to make the manifesto more of a guide. They added the phrase "That is, while there is value in the items on the right, we value the items on the left more" to emphasize that there will be times when lighter approaches are not always realistic or possible, but they should always be the goal.

What does each of these values mean, and how do they influence organizations that are using Agile methodologies? Table 1.2 defines each value and gives an example of how each one can be used in an Agile organization.

Table 1.2 *Agile Values Explained*

Value	Definition	Implementation Example
Individuals and interactions over processes and tools.	It is more important to focus on the contributions that each person brings to the team and the trust and communication that exists within the team rather than the adherence to process or the use of elaborate tools.	People are more effective when they can talk and work together face-to-face. Reduce barriers that inhibit people's ability to get together.
Working software over comprehensive documentation.	Software product development is a creative activity that is difficult to fully envision through the use of static documents. By creating working code that customers can try, you will get better feedback than you would when customers imagine using the documents alone.	Rather than exchanging documents such as test plans and product specifications, Agile teams should build limited capability versions of the product that customers and business users can actually try before signing off on them.

(Continues)

Table 1.2 *Agile Values Explained (Continued)*

Value	Definition	Implementation Example
Customer collaboration over contract negotiation.	It is more important that the customer become intimately involved with the product development team than to focus on the terms and conditions of the project.	Specific project timelines are difficult to predict and commit to. Instead, an Agile project should focus on regular interaction with customers for feedback and work with them to adjust the timelines as the project progresses.
Responding to change over following a plan.	The only thing most teams can be certain about when they start a project is that something will change. Agile teams must be able to respond and adapt to regular change rather than sticking to a plan that was created at the beginning of a project or an iteration.	Product requirements are prioritized at the beginning of the iterations rather than the team agreeing to all product requirements at the beginning of a project.

After developing the list of initial values for Agile software development, the authors decided to add a list of principles that would help teams understand the priorities for Agile practices (see Figure 1.2). They again avoided getting too prescriptive on how to be Agile and emphasized the principles that should guide an Agile team.

As a result of this meeting, the Agile Alliance was formed, and the proponents of lightweight alternatives to Waterfall had a common platform to discuss their ideas. The Agile Alliance (http://www.agilealliance.org/) is a global nonprofit organization whose mission is to advance Agile development principles and practices. The Agile Alliance offers many important benefits to Agile practitioners, including participation in user groups, conference discounts, and volunteer opportunities.

Principles behind the Agile Manifesto

We follow these principles:

Our highest priority is to satisfy the customer through early and continuous delivery of valuable software.

Welcome changing requirements, even late in development. Agile processes harness change for the customer's competitive advantage.

Deliver working software frequently, from a couple of weeks to a couple of months, with a preference to the shorter timescale.

Business people and developers must work together daily throughout the project.

Build projects around motivated individuals. Give them the environment and support they need, and trust them to get the job done.

The most efficient and effective method of conveying information to and within a development team is face-to-face conversation.

Working software is the primary measure of progress.

Agile processes promote sustainable development. The sponsors, developers, and users should be able to maintain a constant pace indefinitely.

Continuous attention to technical excellence and good design enhances agility.

Simplicity—the art of maximizing the amount of work not done—is essential.

The best architectures, requirements, and designs emerge from self-organizing teams.

At regular intervals, the team reflects on how to become more effective, then tunes and adjusts its behavior accordingly.

Figure 1.2 *Agile principles*

Source: © 2001 www.agilemanifesto.org

Each year, the Agile Alliance holds a major conference that covers a wide range of Agile topics. Attendance and participation in the conference have grown extensively each year as a result of the widespread adoption of Agile.

Review 2 At this point, the reader should be able to answer Review Questions 4–7.

Cayman Design

Throughout this book, we use the fictitious company Cayman Design to illustrate how Agile concepts can be implemented in an organization. Cayman Design has been in business for ten years and started as a web design company that specializes in e-commerce web sites. Their headquarters are in Austin, Texas, but they design sites for companies around the world. Their business has grown in the last couple of years to include mobile applications. They have added a development team in Pune, India, to help with the design and test work, but the majority of their team remains in Austin.

Cayman Design's management team decided to start using more Agile methodologies when they entered the mobile application business. Their competitors were using Agile, and they were able to deliver sites to the market faster, with increased customer satisfaction. Cayman Design knew that using Agile techniques with a global team would be a challenge, but they were committed to making it work.

Workers at Cayman Design are a mix of new hires and highly experienced professionals. The management team started down the Agile path by hiring a consultant to train the employees and provide recommendations on transitioning to Agile methodologies. They chose to implement Scrum, Kanban boards, and Extreme Programming. Communication with global team members is done through video conferences, e-mail, and instant messaging. Cayman Design averages six to eight Scrum teams across the e-commerce and mobile applications teams. You will get to know more about Cayman Design's adoption of Agile approaches throughout the subsequent chapters in this book.

Conclusion

Software development has made important shifts since its early days to meet the demands of users. Compared to many engineering disciplines such as mechanical or chemical engineering, software engineering is a relatively new practice and will continue to evolve at the rapid pace technology demands. It is important to understand the roles that Waterfall and Agile methods play in this evolution. We explore specific Agile approaches in Chapter 3, "Understanding the Different Types of Agile."

Summary

- Software development (engineering) is a relatively new field that originated in the 1950s.
- Software development has traditionally been performed using the Waterfall methodology, which focuses on completing each phase of development before the next phase starts.
- Agile methods started gaining popularity for software development in the 1990s, and teams began to experiment with better ways to develop software.
- Waterfall development methods are sequential, prescriptive, and documentation intensive, but Agile methods promote iterative development, flexibility, and intuitive design.
- The Agile Manifesto is a declaration that was developed in 2001 to establish agreement on the values shared by Agile approaches and to advocate for a new way to think about developing software.
- Shortly after writing the Agile Manifesto, the authors created 12 additional principles to explain the basis for the values in the Agile Manifesto.

Interview with Robert Martin (Uncle Bob)

Robert C. Martin (Uncle Bob) has been a programmer since 1970. He is Master Craftsman at 8th Light Inc., and founder and president of Uncle Bob Consulting LLC and Object Mentor Inc., international firms that offer software consulting, training, and skill development services to major corporations worldwide.

Mr. Martin has published dozens of articles in various trade journals, and is a regular speaker at international conferences and trade shows. He has authored and edited many books, including the following:

- *Designing Object-Oriented C++ Applications Using the Booch Method*
- *Pattern Languages of Program Design 3*
- *More C++ Gems*
- *Extreme Programming in Practice*
- *Agile Software Development: Principles, Patterns, and Practices*
- *UML for Java Programmers*
- *Clean Code*
- *The Clean Coder*

A leader in the industry of software development, Mr. Martin served three years as the editor-in-chief of the *C++ Report,* and was the first chairman of the Agile Alliance.

Kristin and Sondra: Alistair Cockburn states in his book *Agile Software Development: The Cooperative Game* that you called the meeting for the Agile Manifesto. What gave you the idea to call the meeting, and how did you decide who should be invited?

Bob: In the summer of 2000, Kent Beck called a meeting of people in the Extreme Programming (XP) community. I think he called it XP Leadership or something. The attendees included myself, Ward Cunningham, Martin Fowler, Ken Auer, and many others from the Design Patterns community. The goal was to set the future direction of XP. At that meeting, I stated that I thought a manifesto and an organization would be a good idea as a way to amplify our message. Martin Fowler agreed, and he and I decided to meet in Chicago to discuss the event and the invitation list.

That meeting took place in the fall of 2000. He and I made a list of the people we thought would be important to invite. Specifically, we invited folks who had contributed to the idea of lightweight processes. Indeed, as I recall, we called the event the Lightweight Process Summit.

One of the invitees was Alistair Cockburn. Apparently he had a similar idea, and our invitation came just a few days before he was going to send his. At least that's how I remember it. He volunteered to do the legwork on finding a venue. He also merged his invitation list with ours, which was a great boon.

Looking back on it, I consider it quite remarkable that so many of the invitees actually came to the event. Apparently the stars were in alignment.

I kicked the meeting off by suggesting we write a manifesto. After that, I was just one of the minor contributors.

Kristin and Sondra: Do you think the Agile Manifesto will need to be updated or changed as Agile development continues to gain greater adoption?

Bob: No, I think it is a statement that points in a direction; and I don't think that direction has changed, or will change. I don't believe the Agile Manifesto is, or should be, a living document. I think it's a milestone on a path, not the path itself.

There have been other manifestos since, which have amplified or extended the direction that the Agile Manifesto began. The software craftsmanship manifesto [http://manifesto.softwarecraftsmanship.org/] comes to mind.

Kristin and Sondra: Do you think Agile methodologies are better than the traditional Waterfall methodology in all cases, or are there situations where Waterfall is more beneficial?

Bob: Agile methods are better in every case, because Agile methods are human methods. We are taught Agile methods when we are in third grade and our teacher tells us to write a story. She helps us with an outline, then a first draft, and a second draft, etc. We learn, from a very early age, that anything worth doing well must be done iteratively through a process of successive refinement.

Kristin and Sondra: Was there a specific event or series of events that led you to recognize the importance of writing clean code and refactoring?

Bob: There was no specific event. Instead, it was a long process of learning and watching and thinking. A critical moment in that process was when I learned TDD—Test-Driven Development [which is described in detail in Chapter 7, "Testing, Quality, and Integration"]—from Kent Beck. As I practiced this critical discipline, it became clear to me that if you have a suite of tests that you trust, then code becomes simple and easy to change. Cleaning code loses the risk that is usually associated with it. Refactoring becomes something you do naturally every day, every hour.

Once you understand that, then the importance of refactoring and cleaning code becomes obvious. When you are afraid to clean, you accept the mess as necessary. When you understand that cleaning can be easy and safe, then the mess becomes unacceptable.

Kristin and Sondra: In your opinion, what is the single most important contribution that Agile development has made to the field of software engineering?

Bob: Agile broke the Waterfall. That, in and of itself, is hugely important because it makes software development into a human activity.

Now I'm waiting for the next revolution, the craftsmanship revolution. We've learned that we must iterate and build our systems through successive refinement. The next thing we have to learn is that we don't really have to make a mess in order to go fast. Our next lesson is "The only way to go fast is to go well."

References and Further Reading

Abran, A., Moore, J. W., et al., eds. (2004). *Guide to the software engineering body of knowledge—2004 version.* Los Alamitos, CA, IEEE Computer Society.

Beck, K., Beedle, M., et al. (2001). Manifesto for Agile software development. http://Agilemanifesto.org/.

Benington, H. D. (1956). Production of large computer programs. Symposium on Advanced Programming Methods for Digital Computers. Washington, DC: Office of Naval Research, Dept. of the Navy.

Bittner, K. (2004). Driving iterative development with use cases. *IBM developerWorks,* http://www.ibm.com/developerworks/rational/library/4029.html.

Carroll, J. M., and Rosson, M. B. (2002). *Usability engineering*. San Diego, CA: Academic Press.

Doshi, C., Doshi, D. (2009). A peek into an Agile infected culture. Presentation at the Agile 2009 conference, Chicago.

Jacko, J., Düchting, M., et al. (2007). Incorporating user centered requirement engineering into Agile software development. *Human-Computer Interaction. Interaction Design and Usability*, 4550: 58–67.

Larman, C. (2004). *Agile and iterative development: A manager's guide*. Boston: Addison-Wesley.

Larman, C., and Basili, V. R. (2003). Iterative and incremental development: A brief history. *Computer*, 36(6): 47–56.

Lehman, M. M., and Belady, L. A. (1985). Internal IBM report, 1969. *Program evolution: Processes of software change.* San Diego, CA: Academic Press Professional.

McConnell, S. (2004). *Code complete: A practical handbook of software construction*. Redmond, WA: Microsoft Press.

Nerur, S., Mahapatra, R., et al. (2005). Challenges of migrating to Agile methodologies. *Communications of the ACM*, 48(5): 72–78.

Sanders, E. (2002). From user-centered to participatory design approaches. In J. Frascara, ed., *Design and the social sciences: Making connections*. New York: Taylor and Francis.

Whiteside, J., Bennett, J., et al. (1988). Usability engineering: Our experience and evolution. In M. Helander, ed., *Handbook of human-computer interaction*. Amsterdam: North Holland, 791–817.

Williams, L., and Cockburn, A. (2003). Guest editors' introduction: Agile software development: It's about feedback and change. *Computer* 36(6): 39–43.

Woodward, E., Surdeck, S., et al. (2010). *A practical guide to distributed Scrum*. Boston: Addison-Wesley.

Zurcher, F. W., and Randell, B. (1968). Iterative multi-level modeling: A metholodology for computer system design. Proceedings from the 1968 IFIP congress, IEEE CS Press.

Review Questions

Review 1

1. How is software engineering defined?
2. How does Waterfall development differ from Agile development?
3. How did the term "Agile" emerge?

Review 2

4. What does the Agile Manifesto encourage Agile teams to value?
5. Why is the term "over" used in the values?
6. What are the key themes in the Agile Manifesto principles?
7. What organization developed as a result of the Agile Manifesto?

Chapter 2

Organizational Culture Considerations with Agile

Learning Objectives

- Understand organizational culture and why it matters in an Agile implementation
- Dive into ways things might be different in an Agile organization from a developer, manager, and executive viewpoint
- Look at successes and failures in behaviors to see the cultural impacts
- Understand how the Agile principles drive different behaviors in an organization
- Investigate the healthy team dynamics of self-organization teams, continuous improvement, frequent delivery, effective seating arrangements, incorporating virtual resources, and adapting to the changing environment
- Explore how an Agile workplace differs for managers and the ways that they must change with regard to teamwork, trust, and transparency
- Review the role of executives and how their behavior can position an Agile transformation for success with executive alignment, respecting priorities, creating supportive environments for the teams, and driving the right behaviors with metrics

Moving from Waterfall to Agile requires an organizational culture transformation in most companies. This chapter delves into the impacts as well as examples of both successful and unsuccessful ways to handle the culture change. First we understand what organizational culture is and how it influences an organization. Then we look through the eyes of three positions in a company to see how Agile changes the way common situations and challenges are addressed.

What Is Organizational Culture, and Why Does It Matter?

Before we dive into the specific impacts of Agile, let's discuss corporate culture. According to Philip Atkinson, corporate culture "is the infrastructure, the glue that binds together people and processes to generate results . . . The culture should become the major force that propels the organization onward" (Atkinson 2012).

How important is the organizational culture in a company's ability to adopt Agile? Critical. In fact, in the VersionOne annual survey of "The State of Agile Development," they found that culture change is the primary barrier to further Agile adoption at companies (VersionOne 2013, p. 9).

Why is it so hard to change a culture? An organization's culture was not built overnight; it is the accumulation of years of interactions and experiences that have formed into a belief system of how work progresses and how decisions are made. To shift the culture, one must create new experiences and reward those who dare to embrace the new and unfamiliar. The organization must be prepared to examine its old practices with a critical eye and try a new way of doing things. When the new experiences are difficult or uncomfortable, it is common to revert to old habits. Driving true culture change, which Agile requires, needs commitment and nurturing from all levels of the organization.

The Team Members' Viewpoint

The first perspective we want to explore concerns the individual team members that are being placed on an Agile team. These people are typically in development and quality assurance (QA) roles but could include others in the organization. The team role is described in detail in Chapter 4, "Describing the Different Roles." Why would team members want to embrace Agile for their projects? Several key principles within Agile are highly desirable to most individual team members.

What Is Different?

To understand the benefits and cultural impacts of Agile, first we should explore what is actually different with the Agile practices and the typical work environments of pre-Agile organizations.

Self-Organizing Teams

Agile advocates for self-organizing teams, which is a big change for many organizations. Many workplaces hire individuals to work on a specific thing, and even though they are part of an organizational structure, they really act alone. They are responsible for their own work, and their performance is measured based on their individual achievements. That all changes with Agile: Employees come together as a team—not just a set of individuals—and they establish themselves as an entity. They become a group of people driving toward a common goal. One of the first manifestations of this newly created team takes the form of a **working agreement**, described in Chapter 4. The team gets to establish their own norms and rules of engagement without management oversight; this offers developers and testers a great deal of autonomy that may not have existed before Agile.

Another desirable outcome of self-organizing teams is that the team members get to actually **select the tasks** they want to work on during the iteration. Before Agile, many organizations distributed work from the manager to the developer, without the developer getting much say at all on the assigned tasks. The pre-Agile assumption was that managers understood the work and how best to deliver it, so they would assign the necessary tasks to individual developers who would execute on their task. There is a high cost of missed opportunities with this method that Agile addresses: The developers might have a better solution for the business problem, and Agile gives them the opportunity to voice their suggestions and alternatives. Also, developers may have skills in a variety of areas, and to be assigned tasks by someone else does not allow them to choose to work on different items. The added variety to their workload is often appealing. Another benefit to self-organizing teams is the ability to organically cross-train. This happens when one developer wants to learn something new and acts on that desire. When selecting the tasks to work on, developers can request those tasks under the guidance of a more experienced developer, or they may ask to shadow an experienced developer so they can learn. The opportunity to choose their own tasks is a dramatic improvement over the pre-Agile environment.

This concept can be demonstrated in university settings as well. If you are put on a team to deliver a class project with no predetermined task assignments, the team can decide how best to distribute the work: One student might be the best researcher, one might be the fastest typist, and another might be best at the oral presentation. By allowing the team to determine how work is distributed, you can play to the strengths of each individual and facilitate new learning, which is the point of the next section.

Continuous Improvement

Another big organizational culture impact of Agile from a team member's viewpoint is the ownership of continuous improvement. Within Agile, each team member is responsible for ensuring that problems from a past or current iteration are not carried into the next one; this creates a higher level of engagement from employees, because they have to determine how best to solve any problems or issues existing within the team. This type of continuous improvement applies not just to their code and the products they produce but also to their sense of teamwork. The best teams actively practice reflection, usually through a meeting called a *retrospective*, which is covered in Chapter 8, "Tracking and Reporting." This meeting is sometimes referred to as a postmortem or "Lessons Learned," and it allows for the team to discuss what went well, what did not go well, and what they need to improve. It is important for teams to step away from the day-to-day activities and spend time discussing the team dynamics. Allowing the teams time to reflect on their actions and progress is important within the fast-paced cycle of iterative development (Cohn 2010, p. 213).

The reason why this is a compelling difference from other methodologies is because individuals are no longer waiting to have their problems solved for them—they are actively engaged in the solutions. In the past, a developer or tester might have relied on the manager or someone else in the organization to resolve issues, improve processes, and relay information. Within Agile, the teams are empowered and encouraged to seek out answers and improvements on their own.

To apply this to a university setting, consider teams that are assigned for the entire semester. Within a team, there may be highly organized, highly driven participants as well as others who are not willing or able to put forth as much time and effort. If one of the team members goes to the professor seeking a solution and the professor rearranges the team assignments, that is certainly one way to solve the problem, but it is not the Agile way. Within Agile, the team members would be asked to resolve their differences themselves first. Of course, if the issue is a true performance problem, then the professor may need to intervene, but the first course of resolution within Agile is always within the team.

Frequent Delivery

When developers move into Agile teams, they may experience a profound shift with the expectations of working software and frequent delivery. In many pre-Agile organizations, developers and testers could work on a project for months and months with very little feedback. This is no longer true in an Agile workplace: Teams are asked to deliver tested code very quickly so that stakeholders can review progress and make adjustments if necessary. This shift in expectations can be significant to some developers and testers—particularly perfectionists—who want everything to be precise and thorough before anyone sees it.

For Alistair Cockburn and the Crystal methodology, this principle is the number one priority: In his 2010 blog, titled "Seven Properties of Highly Successful Projects in Crystal Clear," he states:

> The single most important property of any project, large or small, agile or not, is that of delivering running, tested code to real users every few months. The advantages are so numerous that it is astonishing that any team doesn't do it:
>
> - The sponsors get critical feedback on the rate of progress of the team.
> - Users get a chance to discover whether their original request was for what they actually need and to get their discoveries fed back into development.
> - Developers keep their focus, breaking deadlocks of indecision.
> - The team gets to debug their development and deployment processes, and gets a morale boost through accomplishments.
>
> All of these advantages come from one single property, **Frequent Delivery.** (Cockburn 2010)

Obtaining feedback is critical to an organization's ability to course-correct if something is not quite right or does not meet the needs of the customer. Within Waterfall, because working software was not delivered at regular intervals but rather as a "big bang" after months or years of development, gathering this type of interim feedback was difficult. Becoming comfortable with frequent delivery is important for developers and testers because they must truly desire the feedback and be willing to act on it.

Frequent delivery is not always part of the university experience, because many classes have a team project that is due at the end of the semester; however, projects that allow for feedback throughout the semester are easier to manage. For example, if a critical paper is due after month 1, the team can incorporate the feedback from that paper into future deliverables. If the written presentation is due after month 2, then the team can learn if their proposal resonates and practical ways to improve it. By the time they make their oral presentation at the end of the semester, they are more confident in their work because they have had the opportunity to solicit and incorporate feedback throughout the semester.

Removing the "Us versus Them" Scenarios

In a pre-Agile world, some development teams handed off their code to a testing group, where the QA activities took place; this handoff frequently created an "us versus them" environment, where the developers could criticize the testers based on the types and quality of tests they were running, and the testers could lament the poorly written code that they were expected to debug. By changing the definition of "done"—a concept described in detail in Chapter 6, "Grooming and Planning"—to include testing, the team has a new appreciation for the testing effort. Developers are now collaborating with their testing teammates to create the highest quality software. If an iteration cannot be completed on time because of testing problems, the entire team is responsible.

Testing is one of the most visible manifestations of the Agile concept of teamwork, but many other groups are affected as well. Agile is about working together toward a common goal, and it creates a structure or framework to facilitate collaboration and break down organizational silos. Another area where this is demonstrated is between the product owner and the team. In the past, a lack of clear requirements was often the reason that software was late or inadequate. Now, the product owner, with responsibility for bringing clarity and priority to the requirements, is part of the delivery team. If a developer is unsure of how to proceed, it is his or her responsibility to seek clarity from the product owner, and it is the product owner's responsibility to provide an educated response.

Central to this culture shift is the idea that the team succeeds or fails together. Within Agile, it is impossible for a tester to succeed but the developer to fail, or for the product owner to succeed but the Scrum master to fail. Either the team, the whole team, delivered working software at the end of the iteration, or they did not. If the iteration did not produce working software, it is up to the team to diagnose the problems and work to correct them, previously described as continuous improvement.

In a university setting, this is often demonstrated in group projects where the entire group will receive a single grade. The professor is not likely to entertain conversations about who did what and why the project is difficult—he or she is interested in results, and part of delivering the necessary results is figuring out ways to maximize the talents and motivation of everyone on the team.

Physical Workspace

The collaboration aspect of Agile allows team members to work together and solve problems quickly. When the entire development team is colocated, which is ideal, then how the seating arrangements are managed can greatly contribute to their effectiveness. The best scenario is for the team to sit together in a type of pod arrangement that easily facilitates spontaneous conversations. Cubicle walls (or even offices) can be torn down so everyone can sit together and see one another (see Figure 2.1). This invites collaboration. The founders of Scrum were very direct on this point: "Use open working environments. Such environments allow people to communicate more easily, make it easier to get together, and facilitate self-organization" (Schwaber and Beedle 2002, p. 39).

By allowing the developers and testers to have easy access to one another, questions or issues that may have taken several e-mails or meetings to resolve can be addressed face-to-face for immediate resolution. The speed of clarification and problem solving that comes from being collaborative provides teams with an excellent opportunity to improve their deliverables.

The idea of colocation works in a university setting as well. Many colleges offer remote degree plans today, which is a great alternative for students who live in rural areas or who want to participate in a program that is not offered locally. The challenge with these sorts of arrangements is on the team assignments, where classmates do not have the opportunity to get together regularly to discuss the project progress and roadblocks. These challenges can be overcome, however, using some of the methods described later in the chapter.

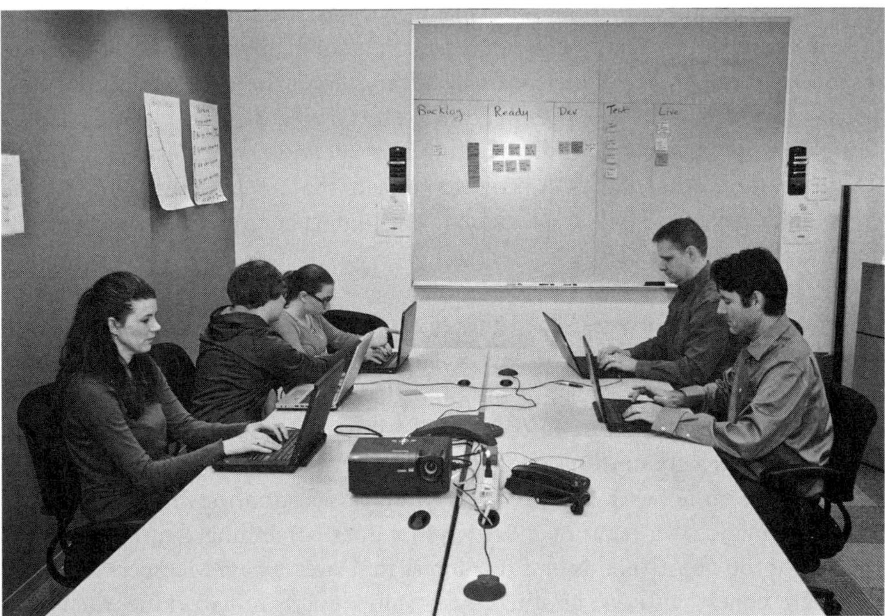

Figure 2.1 *Agile teams working together*

Successes

Now that we understand the differences that Agile brings to individual team members—self-organizing teams, the opportunity for continuous improvement, embracing frequent delivery without organizational silos, and having a collaborative physical workspace—next we examine what organizations do to ensure success or avoid paths to failure.

Team Dynamics

The best self-organizing teams place a high priority on members' knowing each other and creating an environment that plays to the individuals' strengths. What best practices do strong teams use?

First, members get to know one another. Each person has his or her own personality, family situation, areas of expertise, and temperament; by knowing teammates as human beings first and workmates second, team members see themselves as a cohesive unit, poised for success (Adkins 2010, loc. 4841). The most successful team members are the ones who maximize their environment around both personal and professional preferences. For example, if one team member needs to take children to school before work and cannot arrive before 8:30 A.M., then having the mandatory daily stand-up meeting (described in Chapter 8) at 8:15 A.M. would put that team member at a disadvantage. From a professional perspective, if one team member is unskilled at writing documentation, it would be unwise to have that person assume all of the documentation responsibilities. An effective team will address both the personal and professional nuances of their group to maximize everyone's effectiveness and create a desirable work environment; the working agreement described earlier is a great starting place for that clarity. A project and team that are structured around the individuals' personal goals and unique talents will generate the desired commitment (Cohn 2010, p. 216).

The second indicator of success on high-performing teams is their ability to adjust and course-correct. When things do not go as planned, the successful teams find a way to address the conflict in a productive manner.

The most effective teams are the ones that tackle concerns early on, in a respectful and resolution-oriented way. The least effective teams get angry but do not share their frustrations constructively. Ideally, teams operate in a manner that is based on honesty and proactively addresses situations the instant they are problematic. If a team member says or does something that seems disrespectful or too negative, it is best to address that right away. Members of strong teams are honest with one another and if something is not working, the whole team works together for a better alternative.

Incorporating Virtual Resources

Another defining characteristic of high-performing Agile teams is their ability to include virtual and perhaps even offshore (international) resources on their teams. Having team members that are not in your physical location introduces new challenges, and the teams that are able to adapt and incorporate the skills of the virtual team member will enjoy success.

When team members are not colocated, the lack of face-to-face communication is the first hurdle that must be overcome, and this can be accomplished using video tools. Ideally, this means that every meeting is conducted with a video connection so the virtual team members are included in the discussion. Honestly, the structured meetings are the easy part; where virtual team members might miss out is in the organic conversations that happen in the hallway or in the lunchroom. Human beings are always thinking and learning. Sometimes walking away from your desk or leaving the meeting room or bumping into a particular person on the way to the vending machine can spark an idea or help solve a problem. When those moments of inspiration occur, it is vitally important to contact the virtual team members and bring them in on the innovation. Otherwise, the team could advance but the virtual team members would be inadvertently left behind.

How can you create an environment where virtual team members feel as if they are part of the team? The first best practice is to have those people sit with the team at the start of the project for a significant period of time; ideally, this is at least two iterations. It is important for the team to feel as if they "know" the virtual employees, and vice versa; once the initial relationship is established, the virtual team members do not feel so far away. Inside jokes and team banter can happen naturally, with everyone feeling equally involved.

Travel budgets are tight at many companies these days, but having virtual employees come to town for key meetings, such as project kick-offs or quarterly reviews, can help the team bond and can increase the trust between the team members. In fact, to ensure success with distributed teams, companies will likely need to increase—not decrease—their travel budgets (Demarco et al. 2008).

Optimizing the Workspace

Companies and teams that enjoy success in an Agile environment take their workspace considerations seriously and look for options to optimize. Here is a summary of the three key spaces that are required:

- **Individual workstations** should be arranged to facilitate collaboration. Some teams prefer to have distance or walls separating them from other teams to keep noise and distractions to a minimum; other companies place teams with or near the business units that they support so the sense of a common goal is shared in the space.

- An **Agile (Scrum) room** is a discussion area with white boards for times when something needs to be debated or brainstorming of ideas is required. Ideally, this space is not shared with other teams or the rest of the company, because it should be immediately available when something comes up and the team wants to be able to leave their documentation and drawings on white boards for future reference. One innovative company turned old management offices into Scrum rooms so teams had their own dedicated space.
- Access to **company conference rooms** for the larger meetings, such as Sprint demos and backlog grooming sessions, is also necessary (see Figure 2.2). These often have to be scheduled because they are shared spaces, and each conference room needs access to a projector or Smart Board to display the working software at the end of the sprint.

In some companies, moving the physical space will make a powerful statement about the seriousness of the Agile implementation. If you say you are Agile but you stay in cubicles, how Agile are you? By rearranging the office

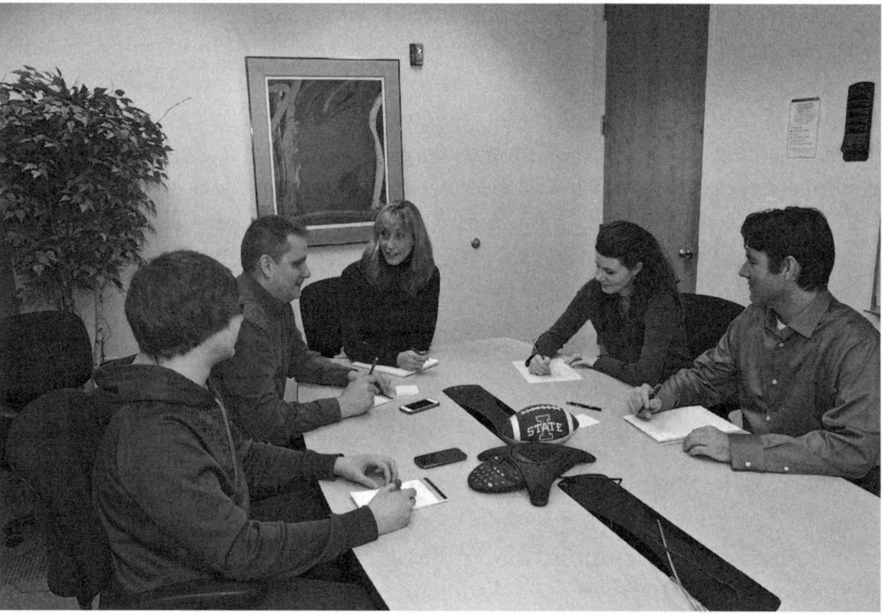

Figure 2.2 *Team workspace*

space, you visibly demonstrate your commitment to change. It is worth noting that the nature of Agile means that the physical requirements will change over time. As teams grow and shrink and traffic patterns change and interdependencies between teams morph, it will be necessary to rearrange the office space again.

> **Exercise**
>
> Consider the most productive team that you have worked on. What were the success factors that contributed? What skill sets did your teammates possess? How did your abilities complement each other? What lessons will you try to incorporate on future teams?

Failures/Risks

What traps or mistakes do team members make that can have a negative impact on the Agile implementation? In many ways, they are similar to the traits of successful teams, but they somehow miss the essence and turn into a liability instead of an asset. Let's explore some common mistakes.

Unhealthy Teams

Unlike the high-performing teams, unsuccessful teams typically fall into one or more of the following situations.

First, they fail to self-organize. There are truly people in the workforce today who are more comfortable being told what to do and simply execute on that order. When we ask those people to become more engaged and be part of the solution process, they are reluctant, or incapable of doing so. Some people are conditioned to this behavior, but over time in a supportive and learning culture, they can transform to being key contributors. For others, it is simply in their DNA to take direction from others and not rise to the level of accountability that Agile requires; these people will not be successful on Agile teams, so the organization needs to either find them a different role or allow them to move on.

Another example of the inability to self-organize is where teams demonstrate hostility, bullying, or demeaning behavior toward one or more of their team members. This aggressive behavior cannot be tolerated, and if the team cannot resolve it on their own, then management needs to get involved. Agile workplaces are safe environments where people are encouraged to learn and grow and take chances and deliver great results; but if there is an unhealthy team dynamic, that can be difficult—maybe impossible—to achieve.

Many people have served on unhealthy teams, and the same dynamics that exist in sports or academia can exist in the workplace. Teammates on unhealthy teams

- are unwilling to help or support one another
- refuse to broaden their role by saying things such as "it is not my job to test" or "he owns that piece of code, so it is his problem"
- withhold helpful information or training because they want to be seen as the expert

These unhealthy team dynamics can sabotage an Agile implementation, and it will take a strong Scrum master, coach, or possibly even manager to break down these bad habits.

Inability to Adapt

Agile requires team members to change, and that is uncomfortable for some people. They need to change how they interact, how they do their work, where they sit, and much more. An inability to adapt is a key reason why some team members fail in an Agile transformation. Looking at a specific example, as already mentioned, having a geographically distributed team introduces challenges, and some teams fail to adapt and accommodate. If the team does not make the effort to include the virtual resources in key conversations and meetings, then their ability to contribute is compromised; this can especially be true with international resources. Having sensitivity to time differences when scheduling meetings, creating a work schedule that allows for overlapping hours, and clarifying requirements so no language barriers impede progress are all efforts high-performing teams make. The ones who fail to have the appropriate sensitivity create a work environment that is polarized between those in the building and those outside.

Another example involves making the transition from cubicles to an open concept. When introducing the collaborative work arrangement, worries may range from a colleague who wears too much perfume, to a germophobe who fears being sneezed on, to concerns about background noise and the ability to concentrate. All are legitimate issues that need to be addressed, but none are worth abandoning the benefits of moving to the open, collaborative space. The teams or individuals that refuse to be open-minded about the seating arrangement and constantly complain are sabotaging their Agile implementation. Like all things, if a legitimate concern is affecting safety, then management needs to address it immediately. Otherwise, being adaptable in the seating arrangements demonstrates a commitment to the greater good. An inability or unwillingness to consider new options and adapt to the evolving needs of the organization can lead to failure.

Lacking Commitment

Another area where team members can experience failure is by lacking a sense of commitment. Within Agile, the team commits to the amount of work that they intend to complete during an iteration. If a team does not feel a sense of obligation to that commitment, the level of success that can be achieved is in jeopardy. Some teams reach the end of an iteration in which they have not completed the required work, but they have an attitude of "oh well, we tried"; these are not successful teams. Failing to honor a commitment should be a disappointment. It should serve as an opportunity to assess what went wrong and how it can be corrected in the future. The teams that are lackadaisical about their commitment will never be truly Agile.

The lack of commitment can reveal itself in a number of ways—failing to complete the work is the most obvious and detrimental—but there are other manifestations as well. Not adhering to the meeting cadence within Agile by grooming, planning, tracking, and demonstrating, all described in Chapter 8, can lead to suboptimized work. It might be easy to become lazy about the daily stand-up meetings and write them off as unnecessary, but that is not in the best interest of the work, the team, or the Agile transformation. Being disciplined about participation and active engagement drives success.

Failing to address issues with team dynamics and allowing bad habits or relationships to continue without proactively confronting them are also examples of lacking commitment. An unwillingness to learn and grow can create a stagnant environment where an individual team member or the entire team stops moving forward and simply becomes complacent. Innovation does not come from places described as complacent or lazy or lacking commitment. Innovation is coupled with true agility, and this comes from dedication, discipline, and a desire for continuous improvements.

Review 1 At this point, the reader should be able to answer Review Questions 1–5.

A Manager's Viewpoint

Agile for team members is full of new opportunities and a chance to contribute in ways that may not have been available in the old environment. The same is true for managers, but they may feel as though their role is shrinking or becoming less important. In many instances, Agile alters their span of control, which can create unease and a lack of clarity regarding expectations and performance measurements.

What Is Different?

The differences for managers center on how their role has evolved. It can be quite positive, but it is definitely different, and some managers are unable or unwilling to let go of their past responsibilities to embrace the new ways that they can help the team.

Questions, Not Solutions

Perhaps the biggest impact to most managers is that they are no longer responsible for defining the solutions—this now belongs to the team. Many managers have prided themselves on being owners of an application or architecture, so adjusting to the idea of team members making decisions about those applications can be difficult.

The manager is in the pivotal position of being able to facilitate how much a team learns and how quickly they embrace their self-organization. The most effective managers will make the shift from telling to asking. When a team member approaches management and asks, "How can we increase the response times with the database?" the manager in a pre-Agile world would provide an answer or at least a suggestion. In an Agile environment, the best managers will ask questions: "Why do you think the response time is bad?" "What is the customer expecting?" "What data is being retrieved?" "Is that the right amount of data?" "Are any business rules being applied to the query?" And so on. This allows the team to think through the situation to arrive at their own solutions. It might take a bit longer, but by enabling the team to derive the solution, the manager is truly being Agile and positioning the team for success and continuous improvements.

Applying this concept to a university environment often brings memories of favorite professors or key learning moments. When you struggle with a concept and visit the professor, the Agile-minded ones will ask you numerous questions until you arrive at the answer on your own; the less engaged professor might just give you the answer. By asking questions and allowing you to reach the answer on your own, your professor is demonstrating confidence in your intelligence and problem-solving capabilities. Taking the time to work with you to arrive at the answer—rather than just telling you—is an investment of the professor's time and will enable you to feel empowered and capable of reaching the right conclusion in the future. Professors are often used to this teaching role because they purposely chose their profession; managers may not be inherently good teachers, and displaying this type of faith and investment in employees might feel foreign and unnecessary. The good Agile managers are the ones who adopt a professor-like mind-set focused on continuous improvement and learning.

Clearing Roadblocks

The manager's role shifts to one of clearing roadblocks for the team to enable their success. This is a different role for a manager, and although it is vitally important to the organization, it might not feel very rewarding, at least not at first. If the team has an issue with training or tools or collaboration with other departments, the manager can be a great help navigating the political environment to solve the problem. The difference is that the manager used to be deeply involved in the problem solving, but now he or she is clearing roadblocks to allow the team-led solution to come to fruition. Some managers view this negatively, as though part of their job—or even their worth to the company—has been diminished. This should not be the case: Effective managers in an Agile environment are a tremendous asset. Since they no longer have to focus on every day-to-day detail associated with the project, they can devote time to higher-level activities such as technology architecture and true employee development—areas that are often neglected in the pre-Agile environments. Managers can assist with mapping the business process flow and then make recommendations to improve performance and drive toward simplicity. They also can spend time creating career development plans for employees based on their skills and desires, and they can devote meaningful time and attention to recruiting and making sure each hire adds to the cohesiveness of the team and further position them for success. It is a new role of clearing roadblocks and focusing on higher-level activities, but when done well, it is meaningful and delivers significant value to the organization.

Trusting the Team

Some managers are predisposed not to trust those beneath them in the organization. Douglas McGregor captured this management style in his X-Y theory of management. The Theory X manager believes that employees are inherently lazy and therefore need authoritative supervision and a comprehensive set of controls to manage them (McGregor 1960). Thus, Theory X managers will have a very hard time with an Agile implementation, because they fundamentally believe that self-organizing teams cannot exist. These people tend to act as "command and control," meaning that they dictate the work to be done and even how it will be done, and they tightly control the environment for that work. Clearly, this type of management attitude directly conflicts with the very core of Agile values. This belief system still exists in the modern workplace and must be addressed to ensure Agile success. If an organization has Theory X types of managers, they may need to move to new positions to not interfere with the Agile implementation. Departments that are very operational in nature often thrive with this type of management; self-organizing development teams do not.

Even if the manager is not a Theory X manager, he or she may still need to make adjustments in trusting the team. For some period of time (perhaps years), the manager has evaluated staff aptitudes based on a non-Agile measure. Often, managers have a hard time envisioning their employees stepping into and embracing new responsibilities and problem-solving techniques. The most effective Agile managers are those who know that the best way to truly embrace Agile is by letting go of their control and allowing the team to learn, and perhaps fail.

A nonworkplace example of this comes with parenting. When children are small, their physical, emotional, and intellectual capabilities are limited, but as they grow, these things obviously evolve. Imagine if parents kept acting as though their children were three-year-olds, even as they grew: The parents would still cut their food into tiny bites, would never dream of allowing them to ride a bike, and would certainly not allow them to bathe themselves. As the children grew, they would become increasingly frustrated with the limited expectations and would either lash out or disengage. The same is true in our workspace: Employees are constantly learning and evolving, and they can and should take on increasing levels of responsibility for their work. Agile supports this evolution, but some managers cannot move beyond their initial assessment of an employee's abilities. If a manager is struggling with an Agile transformation, this is an area to apply some self-reflection: Is the manager actually holding the employees back? If so, a little bit of trust can go a long way.

Successes

Can managers survive the changes in their roles in an Agile environment? Of course, and the successful ones display a few common traits. The best managers embrace the Agile values and principles by endorsing teamwork and trust.

Teamwork

The ideal manager is going to do everything in his or her power to ensure the success of the team. This includes staffing the team for success and ensuring that all roles are covered, assigning the team members full-time, and making sure they have the necessary tools and environment to deliver on their commitments.

One example that Cayman Design encountered needed management assistance to ensure team success. When creating the Scrum teams, there were not enough testing (QA) resources for every team to have a dedicated tester, so the decision was made for two teams to share testing resources. The first iteration went well, and both teams received the testing support that they needed. But in a subsequent iteration, one team ran into a problem, and they relied heavily on the tester to help them diagnose the issue. The other team, therefore, received no QA support during their iteration, and they were unable to deliver working software. Solving this problem was outside of the control of the individual teams because it required a reallocation of resources. The successful Agile manager took ownership of this problem and worked through budget and head count issues with senior management to allocate a dedicated QA resource to each team. The manager's proactive ownership of the situation positioned the teams for success.

A strong Agile manager also allows and encourages team members to work on their own differences. Members of a certain team at Cayman Design visited the manager, complaining of communication issues on the team: They did not know what their team members were working on, they were surprised when things were not completed, and they did not feel informed on roadblocks that were impeding their teammates' progress. Rather than addressing this in the typical management fashion, by calling the team together to discuss it or by speaking to everyone individually, the successful Agile manager pushed the issue back to the team to solve. Agile provides a structure to facilitate team success, and teams need to use those mechanisms on their own.

Trust

An effective Agile manager fundamentally trusts the team to do good work; this is evident in allowing team members to truly own issues and resolve them on their own. Trust is a bit like allowing your children to explore their own ideas, even if you are skeptical that they will work. Here is an example:

Your Scrum master comes to you and says that the team would like to work from home four days a week and be in the office only the one day that they host their Scrum meetings. You, as their manager, have serious reservations about this idea: It contradicts one of the Agile principles about the importance of face-to-face communication, and it will likely reduce the team's ability to collaborate. A non-Agile manager might immediately respond with, "That is out of the question. We would lose far too much collaboration if no one was in the office. Plus, what would our business partners think if they came into our workspace and no one was here?"

A successful Agile manager would likely respond with a question: "That is an interesting proposal. What is the business problem that you are trying to solve with the work from home idea?" Through this response, the Scrum master can share additional facts and drivers that led the team to think that this was a good idea. The manager can then react to the additional information with more accurate guidance and may even—through asking questions—guide the team to a different alternative. The successful Agile manager assumes the team is trustworthy and that their ideas are valid.

Failures/Risks

The managers that fail to make the transition to an Agile organization typically display common characteristics.

Command and Control

There are managers who simply cannot give up their command and control demeanor; it is how they manage, and it is inherent in their style. It can be similar to asking a Marine drill sergeant to let recruits decide how far they are going to run and how clean their barracks need to be—it is just unnatural to them. When working with a company recently, we encountered this type of personality in the Project Management office. When asked what he liked about his current (non-Agile) role, this person said, "I like being able to manage people, control the environment, and manipulate the teams to get the deliverable that I want." A person with this type of philosophy will have a very hard time adjusting to an Agile environment.

How can managers overcome their command and control tendencies? First, we must accept that some are willing and able to change and some are not, and that the organization must respond accordingly (see the discussion of executive roles in the next section). Many previously controlling personalities have successfully shifted to Agile by understanding its benefits and the important role that they can play in optimizing the team. Some of these techniques have already been mentioned; here are some additional details.

- **Ask questions instead of offering solutions.** If a manager can shift into a questioning mode, he or she can help the team to self-organize and establish trust. This could be as simple as asking "What do you think we should do next?"
- **Direct others to the team.** If someone from another organization has a question or needs information, instead of immediately answering, as command and control personalities tend to do, a manager can encourage that person to ask the team directly. This will position the team as the authoritative source of information.

- **Do not talk.** When a command and control manager attends a meeting, typically the first impulse is to actively contribute to the meeting to advance the discussion. As a start to break down this tendency, a manager can try not to speak during an entire meeting. The silence might be profound, particularly if the team is conditioned to receiving direction. The manager can embrace the silence and let the team members fill it with their ideas and suggestions.

It is difficult to change a way of thinking that likely served managers well throughout their careers, and that is why Agile asks people to stretch outside of their comfort zones. The results can speak for themselves when empowered and self-organizing teams deliver amazing business results to the organization.

Territorial

Some managers truly believe that they "own" a process or an application and that no one should make decisions on that process or application without their involvement and consent. Agile is very collaborative and customer-focused, and if a solution is presented that crosses systems or changes workflows to enhance the experience for the customer, that effort needs to be allowed to proceed without deference to artificial organizational boundaries.

As an example, we had a situation where a manager believed that he owned a gateway service, and to maximize the speed of the gateway application, no business rules could reside in the gateway; all business rule logic needed to be performed by other systems. This is actually a wise architectural guideline to drive performance, but if a team has a need where putting business rules into the gateway might make the most sense, then that discussion needs to be able to proceed without territorialism. The decision may not change, but the ability to have a productive and value-focused conversation is critical to the organization.

Ownership is a difficult challenge within Agile because we want people to feel accountable for their work. Some could view territorialism as ownership, which implies accountability. The difference that Agile presents is that territorialism for the sake of ownership is bad; accountability for the sake of delivering business value to the organization is good. Whenever managers find themselves feeling uncomfortable about what is being suggested for "their" application, the best course of action is to step away from the technical details of the situation and dive into the business problem that they are trying to solve. The better we understand the end users' pain point, the better we can devise solutions, without undue deference to a particular system or workflow. Looking through the eyes of the customer can tear down territorial boundaries quickly.

Team Oversight

Another failure that comes up from time to time involves managers who simply cannot let go of the team: They continue to distribute work to team members, thwarting their ability to self-organize. Managers who attend and actively participate in the daily stand-up are not allowing the team to self-organize, and those who dictate roles on the team are not helping the Agile environment.

How can managers overcome their need to get involved in day-to-day decisions and team oversight? One of the fastest cures to this problem is to stop attending the meetings. This happened at Cayman Design, where a manager chose to stop attending the meetings and would get the necessary information from the transparency Agile afforded. At first, the manager's absence slowed the team down because they believed they needed her to make key decisions. Over time, the team realized that the manager was not going to attend the meetings, so they needed to solve their own problems and come up with their own recommendations. It can be a difficult transition, but there are simple ways to become more Agile. It is important to note that an Agile transformation does not happen overnight: Managers do not move in one motion from being controlling and territorial to being collaborative and enabling, nor do teams accept the accountability of becoming self-organizing and decisive in short order. Organizations must be thoughtful and deliberate with the Agile adoption, always striving to embrace the Agile principles and continuously improve.

> **Review 2** At this point, the reader should be able to answer Review Questions 6–10.

An Executive's Viewpoint

Executives play a critical role in an Agile transformation, because they hold the power in terms of budget and personnel resources to either back the Agile transformation or reinforce the ways of the past. They also have the opportunity (and obligation) to lead by example, because others in the organization are surely watching to see if situations are handled differently, now that they are an "Agile" organization.

What Is Different?

How an executive's role changes within Agile is interesting. Many executives are the sponsors of the Agile transformation without a deep realization that their role will also be altered. Outlined next are several examples of how executives are asked to stretch and evolve in an Agile environment.

Embracing Evolving Requirements

Executives are tasked with budgets, milestones, and reporting progress to the board of directors, shareholders, and others who have invested in the success of the company. The executives need to be wise stewards of the financial resources that they control to ensure company success; that is a heavy responsibility, which makes many executives want to chart a clear path before a dime is spent. This type of thinking works well in a Waterfall environment, where we complete our requirements before we utilize our often expensive development resources. However, the ever-increasing pace of change in the marketplace makes it increasingly difficult to map out an entire project before we even begin. Agile asks executives to shift from operating capital budgets with robust (though often inaccurate) business cases to an environment of rapid delivery and inspection. For example, a company wants to replace its mainframe system with a more modern, scalable architecture. In the past, a project would be kicked off to assess every application on the mainframe and what it would take to move that application elsewhere. What are the integration points? the risk factors? the expense? the required resources? the schedule? And much more. The project management team would pore over documentation, create massive spreadsheets, and make thousands of assumptions to present a plan to the executive team. It would likely be a multimillion-dollar project with a lengthy timeline. This type of activity provides security to the executives because they can see the entire project laid out, and they believe they can anticipate the cost to completion. The problem with this approach is that assumptions have been layered onto assumptions within the business plan because there is no way to answer all of the complex questions before beginning an effort of this size.

Agile advocates for a different approach. Let's just try to replace one minor application in the mainframe. We will keep the scope very small, we will deliver frequently, and we will inspect our results often, allowing us to course-correct if necessary. With the learning gained from the first effort, we will embark on the next effort, and so on. The organization gains much more predictability in the incremental deliverables, and the wise Agile executives are courageous enough to present this new philosophy and information flow to their investors.

Respecting the Priorities

Executives in all organizations participate in different conversations than the developers and managers, and this leads to slightly different perspectives. If an executive has just been grilled by an existing customer over a problem in the product, or by a high-margin prospect who will sign the contract only if a specific feature is added, it is common for the executive to place high priority on that immediate feedback. Keeping customers happy and gaining new business are critical to the organization and its longevity, so executives are justified in their sense of urgency. This becomes detrimental in an Agile organization when the executive priority disrupts the current work that has been fully groomed, as described in Chapter 6, and has been committed to by the development team. Stopping their work in progress is hazardous and often unnecessary. What an experienced Agile executive will do is understand and respect the current priority projects being delivered and will send the request to the appropriate product owner to begin exploring all of the details of the new request. The executive that says "stop everything and work on this" when "this" is likely ill-defined and not fully understood creates a chaotic environment where the teams are not able to deliver on their commitments.

Executives came to be in their positions because they are decisive, action-oriented and results-driven, so their first impulse is to mandate an immediate response. However, respecting the existing priorities, providing the team with an opportunity to clarify the details and examine the best solution, and allowing the team to finish the work currently in flight will lead to much more consistent and predictable results.

Staying the Course

An Agile transformation is challenging for most organizations. Some command and control managers will fight the change, offering dire predictions of failed projects as examples of why this is a bad idea. Developers may not embrace the increased accountability and transparency, and some may choose to leave the organization. There are new expenses in the form of seating arrangements, training, and Agile tools that may stress the budget. Agile transformations also have a history of bringing chronic issues that the organization has ignored for years to the surface where they must be confronted. All of these are reasons why an executive might abandon the effort and simply revert to what is comfortable (but ineffective). Any change worth making is going to require effort, and Agile is no different. The strong Agile executive will work through these issues without wavering on the commitment to Agile.

Let's examine these instances individually to identify the best reaction by a truly Agile executive.

- **The command and control manager is uncomfortable.** This often takes the form of bringing up the multitude of ways that Agile could fail—the teams cannot self-organize, our clients are too demanding, our software is too complex, we are impeded by government regulations, our business partners are too inexperienced, and so on. Each of these hurdles, and many others, has been overcome by organizations with Agile. The Agile executive needs to resist the urge to slow down the implementation and carefully think through every possible scenario. Instead, he or she should embrace the "inspect and adapt" mantra of Agile by moving rapidly and carefully forward and learn from every decision. Constantly inspect the implementation and make course corrections as necessary. Do not let fear of what *could* happen delay the positive outcomes of what *will* happen.

- **Developers self-select out of the organization.** There are certainly people in every organization that we believe we cannot live without; their domain expertise or years of experience make them assets to the organization. Agile supports these experts and provides them with opportunities to contribute in ways they may never have before. The employees that see and desire the collaboration and accountability associated with Agile are critical to the longevity of the organization. Those that are threatened by Agile and want to withhold their expertise or refuse to try new alternatives will ultimately hold the organization back. Certainly, their departure is disruptive, but it can and should be managed by an Agile executive. Creating an environment of continuous learning involves identifying and rewarding those who want to join the transformation.
- **New expenses.** Agile does not break a budget, nor does it come for free. If you are truly committed to changing an organization's culture, then spending money on training and tools and possibly even new hires is an investment—not an expense. Asking an organization to convert to Agile without any additional budget is not demonstrating the necessary commitment to the change. Agile executives need to "put their money where their mouth is" and authorize the appropriate expenditures to ensure success.

An Agile executive will stay the course when confronted with issues and concerns. Making an Agile transformation cannot be optional to the organization: Either the executives are committed or they are not. There can be no wavering, because the minute an executive indicates that it is acceptable to continue with the old ways of doing business, many people will fall back into their old, comfortable patterns that will not deliver the desired results.

Successes

Agile executives that are committed to the transformation can chart a meaningful path for their teams by focusing on the right things that will drive true culture change.

Focus on Sustainability

One of the 12 Agile principles states that "Agile processes promote sustainable development. The sponsors, developers, and users should be able to maintain a constant pace indefinitely." Promoting this is a critical success factor for Agile executives.

We need to avoid burnout amongst the teams. When organizations adopt Agile, there is typically a good deal of enthusiasm and a desire to work hard and deliver compelling results. Then as the Agile implementation continues, some teams can suffer from long hours, which can create an unsustainable environment. Bob Hartman wrote about this in a July 2009 blog:

> If the pace of the team is not sustainable several undesirable effects are likely to occur:
>
> - Defects will increase. Tired teams let more defects through.
> - Work output will decrease. Tired teams do less work in more time!
> - Morale will drastically decrease. This may lead to employee turnover at a most unfortunate time in the project.
> - The blame game will become common. (Not our fault you didn't say X. I said X. Did not. Did so . . .)
> - The team starts to abandon good practices for those that "seem" faster. Sorry, but test-driven development (TDD) is actually faster than just writing the code and throwing it over the wall to QA! (Hartman 2009)

The responsibility for sustainability often lies with executives because they can control the resources and, to some extent, the expectations of the organization. If executives make commitments to customers that are unreasonable or fail to provide teams with the tools and training that they need, then the executives are contributing to an unsustainable environment where good people can become frustrated, which either affects the quality of their work or may even encourage them to leave the organization. Most employees want to work hard and accomplish significant goals, but they require an environment that facilitates their success.

Focus on Technical Excellence

Another of the 12 Agile principles focuses on technical excellence by stating: "Continuous attention to technical excellence and good design enhances agility." A strong Agile executive can have a tremendously positive impact on this idea by making sure the teams have both the time and the resources to make wise architecture decisions that will allow the application to scale and perform. Executives who want teams to rush to designs or build point solutions are not allowing them to do their best work. Technical excellence pays dividends not just today but into the future, because a well-designed platform can handle evolving requirements and additional features. A poorly architected solution will result in convoluted designs to accomplish future goals. Jeff Sutherland, a signer of the Agile Manifesto and a creator of these principles, finds that one of the biggest remaining problems for Agile teams is that they do not demand technical excellence (Sutherland 2011).

An Agile executive has an opportunity to influence this, just as a university professor does. By forcing team members to slow down enough to think things through—and giving them the time and latitude to do so—both professors and executives encourage thoughtfulness and deliberate decision making. Rushing and setting unrealistic expectations compromise technical excellence.

Focus on Simplicity

There are many wonderful quotes about the value of simplicity and how hard it is to achieve, including one by Leonardo da Vinci: "Simplicity is the ultimate sophistication" (Goodreads 2013).

An Agile executive that understands and values simplicity can propel the organization forward. Simplicity can be utilized in an Agile implementation in several ways. The first is with the implementation itself. Being flexible in an Agile implementation means embracing the unknown and trying new things. If an organization tries to overplan an Agile transformation and think of every possible roadblock that could be encountered, they will strive for perfection and get stuck in a lengthy (and Waterfall-like) planning stage.

The Agile organization that understands simplicity will try different small steps to learn what will work best for the organization. Continuous learning by inspecting and adapting allows for a simple approach to Agile.

The second way that an Agile executive can embrace simplicity is with the corporate or product objectives. When goals are too ambitious or expectations are too varied, it leads to an organization that is fragmented and chasing too many disparate deliverables.

Steve Jobs once said, "People think focus means saying yes to the thing you've got to focus on. But that's not what it means at all. It means saying no to the hundred other good ideas that there are" (Griggs 2012).

An Agile executive knows that simplicity and precise focus enable the teams to deliver great work.

Failures/Risks

How can Agile executives fail when it comes to an Agile implementation? There are many things that even well-meaning executives do that sabotage the Agile efforts of their teams.

Not Honoring Commitments

One of the most common mistakes that executives make is not allowing the teams to honor their commitments. Looking at Scrum as our example, executives need to adhere to the sacredness of the sprint. What does this mean? It means that once a sprint goal is committed to, there should be no changes to that goal. This is especially difficult for executives because there is always some crisis or customer request or great idea that an executive wants the team to investigate immediately, and there is a tendency for executives to pull the team off their sprint commitment to work on the latest critical task. The executives that refrain from allowing their urgent requests to disrupt the team are more successful in their Agile adoptions. Truly, it is a sign of executive commitment to the process and the methodology if they honor this one aspect. Mike Cohn (2010) is very firm on this issue: "Nothing is allowed to change within the sprint. The team commits to a set of work on the first day and then expects its priorities to remain unchanged for the length of the sprint" (p. 279).

Are there instances where the sprint must be interrupted? Absolutely. If one of your production servers goes down and your developers need to restore the system, then that is clearly a priority over new development. If you are under attack from hackers (such as a DDoS attack), then the developers may need to work on an immediate patch. Those situations notwithstanding, there are many more instances where the "crises" can and should wait while the team works on their current sprint commitment.

A strong Agile executive should have the power and conviction to keep fellow executives in line so the sacredness of the sprint can remain intact. Executives who have not fully embraced Agile or do not appreciate the impacts of their decisions on the organization can create chaos and confusion by not honoring the teams' commitments.

Not Engaging the Rest of the Organization

Another common failure of an Agile executive is not enlisting the support of the other departments within the company. Often the Agile executive sponsor is the chief information officer (CIO) or another leader in the IT organization, which is where most Agile implementations start. It is imperative that the CIO or Agile sponsor capture the attention and support of the other department leaders to ensure the success of the implementation. This is particularly critical with "the business": If the Agile implementation is viewed as an IT-only endeavor, then the organizations that need to contribute clarity regarding business value and priority may not actively participate, which can doom the Agile efforts. The people in marketing or product management or various customer-facing departments have the best sense of the marketplace, competitive environment, and customer behavior, and therefore are the best people to make the prioritization decisions so the most important and valuable efforts are worked on first. If those organizations do not participate in the Agile transformation, then the opportunity for success is greatly diminished. The Agile executive sponsor needs to illustrate to peers the importance of their involvement and the value that they will derive from participating. Gaining their commitment often requires executive alignment and usually cannot be accomplished by those lower in the organization. The time commitment and the changes to the way that work progresses through to completion will affect many organizations, and their buy-in is absolutely critical. An ineffective Agile executive may ask the team to solicit the necessary involvement from the other organizations, but this passive approach typically does not deliver the appropriate visibility and alignment. The Agile executive sponsor needs to convince his or her peers that Agile is right for the whole organization.

Valuing the Wrong Metrics

Executives play such a critical role in an Agile transformation, and often they may not realize the messages that are sent to the organization when decisions are made, even with the best intentions; metrics are a perfect example of this concept. A well-meaning executive can completely derail an Agile implementation by trying to measure the wrong things. Let's look at a few examples.

- Actual time taken to complete a task vs. estimated time
- Velocity of Team A vs. Team B
- Number of stories with acceptance criteria vs. those without

Each of these metrics may sound reasonable, but they could drive the wrong behavior. With the first example, one might wonder: What does the organization value, working software? or precise estimates? Of course, Agile would like the estimates to be relevant and close to the level of effort required, but we want our developers to spend their time writing great software, not doing extensive research to ensure accuracy in their estimates. Defining the wrong metric could force developers and testers to spend time in unproductive efforts.

In the second example, velocity, or the amount of work that a team can accomplish during a sprint (described in detail in Chapter 6), is a tool used to predict the amount of work that a team can commit to, not as a measure of productivity. First, two teams could use different measures of effort—a medium-sized task or an eight-point story (also described in Chapter 6) might mean very different things to different teams. Second, a dip in velocity might have nothing to do with productivity: If Team B has three developers at a training class, then the amount of work they can accomplish is reduced, but not because the team is less productive.

Finally, with the third example, the premise behind Agile requirements gathering is that we are learning and negotiating on the best way to deliver maximum business value. If we are measuring the performance of how stories are written, we may unknowingly reduce the conversation about that story.

Agile executives need to be very careful about the metrics they choose to ensure that incentives are provided for the correct behaviors. Measuring success in an Agile environment is different from traditional metrics, as we now place a heavy emphasis on customer satisfaction, frequent delivery of working software, and continuous learning.

Review 3 At this point, the reader should be able to answer Review Questions 11–15.

Conclusion

The organizational culture impacts to an Agile transformation are profound. Successful implementations need support from the team members, management, and executives to embrace new ways of completing work and collaborating. Every role in the organization will be affected in some way, and by understanding what is different and what drives success in each role, we are better positioned for the increase in productivity, responsiveness, and customer satisfaction that can be delivered by becoming Agile.

Summary

- Organizational culture is the accumulation of years of interactions and experiences that have formed into a belief system of how work progresses and how decisions are made. To shift the culture to Agile, the organization must be willing to embrace new roles, workflows, and definitions of success.
- Self-organizing teams have working agreements, select the work that they will own, cross-train and support one another, and create a dynamic that plays to the strengths of each individual.
- Continuous improvement on teams means that members can solve their own problems without outside intervention and they are working to improve not only the product but also team effectiveness.
- Frequent delivery of working software is central to Agile success. This creates a meaningful feedback loop for the team to incorporate.

- Agile breaks down organizational silos and creates teams where developers, testers, and requirements owners all depend on each other for shared success.
- In Agile, teams should be colocated to facilitate collaboration. This can be challenging for teams with virtual or international participants, so optimizing the physical workspace and collaboration tools is a priority.
- High-performing teams have excellent team dynamics where individuals know and respect each other and can resolve differences productively.
- Effective teams are adaptable to the changes that come with continuous improvement in Agile, and they demonstrate a commitment to completing the deliverables even when circumstances are not ideal.
- Managers in an Agile transformation have to make adjustments as well, and some managers will struggle to embrace their new roles and enable the teams.
- One area where managers can assist an Agile implementation is to refrain from offering solutions to the teams. Instead, they should ask thoughtful questions to help the teams reach their own conclusions.
- Another way that managers can accelerate an Agile deployment is to clear roadblocks for the team. This is particularly helpful when it comes to resource and staffing discussions, because the manager may be able to address impacts to the budget more effectively than the team can.
- When it comes to trusting the team, some managers follow Douglas McGregor's Theory X style of management, where they believe employees are lazy and need oversight to monitor their performance and behavior. This style of management will struggle to adopt Agile.
- Executives in organizations adopting Agile will find that their roles have changed too. Since executives often hold the budget resources and the decision-making power, their involvement in the transformation is critical.
- Executives can support Agile by understanding and embracing evolving requirements. Those that want comprehensive plans and business cases will fail to reap the benefits of iterative development, rapid feedback loops, and continuous learning.
- Executives are in a unique position with Agile to respect the commitments and priorities. They hear complaints and feedback from a wide variety of stakeholders and may be inclined to immediately act on that feedback without understanding the disruption and negative impacts to the team.
- Executives that truly want Agile to be a part of the ongoing organizational culture need to dedicate budget dollars to its implementation; it

might be with regard to tools, training, staffing, consulting, or a number of other things. A transformation of this magnitude requires investment.

Review 4 At this point, the reader should be able to answer Review Questions 16–20.

Interview with Scott Ambler

Scott W. Ambler is the Senior Consulting Partner of Scott Ambler + Associates, working with organizations around the world to help them to improve their software processes. He provides training, coaching, and mentoring in disciplined Agile and Lean strategies at both the project and organizational level. Scott is the founder of the Agile Modeling (AM), Agile Data (AD), Disciplined Agile Delivery (DAD), and Enterprise Unified Process (EUP) methodologies. He is the (co)author of several books, including *Disciplined Agile Delivery*, *Refactoring Databases*, *Agile Modeling*, *Agile Database Techniques*, *The Object Primer* (3rd ed.), and *The Enterprise Unified Process*. Scott is a senior contributing editor with *Dr. Dobb's Journal,* and he blogs about DAD at http://DisciplinedAgileDelivery.com. Scott is also a Founding Member of the Disciplined Agile Consortium (DAC), the certification body for disciplined Agile. He can be reached at scott@scottambler.com, and his web site is http://scottwambler.wordpress.com.

Kristin and Sondra: How do you know when a company is culturally ready to adopt Agile?

Scott: My initial thought was "you just know," but clearly that's not the answer you're looking for. People, at all levels of IT and at least in key positions within the business, need to recognize that they need to deliver IT solutions more effectively. They need to recognize that the old, documentation-heavy ways simply aren't working, and in many cases they need to stop lying to themselves about this. They need to recognize that greater collaboration, greater flexibility, and the need to embrace some kinds of uncertainty are the order of the day.

Kristin and Sondra: What are the most significant differences between Agile and Waterfall, from a cultural perspective?

Scott: Agile focuses on collaborative, iterative, high-value activities that focus on producing solutions that meet the needs of stakeholders. The challenge is that Agile teams need to be skilled and disciplined enough to pull this off, while the stakeholders need to be actively involved with the Agile teams. Waterfall teams often take documentation-heavy approaches in the name of risk reduction. The challenge is that Waterfall strategies prove to be higher risk in practice, but because they involve so many perceived "checks and balances," the people involved are unable to recognize the very clear risks they are taking on.

Kristin and Sondra: How important are things like the seating arrangements for a successful Agile adoption?

Scott: Communication and collaboration are key success factors on Agile projects, so how people are physically organized is important. I've explored this issue in several surveys [see http://Ambysoft.com/surveys/], and it's clear that the closer people are to one another, including to stakeholders, the higher the success rates of project teams. Even something as simple as putting people in cubes can lower the success rate.

Kristin and Sondra: How do successful teams integrate virtual (and perhaps global) team members?

Scott: The best strategy is to not take on these sorts of risks at all. If you choose to, do so with your eyes wide open. Try to have distributed subteams, not dispersed individuals. Fly key people around between sites. Fly key people together at critical times in the project, particularly at the beginning when you're making fundamental strategy decisions. Adopt communication technologies, in particular video conferencing. And finally, adopt distributed development tools, such as IBM Jazz or Microsoft TFS.

References and Further Reading

Adkins, Lyssa. (2010). *Coaching Agile teams: A companion for Scrum masters, Agile coaches, and project managers in transition.* Boston: Addison-Wesley. Kindle edition.

Ambler, Scott, and Lines, Mark. (2012). *Disciplined Agile delivery: A practitioner's guide to Agile software delivery in the enterprise.* Boston: IBM Press.

Atkinson, Philip. (2012). Creating culture change. http://www.philipatkinson.com/Philip-Atkinson-CreatingCultureChange.pdf.

Beck, Kent. (2000). *Extreme Programming explained.* Boston: Addison-Wesley.

Cockburn, Alistair. (2006). *Agile software development: A cooperative game* (2nd ed.). Boston: Addison-Wesley.

Cockburn, Alistair. (2010). Seven properties of highly successful projects in Crystal Clear. http://alistair.cockburn.us/7+Properties+of+Highly+Successful+Projects+from+Crystal+Clear.

Cohn, Mike. (2010). *Succeeding with Agile: Software development using Scrum.* Boston: Addison-Wesley.

Demarco, Tom, et al. (2008). *Adrenaline junkies and template zombies.* New York: Dorset House.

Derby, E., Larsen, D., and Schwaber, K. (2006). *Agile retrospectives: Making good teams great.* Frisco, TX: Pragmatic Bookshelf.

Goodreads. (2013). https://www.goodreads.com/author/quotes/13560.Leonardo_da_Vinci.

Gower, Bob. (2013). *Agile business: A leader's guide to harnessing complexity.* Boulder, CO: Rally Software Development.

Griggs, Brandon. (2012). Ten great quotes from Steve Jobs. http://www.cnn.com/2012/10/04/tech/innovation/steve-jobs-quotes.

Hartman, Bob. (2009). New to Agile? Work at a sustainable pace. Blog entry, July 24. http://www.agileforall.com/2009/07/new-to-agile-work-at-a-sustainable-pace.

Layton, Mark C. (2012). *Agile project management for dummies.* Indianapolis, IN: Wiley.

McGregor, Douglas. (1960). *The human side of enterprise.* New York: McGraw Hill.

Schwaber, Ken, and Beedle, Mike. (2002). *Agile software development with Scrum.* Upper Saddle River, NJ: Prentice Hall.

Schwaber, Ken, and Sutherland, Jeff. (2012). *Software in 30 days: How Agile managers beat the odds, delight their customers, and leave competitors in the dust.* Hoboken, NJ: Wiley.

Sutherland, Jeff. (2011). Ten year Agile retrospective: How we can improve in the next ten years. http://msdn.microsoft.com/en-us/library/hh350860(v=vs.100).aspx.

VersionOne. (2013). 8th annual state of Agile survey. http://www.versionone.com/pdf/2013-state-of-agile-survey.pdf.

Review Questions

Review 1

1. In what ways does self-organization change the day-to-day life of a developer?
2. Who should the team look to first to solve their problems?
3. Why would frequent delivery of working software make a developer uncomfortable?
4. What do successful teams do to incorporate virtual team members?
5. How does altering the seating arrangements change team dynamics in Agile?

Review 2

6. Instead of offering solutions to the team, what should an Agile manager do?
7. What is an example of a type of roadblock that an Agile manager could clear?
8. What are the characteristics of a Theory X manager, according to McGregor?
9. How can an Agile manager demonstrate trust in a team?
10. What are some managerial traits that are incompatible with Agile?

Review 3

11. What are examples of items that require additional budget from an Agile executive?
12. How can executives help with sustainability on Agile teams?
13. Why might an executive want to change the priorities for an Agile team immediately?
14. Who typically serves as the executive sponsor of an Agile implementation?
15. What are examples of metrics that drive the wrong behavior, and why?

Review 4

16. What are some of the practices to ensure that international resources are effectively integrated into the team?
17. Identify several roles outside of the IT organization that are affected by an Agile transformation.
18. Why is it so important to enable teams to honor their commitments?
19. Why would someone choose to leave the organization (resign) rather than move to an Agile environment?
20. What should be done when an aspect of the Agile transformation is not working or delivering the desired results?

Chapter 3

Understanding the Different Types of Agile

Learning Objectives

- Understand the meaning of an Agile organization
- Become familiar with the Agile approaches and tools that are available
- Review the Agile certifications that are available
- Read an interview with the creator of the Crystal Family

This chapter describes some of the more widely used Agile tools that are available, describes the similarities and differences between Agile methodologies, and illustrates how Cayman Design has implemented these techniques. Table 3.1 on the following page provides an overview.

How do you know when a software development organization has become Agile? Is there such a thing as a completely Agile organization? An **Agile organization** is quite simply one that is adaptive to change. This could be the software development arm of a company or any other area, such as marketing or finance. These areas have put policies and tools in place that enable them to be highly reactive to issues and opportunities as they arise.

An **Agile software development organization** is one that uses Agile tools, techniques, and cultural norms to develop their products. Becoming an Agile organization is more of a journey than a destination. Most organizations use a

Table 3.1 *Comparing Agile Methodologies*

Agile Methodology	Emphasis	Founder(s)
Extreme Programming (XP)	Efficiency, customer focus and feedback, and quality	Kent Beck
Scrum	Teaming, organizing work	Jeff Sutherland and Ken Schwaber
Feature-Driven Development	Iterative development of user-focused features	Jeff De Luca
Dynamic Systems Development Method (DSDM)	Structured approach to rapid development, collection of best practices	DSDM Consortium
Lean Software Development	Eliminate work that does not create customer value	Mary and Tom Poppendieck
Kanban Method	Visualize and manage workflow, just-in-time development	David J. Anderson
Crystal Family	People, communication, process rigor maps to product and organizational dynamics	Alistair Cockburn

combination of Agile tools and methodologies that best support their goals and objectives. To date, there is no certification process that an organization can undergo to become an official Agile-certified software development organization. There are, however, Agile certifications that individual team members can pursue to distinguish them as Agile experts, such as the Scrum Master certification and the Agile Certified Professional from the Project Management Institute. More details on such certifications are covered at the end of this chapter.

Extreme Programming (XP)

The idea of Extreme Programming started at Chrysler Motors in 1996 with a payroll project named the Chrysler Comprehensive Compensation System (C3). The project team, led by Kent Beck, was struggling with how to release high-quality code much faster and more efficiently, and as a result morphed their development process to be efficient, with a quality focus. In 1999, the popularity of Extreme Programming took off when the ideas developed during the C3 project were documented in a book written by Beck called *Extreme Programming Explained*.

Techniques and principles from Extreme Programming are now some of the most popular in Agile software development and focus on the following key themes:

- Frequent releases, short development cycles
- Pair programming
- Regular builds and integration tests
- Quality and avoiding code breakage
- Simplicity of code, coding only what is needed
- Rapid and regular feedback

Frequent Releases, Short Development Cycles

One of the most fundamental changes that XP introduced was the idea of smaller and more frequent development cycles. Traditionally, software had been developed using a lengthy design proposal and modification phase followed by the coding of all of the requirements for the new version of the product. Figure 3.1 provides a summary of the traditional and XP approaches to software development. In contrast, XP practitioners argued that code is more useful than extensive documentation and that developers should put their focus on developing quality code rather than on documenting what they plan to code.

The process also relies heavily on an automated unit-testing strategy known as **test-driven development (TDD)**. When practicing TDD, developers write automated unit tests before writing the corresponding production code; code is not considered complete until all automated tests pass. Test-driven development is discussed in more detail in Chapter 8, "Tracking and Reporting."

Pair Programming

Pair programming is an exercise where two developers work together to create production-ready code (see Figure 3.2). Ideally, paired developers would write all production code. When pairing is not possible, a developer should write nonproduction code. Pair programming has become a popular XP tool because code is regularly reviewed by more than one person, resulting in higher-quality code. It also exposes team members to a broader range of the product's code, which aids in cross-training and learning development best practices from one another. Some teams pair developers and testers so the code gets an early review and to also help testers learn more about new fixes or features.

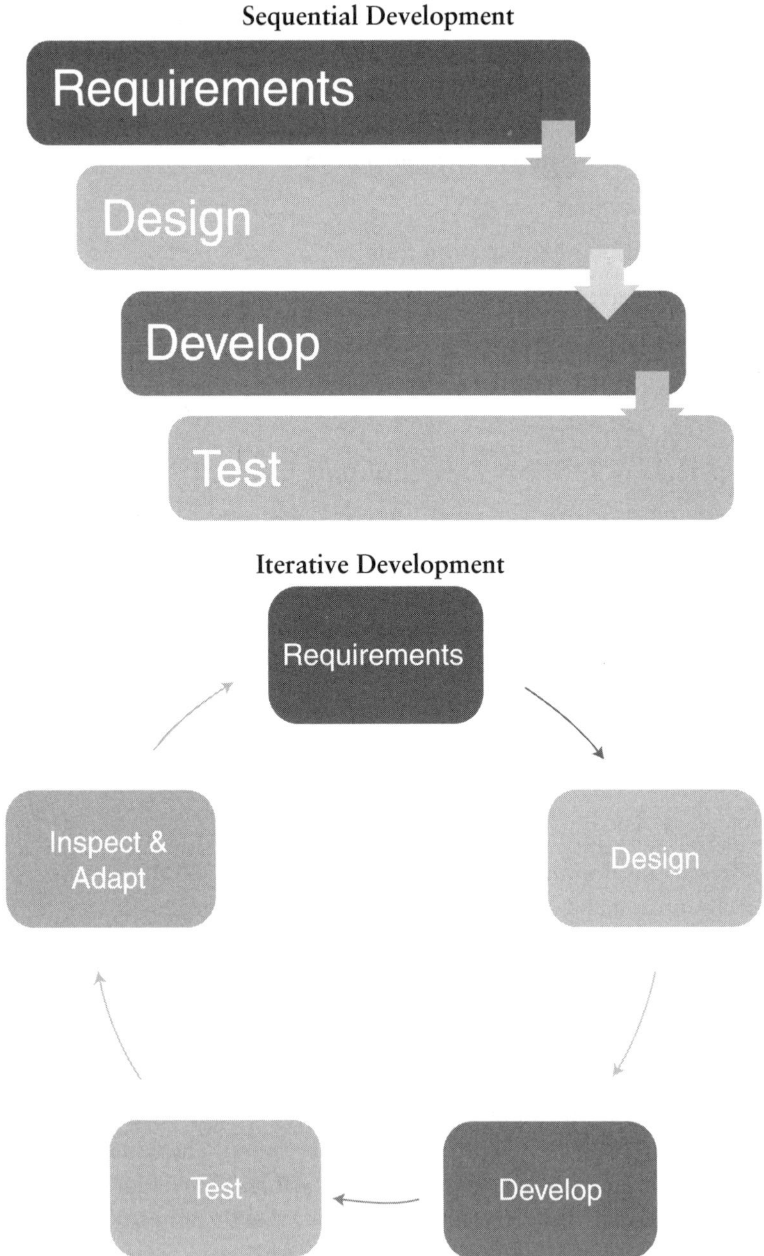

Figure 3.1 *Sequential versus iterative software development*

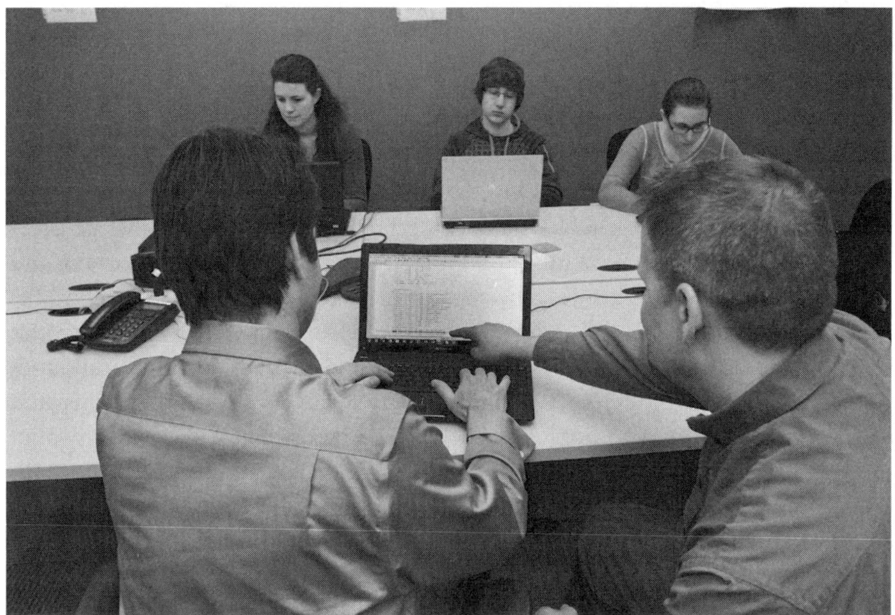

Figure 3.2 *Software engineers pair programming*

There are some basic guidelines that programmers should follow when they are pairing. The first is that the development space should accommodate two developers working side by side. The developers share a keyboard and either use dual screens or share a large screen. Both developers should be active participants in the creation of the code, and the pairing should end when one or both developers feel tired and unable to concentrate.

Regular Builds, Integration Tests, and Rapid Feedback

Regular builds and integration tests were introduced in XP to alleviate the problem of high defect counts during builds and code integration. Previously, it was not uncommon to have a weekly build or code integration at the end of the development cycle. XP encourages a minimum of a daily build with code integration happening every time a developer checks in new code. Some organizations that have adopted this XP technique use a flashing light or a siren if new code that is checked in to the code build introduces an error; this rapid feedback enables the developer to respond quickly to the error so that quality builds can be maintained. This also makes fixing errors easier because developers are working with code they recently developed.

Scrum

According to the Webster dictionary definition, a "scrum" is a rugby play in which the forwards of each side come together in a tight formation and struggle to gain possession of the ball using their feet when it is tossed in among them. Rugby is a game that cannot be won by a single superstar; it takes a full team, working closely together, to be successful. The same is true with Scrum software development. Each member of the Scrum team is vitally important and must contribute if the team is to be successful. When referencing a method for developing products, four founders are credited with the use of the term **Scrum**: Ken Schwaber of Advanced Development Methods as well as Jeff Sutherland, John Scumniotales, and Jeff McKenna of Easel Corporation. Jeff Sutherland developed the Scrum methodology in 1993, and he teamed with Ken Schwaber to take the idea of Scrum development public when they presented their methodology to fellow product developers at the 1995 Object-Oriented Programming, Systems, Languages, and Applications (OOPSLA) conference. From there, Schwaber and Sutherland continued to combine their ideas into a joint methodology. Eventually Schwaber partnered with Mike Beedle to write *Agile Software Development with Scrum,* which helped to launch Scrum into a more commonplace toolset in the Agile development movement.

Despite Scrum's overwhelming popularity with companies that decide to adopt Agile methodologies, many are still uncertain about what it entails. Many consider XP to have a technical or developer focus, but Scrum tends to address more of the project management and teaming aspects of software development.

Scrum emphasizes the importance of organizing a project into specific durations, known as **time boxes**, that help the team know what they need to focus on each day and encourage a sense of urgency. Work requirements are grouped into chunks of work that can be completed in one- to six-week time frames called **sprints**. All design, development, test, and customer validation work is contained within the sprint; the goal is that by the end of the sprint, the new functionality is ready to deliver to customers.

The product owner selects work requirements for each sprint. The product owner maintains a prioritized list of requirements for the product called a **product backlog**. The requirements are written in the form of **user stories** or stories about the problem that needs to be solved by the requirement. User stories are covered in more detail in Chapter 5, "The New Way to Collect and Document Requirements."

Tracking is also an important part of the Scrum approach. Scrum teams meet daily in what is commonly referred to as a **daily stand-up** or **daily Scrum**

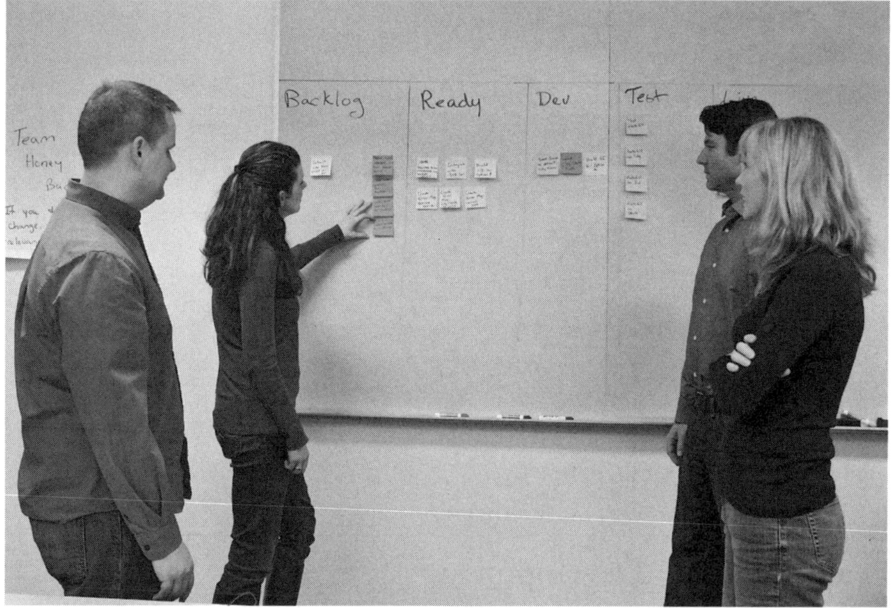

Figure 3.3 *Daily stand-up meeting*

meeting (see Figure 3.3). A **Scrum master** is assigned to lead these meetings to ensure that they remain brief and focused and that all team members have a chance to contribute. These meetings are designed to be short (usually around 15 minutes), and each team member answers the following questions:

- What have I done since yesterday?
- What am I doing today?
- Any roadblocks?

The team also uses **burn down** or **burn up** charts to track progress through the sprint. More information on tracking is covered in Chapter 7, "Testing, Quality, and Integration."

The diagram in Figure 3.4 depicts the general flow of a project using the Scrum methodology.

The future chapters in this book emphasize the Scrum process, because it is the most widely adopted Agile methodology.

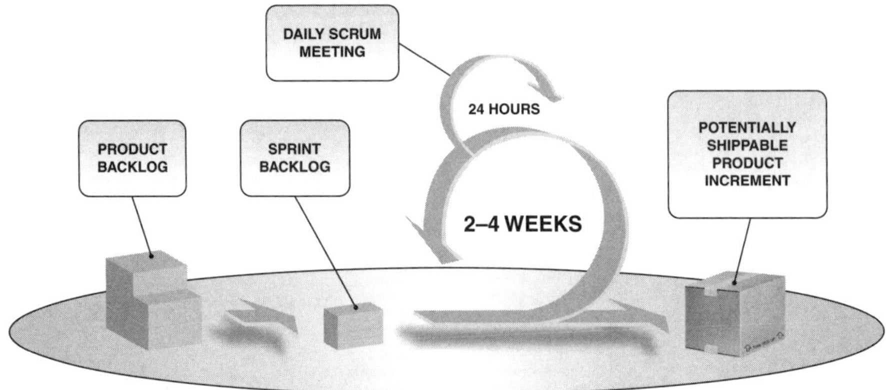

Figure 3.4 *Flow in a Scrum project*

Source: Mountain Goat Software (Mike Cohn).

Feature-Driven Development

Jeff De Luca conceived Feature-Driven Development (FDD) in 1997 in an attempt to deliver software to a customer in Asia using an iterative and efficient approach. De Luca found that by incorporating aspects of Peter Coad's object modeling and blending processes, he could achieve the objective of incrementally delivering user-focused functionality. This methodology is called Feature-Driven Development because the planning and development focus on the specific features that address customer requirements. At his nebulon.com web site, De Luca states that the value of FDD is "to enable the reliable delivery of working software in a timely manner with highly accurate and meaningful information to all key roles inside and outside a project."

The success of this initial use of FDD encouraged De Luca to document the best practices of his approach and share them with other software development professionals. In 1999, he began by teaming up with Peter Coad and Eric Lefebrve on their book, *Java Modeling in Color with UML,* and dedicated a chapter to describing the FDD methodology. He has also published extensive information on his web site (http://www.nebulon.com/fdd/index.html). A few years later, in 2002, Stephen Palmer wrote a more comprehensive book on FDD with Mac Felsing entitled *A Practical Guide to Feature-Driven Development.*

FDD has been adopted by the Agile Alliance as a recognized Agile methodology. Product features are developed in two-week iterations and focus on the following activities:

1. **Create the model**—Perform an initial customer walk-through that determines scope and context and creates the model.
2. **Develop the feature list**—The model determines the features. Features are often described as a sentence in a format that looks something like this:

   <verb> the <something> for/of/to a(n) <something else>.
   <verb> the "<result>" by|for|of|to a(n) <object>

   For example, for a movie review site, the features might say:

   a. Calculate *the* average star rating *for* a movie
   b. Calculate *the* "go" or "don't go" recommendations *for* a movie
   c. List *the* local movie theaters *to* show the current movie locations <calculate> the <average star rating> for a <movie>

Features are then ordered and assigned to classes.

1. **The plan is determined by features**—Unlike other Agile methodologies, FDD advocates that teams create a development plan that is based on ordering features and assigning them to classes. Classes are then assigned to an owning developer.
2. **The design is based on the features**—The owning developer assigns a small set of features that can be developed in two weeks. Detailed sequence diagrams are created based on features, and the overall model is updated to reflect the changes. Classes are written, and a design review is held.
3. **The build is based on the features**—Code is developed based on feedback from the design review. Once the developer completes the code and unit testing, then a code review is held to analyze whether final changes are needed. Final updates to the code are made and the code promoted to the current build.

Dynamic Systems Development Method

Dynamic Systems Development Method (DSDM) was introduced in 1994 as a framework to provide more structure to rapid application development (RAD).

RAD is a product development approach that focuses on creating working prototypes as efficiently as possible by minimizing process rigor and overhead. The DSDM Consortium was formed in London to bring together best practices from practitioners and vendors with a vision for "jointly developing and promoting an independent RAD framework." The DSDM Consortium has remained a nonprofit organization that seeks to promote Agile best practices to its members and the wider development community. They are the owner of the DSDM method and regularly publish updates to the methodology. Their most recent version of the framework, Atern, touts that it helps organizations "deliver the right product at the right time." Project teams must decide which requirements are "musts, shoulds, coulds and won't haves" to meet that objective.

DSDM is part of the Agile Alliance and focuses on the project management aspects of Agile software development and non-IT projects; it is often considered a complementary approach to Extreme Programming. DSDM relies on nine core principles, all of which must be followed to ensure the best chances of a successful project:

1. Active user involvement is critical for any project.
2. Teams must be empowered to make decisions.
3. Teams need to focus on frequent product delivery.
4. Criteria must be in place for an approved deliverable.
5. All development must be done iteratively and delivered incrementally.
6. Any change introduced during development must be reversible.
7. Product requirements are baselined as high-level themes rather than low-level changes or improvements.
8. Product testing is performed throughout the project life cycle.
9. Team interactions are collaborative and cooperative.

In addition to the nine principles, four major phases are used to iterate through during the project, including

1a. **Feasibility Study**—The project team identifies the functionality that will be included, creates and tests a functional prototype, and develops a timeline for the project.

1b. **Business Study**—The business processes and associated requirements are analyzed by the project stakeholders using the MoSCoW requirement prioritization method. MoSCoW prioritizes requirements based on what the product "must have," "should have," "could have," and "won't have." Schedules are developed using the time boxing method to create and schedule and ensure quality can be maintained throughout the project.

2. **Functional Model Iteration**—Requirements from the business study are translated into functional models that are tested and reviewed by user groups. The project team iterates on the functional models with users until there is agreement that the models are ready to proceed to a design prototype.

3. **Design and Build Iteration**—All of the functional models are brought together to create a design prototype; this prototype incorporates all product functions and again is tested and reviewed by user groups. The result is a working prototype that includes user documentation.

4. **Implementation**—The final phase includes user acceptance of the product and implementation in their environment. Users are trained, and the project team reviews the business objectives to ensure the user goals have been achieved.

DSDM relies heavily on time boxing, prototyping, and the MoSCoW rules during the project phases. These tools are discussed in more detail in later chapters. Visit http://www.dsdm.org/ for the latest DSDM framework and best practices.

Lean Software Development

Lean software development stems from the world of manufacturing, which has widely adopted the idea of Lean manufacturing. Lean manufacturing is built on the idea that all processes and resources must directly contribute to creating something of value to the customer; *customer value* is defined as anything that a customer is willing to purchase. Anything outside this scope is considered wasteful, and every effort must be made to eliminate the waste. Lean software development subscribes to the same principles but relates them to the development of software.

In 2003, Mary Poppendieck and Tom Poppendieck penned the first book on this topic, entitled *Lean Software Development: An Agile Toolkit*. Their book describes the seven principles that guide Lean software development; these principles are close derivatives of the Lean manufacturing principles. They offer an additional 22 tools that software developers can use, and illustrate how the Lean principles are applicable to Agile development environments.

Following are the seven principles of Lean software development:

- **Eliminate waste**—Remove anything that does not add customer value
- **Amplify learning**—Regularly test code, learn by doing rather than documenting or planning, gain customer feedback through prototypes
- **Decide as late as possible**—Wait to get facts rather than making assumptions
- **Deliver as fast as possible**—Focus on speed to market
- **Empower the team**—Managers allow team members to make key decisions
- **Build integrity in**—Pieces work together as a whole
- **See the whole**—Focus on the entire product experience rather than the pieces

Lean principles and tools are covered in more detail in Chapter 5.

Review 1 At this point, the reader should be able to answer Review Questions 1–5.

Kanban Method

The **Kanban method** was developed by David J. Anderson, who was interested in "just in time" software delivery and evolving the process to create an optimal system. The word *Kanban* loosely translates to "signboard" in Japanese. A **signboard** is traditionally described as a visual process-management system that tells teams what to produce, when to produce it, and how much to produce.

The visual signboard and work-in-progress pull method, also known as the **Kanban system**, is the most popular tool that organizations adopt when they use the Kanban method. The Kanban system is covered in more detail in Chapter 8.

The Kanban method is based on four key principles:

- **Foster leadership at all levels of the organization**—Everyone in the organization is encouraged to act as leaders, from the entry-level employee to the executive team.
- **Start with what you know**—Kanban is not prescriptive in nature and assumes that organizations are not all the same. Instead, it is important to

understand where you are today and use change management approaches to evolve from that point.

- **Focus on incremental and evolutionary change**—The goal is not to overhaul the process, culture, and product overnight. Instead, it is important to make small but impactful changes often.
- **Respect current methodologies and roles**—The current process was put there for a reason; something about it has worked, and that is why people have continued to use it. It is important to preserve what has worked and to change what is no longer helping the team achieve their goals.

Six core practices are central to the Kanban method:

- **Visualize workflow**—Teams need to visually understand their work so that they can optimize their workflow. The Kanban method often uses a board with columns and cards to show the workflow (see Figure 3.5).
- **Limit work in progress, and pull in new work only when time becomes available**—The team cannot be efficient and focused if too much work

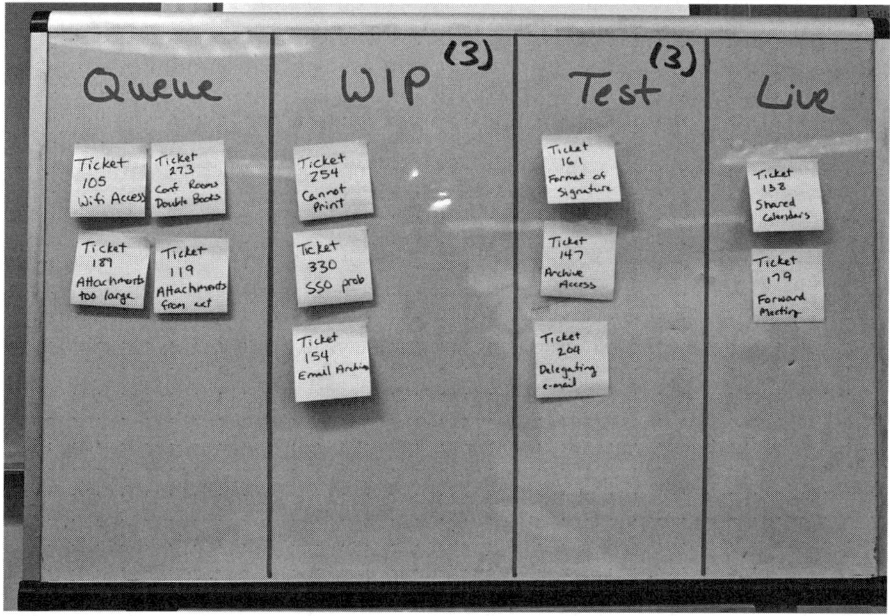

Figure 3.5 *Kanban board*

is on their plate; it is important to focus on one task at a time and not to start a new task until the current task is completed.

- **Manage the flow through the system**—Just as with a relay race, the team needs to understand how the work progresses toward the goal. The team needs to ensure that the appropriate level of work is flowing through the system and that bottlenecks are being kept to a minimum.
- **Provide explicit policies**—The team needs to understand how to work within their organization in order to eliminate ambiguity. For example, a team may enact the policy that they do not pull a new feature until the current feature has been through unit test.
- **Improve collaboratively and evolve experimentally**—A team can best improve if members first have a shared vision and work together to generate ideas for improvement. Evolution cannot happen through guesswork or intuition; the team needs to try new approaches and objectively evaluate their merit.
- **Ensure feedback is part of the process**—Both positive and negative feedback are essential in understanding how the organization needs to change and evolve.

One important difference of Kanban from other key approaches such as XP or Scrum is that it does not rely on iterations. Kanban allows the team to focus by limiting the work that is in progress and advocates a continuous flow of work. Kanban does not prohibit the use of iterations or time boxes, and it is common for teams to use these tools with Kanban, but specific time frames are not considered a necessary element of this approach.

Crystal Family

Alistair Cockburn created the Crystal Family, which advocates that when a team is using an iterative process, the amount of structure should be tailored to the dynamics of the team. It favors choosing the best method for the situation rather than a "one size fits all" approach. This methodology differs from other methodologies in that it focuses on the people over the specific processes or features but shares the belief of other Agile methodologies by emphasizing frequent delivery to users, colocation of teams, and a focus on adaptation through regular reflections.

Cockburn used the term "crystal" for the methodology because no two crystals are exactly the same, based on their unique colors and hardness; the analogy is that no two projects are the same. Also, a color (x) continuum is used to select the number of people needed for the project team and the project "heaviness" that is required: The darker the color, which ranges from clear (quartz) as the lightest to the deepest (sapphire) as the heaviest, the more team members and heavier process would be needed for the project. For example, you would expect a ruby project to have significantly more team members than a quartz project, and it would also require a heavier process (more communication, documentation, coordination). The y continuum signifies the hardness of the project: The higher the number, the more hardness or robustness of the process required. In Crystal, the hardness represents the severity of damage if the system fails to operate properly. Figure 3.6 shows how a project can be evaluated for color (number of team members) and hardness (criticality).

For example, if an organization were working on software that shows a patient's heart rate, then there would be dire consequences if the program failed to show a spiking heart rate and did not warn doctors of an impending heart attack; a project with such serious consequences would rate high on the hardness (criticality) scale. This project would have a low tolerance for error because it is life critical (L), but may not require a large team to develop the product, rating it lower on the color (people involved) scale, in the 20-person range. Given these criteria points, it would fall in the L20 (orange crystal) methodology range. An orange crystal project would likely involve a lot of face-to-face communication, but it would not be as formal because it would not require the formalities of a 500-person team. The fact that it rates high on criticality would introduce the need for extensive testing, more documentation, and close collaboration with the target users.

Rather than give a specific set of guidelines for each color, Cockburn uses case studies to illustrate common approaches that are used for a specific color.

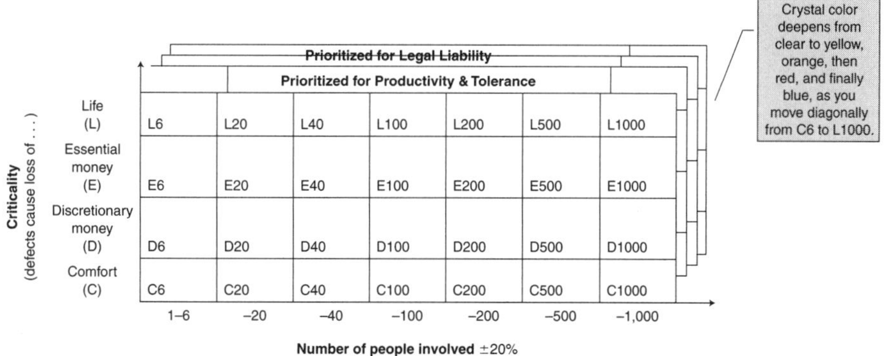

Figure 3.6 *Plotting a Crystal project*

Source: © Alistair Cockburn

There are, however, specific values and rules that are applicable to the entire Crystal Family:

- Values
  - High tolerance
  - Focus on people and communication
- Rules
  - Development must be incremental and last less than four months.
  - The team must conduct reflection sessions before and after the project. Holding a mid-project reflection meeting is also encouraged.

Examples of Crystal projects can be found in Cockburn's 2004 book, *Crystal Clear,* and also in *Agile Software Development: A Cooperative Game,* which was published in 2001 and revised in 2006.

Certification

Certifications are available for practitioners who are interested in identifying themselves as experts in Agile methodologies or in a specific Agile methodology, such as the Rational Unified Process (RUP). Most Agile certifications require documented experience with Agile, the completion of Agile coursework, and in some cases a test. Table 3.2 lists some of the available Agile certifications.

Table 3.2 *Certifications*

Certification Name	Specialty	Granting Organization
Scrum Master (CSM)	Scrum team leadership	Scrum Alliance (http://www.scrumalliance.org/certifications/practitioners/certified-scrummaster-%28csm%29)
Product Owner (CSPO)	Agile product owner	Scrum Alliance (http://www.scrumalliance.org/certifications/practitioners/cspo-certification)
Scrum Developer (CSD)	Scrum development	Scrum Alliance (http://www.scrumalliance.org/certifications/practitioners/csd-certification)
Scrum Professional (CSP)	Scrum methodology	Scrum Alliance (http://www.scrumalliance.org/certifications/practitioners/csp-certification)
Agile Certified Professional (PMI-ACP)	Agile project management	Project Management Institute (http://www.pmi.org)
DSDM (Foundation, Advanced Practitioner, Trainer/Coach/Consultant)	Dynamic Systems Development Method (DSDM)	DSDM Consortium (http://www.dsdm.org/prof-development)
Certified ICAgile Professional	The fundamentals of Agile methods	International Consortium for Agile (http://www.icagile.com/)
Certified FDD Practitioner Certified FDD Project Manager	Feature-Driven Development	Nebulon (http://www.featuredrivendevelopment.com/certification)
Certified Kanban Practitioner	Kanban	LeanKanban University (http://www.leankanbanuniversity.com/certified-training)

Review 2 At this point, the reader should be able to answer Review Questions 6–10.

Implementing Tools and Techniques at Cayman Design

The managers at Cayman Design had heard from colleagues and designers at the company about the benefits that Agile software development had brought to other similar organizations. They decided to send their lead project manager, product manager, developer, and tester to an Agile training course so they could provide recommendations on how to introduce Agile techniques in their design process.

The team returned from the course excited to try some new techniques and recommended that they start with three of the more common tools from Extreme Programming, Scrum, and Kanban. The Cayman Design team brought in an Agile consultant to teach the team the basics, and they got started by reorganizing their work environment to implement these techniques. The team installed Kanban white boards on the walls and arranged pairing stations for team members to use during the workday, and they assigned team members to Scrum teams and developed a code repository that could create daily code builds.

Conclusion

This chapter provides a brief overview of some of the more widely adopted Agile methodologies that are currently being used by software development teams. It is important to understand that one method is not generally better than another; instead, organizations need to understand which method(s) will best help them achieve their goals. Most organizations use a combination of Agile methods and leverage best practices from each; Agile methods are adaptive by nature and encourage experimentation with a variety of approaches. Other methodologies such as RUP and Scalable Agile Framework (SAFe) are linked to Agile methodologies, but are not covered as focus approaches in this book. As Agile methods continue to become mainstream, we expect new methods and tools will be introduced and current methods will evolve.

Summary

- There is not one specific formula for becoming Agile. Agile is a collection of tools and methods that encourage adaptability and best practices.
- Extreme Programming is an Agile approach that encourages rapid development, high-quality code, and close interaction with users. Paired

programming is a widely used technique where team members code together to offer real-time code reviews and cross-training.

- The Scrum methodology focuses on teaming, organizing, and prioritizing the work.
- Feature-Driven Development focuses on the specific features that address customer requirements during the planning and development phase. This method emphasizes timely delivery of working software and strong internal and external communication about the project.
- Dynamic Systems Development Method is a project delivery framework that uses a structured approach to rapid development. A collection of nine principles and four major project phases guides this approach that is often considered complementary to Extreme Programming.
- Lean development derives from the idea of Lean manufacturing. This method encourages teams to eliminate wasteful activities, create a learning environment, and take a holistic view of the product.
- Kanban method uses a pull approach to keep a continual flow of work through the system. The Kanban board is a popular tool that helps teams organize their work into a flowing and visible system.
- Crystal Family advocates that when a team is using an iterative process, the amount of structure should be tailored to the dynamics of the team. It favors choosing the best method for the situation rather than a "one size fits all" approach and uses a color and hardness scale to determine the appropriate amount of structure.
- A variety of certifications are available for a general practitioner (e.g., PMI-ACP); for specific methods, such as a Certified Kanban Practitioner; and for specific roles on Agile teams, such as a Certified Scrum Master (CSM).

Interview with Alistair Cockburn

Dr. Alistair Cockburn, consulting fellow at Humans and Technology, is responsible for helping companies succeed with software development. This includes setting corporate strategy, injecting Agile methods into existing situations, mentoring and coaching staff, designing new processes, improving design quality, managing projects, and assisting in technical design. Dr. Cockburn has been designing hardware and software systems since 1974, leading projects in hardware, software, research, and application systems. He is an internationally recognized expert on Agile and object-oriented software development, appreciated as a collaboration facilitator, and famous as a teacher and speaker.

Kristin and Sondra: Has anything surprised you about the adoption of Agile methodologies in general? Have you experienced any unexpected responses specific to the Crystal Family?

Alistair: Probably what surprised me is not what you might expect. People generally think that I (we) would be surprised by how badly people adopt the Agile methodologies, how they misinterpret the message. This certainly didn't surprise me, and I don't think it really surprised the other authors very much. My view is that you will either be misquoted or ignored, that there isn't a sweet spot in the middle where people understand your message and follow it.

That having been said, one thing did surprise all of us who wrote the manifesto, and that is how quickly it was picked up by the industry—literally within months. We wrote it in February of 2001, and already by summer there were panels on it and a conference already in 2002. It appeared as contractual terms in a contract between two large companies already in late 2003. This is very fast adoption, even though the PMI and IEEE waited almost ten years to pick it up.

The other surprise, to me, personally, was the adoption of reflection workshops and methodology adaptation as core to the Agile approach by the industry. At the time of the 2001 meeting, the idea of holding monthly reflect-and-improve meetings was, to my mind, a long stretch for most teams. The methodologies presented at the 2001 workshop were largely fixed in form, not as malleable as Crystal—they were "agile" but not particularly "adaptive" (for an example to see the difference, RUP was "adaptive" but not particularly "agile"). The surprise to me is that by five years later, most practitioners had associated Agile with making changes to their methodology, as a core concept and practice. This surprise was a welcome and happy surprise to me, since adaptive methodologies have been in my blood since the very beginning, back in 1991.

Kristin and Sondra: What is the most important idea you would like people to take away from the Crystal Family methodology?

Alistair: Start lighter than you think you need, focus on the quality of conversations between people, change something every month to experiment with ways to get better.

That may look like three things, but there is no part of that you can remove and get Crystal.

Kristin and Sondra: What recommendations do you have for practitioners who are new to using Agile approaches?

Alistair: Deliver to real users early and often, focus on the quality of conversations between people, change something every month to experiment with ways to get better.

Kristin and Sondra: What is your vision for Agile methodologies as we look toward the future of software development?

Alistair: I don't know if it is a vision or an aspiration. In the 1990s, we suffered under the burden of the NATO 1968 and 1969 conferences on software engineering and all the resulting discussion, which gave us Waterfall development and heavy, impersonal, predictive methodologies. With the Agile Manifesto, we broke free from that burden. My, and other, research has shed a lot of light on what improves team results in design tasks, so we now know why Agile works and what needs adjustment.

The shortfall in Agile adoption is shoddy thinking practices and sloppy behavior and pretending that Agile makes all that okay. It doesn't. My aspiration is that people will keep the people aspects and learn to sharpen their thinking to get even better results (I write this up these days as "Disciplined Learning"; see my web site). Then we can get the best of both worlds.

Will it happen? I don't speculate on things like that. We'll see.

Kristin and Sondra: Do you think there will be a point where all software development will be done using Agile methodologies, or do you think traditional methodologies such as Waterfall will always have an important role in software development?

Alistair: Waterfall is a scheduling and staging strategy in which there is only one integration and delivery at the end. There are still projects (rarely in software) where there can be only one integration and delivery at the end, and so the need to keep knowledge of how to behave in such situations will remain. There will also remain, in all likelihood, people who simply refuse to switch over, and so the topic will plague us for decades to come, as far as I can see.

References and Further Reading

Anderson, David J. (2010). *Kanban: Successful evolutionary change for your technology business*. Sequim, WA: Blue Hole Press.

Astels, David, Miller, Granville, and Novak, Miroslav. (2002). *A practical guide to Extreme Programming*. Upper Saddle River, NJ: Prentice Hall.

Beck, Kent. (2000). *Extreme Programming explained*. Boston: Addison-Wesley.

Beck, Kent, and Fowler, Martin. (2001). *Planning Extreme Programming*. Boston: Addison-Wesley.

Cockburn, Alistair. (2004). *Crystal clear: A human-powered methodology for small teams*. Boston: Addison-Wesley.

Cockburn, Alistair. (2006). *Agile software development: The cooperative game* (2nd ed.). Boston: Addison-Wesley.

Highsmith, James A. (1999). *Adaptive software development: A collaborative approach to managing complex systems*. New York: Dorset House.

Palmer, Stephen, and Felsing, Mac. (2002). *A practical guide to Feature-Driven Development*. Upper Saddle River, NJ: Prentice Hall.

Poppendieck, Mary, and Poppendieck, Tom. (2003). *Lean software development: An Agile toolkit*. Boston: Addison-Wesley.

Schwaber, Ken, and Beedle, Mike. (2002). *Agile software development with Scrum*. Upper Saddle River, NJ: Prentice Hall.

Review Questions

Review 1

1. What are the key themes for Extreme Programming?
2. What three questions are typically covered in a daily stand-up meeting?
3. What five activities need to be performed in an FDD project?
4. What four requirement categories are used for DSDM?
5. What are the seven principles of Lean software development?

Review 2

6. What is a "signboard"?
7. What are the four key principles of Kanban?
8. Why was "crystal" used to name the Crystal Family?
9. What two factors are considered when assessing a color level in Crystal Family?
10. What Agile certification is available through the Project Management Institute?

Chapter 4

Describing the Different Roles

Learning Objectives

- Understand the roles in Scrum with their specific responsibilities—product owner, Scrum master, and team
- Identify the attributes and personality types that are most successful in the various roles
- Learn the Agile definitions of "chickens" and "pigs"
- See how extended team members interact with the team
- Compare and contrast the roles in Scrum and the other methodologies
- Walk through practical examples of how the roles are filled in different-sized organizations

It is important to understand the different roles that are used in Agile because they lay the foundation for how the work is delivered; detailing the responsibilities of each role shows how the Agile principles are brought to life in organizations of various sizes and complexities. In this chapter, we first explore the roles within Scrum, the most widely used Agile methodology (VersionOne 2013) and deep dive into the descriptions of the product owner, the Scrum master, and the Scrum team. With that foundation, we can then discover other roles and methodologies and how they approach the delivery of working software to key stakeholders and customers.

Deep Dive into Scrum Roles

To provide a more in-depth review of roles within Agile, we dive into the roles with the Scrum methodology—the product owner, the Scrum master, and the team.

Product Owner

The first critical role to understand in Scrum is the product owner. This role gets right to the heart of two of the twelve Agile principles: #4, "Business people and developers must work together daily throughout the project," and #1, "Our highest priority is to satisfy the customer through early and continuous delivery of valuable software." To satisfy the customer, Scrum requires active engagement from "the business," and that engagement is found through this role. The product owner must have a vision for what the product is supposed to do and must be able to convey that vision to the development team (Cohn 2013).

Roman Pichler, who has published many articles and books on the topic of the product owner, and who is also one of the interviewed guests for this chapter, describes the role as follows: "As the name suggests, a product owner should own the product on behalf of the company. You can think of the product owner as the individual who champions the product, who facilitates the product decisions, and **who has the final say about the product**, for instance, if and how feedback is actioned, or when which features are released" (Pichler 2010a).

Turning the product vision into an actionable project is accomplished by creating and maintaining the product backlog, which is the core responsibility of the product owner. The product backlog contains all of the requirements for the project in priority order to ensure that the team is always working on the most important things. The product backlog is described in detail in Chapter 5, "The New Way to Collect and Document Requirements." One of the key differences with Agile, and specifically Scrum, is that the requirements are broken down into small units of work called "user stories"; the product owner writes these user stories to capture the most urgent needs of the desired customer. As the marketplace, competition, and customer expectations change and evolve, the product owner can easily react by changing the priority of the work units in the backlog. The ability to seamlessly respond to change without disrupting the development process is one of the things that make Agile so enduring.

Setting the Priorities

Therefore, one important part of the product owner role is the responsibility of setting the priorities, and this can belong to only one person. If you have two or more people tasked with setting the priorities, then you are likely to incur a conflict. In the business world, it is very common to have more work to do than the team can reasonably get done, so there are often multiple top priorities; having one person tasked with being a tie-breaker can make the difference between success and failure within a project. Ken Schwaber and Mike Beedle noted this as early as 2002:

> The practice Scrum adds is that only one person is responsible for maintaining and sustaining the content and priority of a single Product Backlog. Otherwise, multiple conflicting lists flourish and the Scrum teams don't know which list to listen to. Without a single Product Owner, foundering, spin, contention and frustration result. (Schwaber and Beedle 2002, p. 34)

Cayman Design Example

Our company, Cayman Design, has built a web site to tell people the weather. Thus far, we have developed the following:

- Built a landing page for site visitors to come to
- Added a way to pull in or import the latest weather information
- Created a page to display that information

It may seem a bit simplistic, but we wanted to start with the basics and get our product to market quickly, knowing that we can add features in future sprints.

The product owner knew that, for the initial launch, the target market was largest in New York City, and Cayman Design needed to provide only weather for New York City to satisfy the most urgent business need. Then following the initial launch, the product owner will prioritize other features that can be released in a more iterative manner. The concept of being able to iterate, continuously grow, and improve an application is central to the benefits of Agile.

Prioritization by Business Value

What should Cayman Design work on next? We have a number of conflicting priorities.

- We want to add more cities so our application will appeal to a broader audience.
- We want to add features that will drive revenue and help monetize the site, such as selling weather-related calendars.
- Our IT teams have found that the code they have written to import the weather data is too slow, and they need to "refactor" the code to increase the processing speed.

Each one of these three efforts is important and valid, so how do you know which one to work on first? Within Agile, the main driver of priorities should be **business value**. Business value can take a number of forms, such as the following:

- Increased revenue
- Expansion of addressable market (i.e., with this new feature, more people will be interested in buying it)
- Decreased cost
- Increased customer satisfaction
- Increased processing speed
- Increased stability of the application
- Improved usability

The important thing about business value is that it is understood, articulated, and measured (when possible.) The reality of the workplace is that subjective measures may come into play, such as political pressure, executive opinions, or power within the organization. Although these types of things certainly happen, the goal of Agile is to be as objective as possible, always striving to *increase business value*.

The product owner must balance all of these inputs to determine the next effort that the Scrum team will work on, thereby setting the priorities. It is important that the product owner be precise in the prioritization setting as well, truly defining the number 1 and number 2 priorities, and so on; simply bucketing work into high, medium, and low categories is not detailed enough (Cohn 2004, loc. 2102).

Sprint Results

Another responsibility of the product owner is to accept or reject the work at the end of the sprint or iteration. Although that is a technical description of the product owner's responsibilities, it is not in the spirit of Agile to simply reject the work, because that is not being collaborative. The more likely scenario is that if the results of the sprint do not meet the product owner's expectations, then he or she will add new user stories to future sprints to correct the imperfection. It is also the product owner's responsibility to make sure all of the necessary work was completed on a story. If the team says that a story is done and yet the code is filled with bugs or the documentation is lacking, the product owner needs to hold the team accountable for the quality of their work. The definition of "done" is another Agile concept to help with this process, and that is described in detail in Chapter 6, "Grooming and Planning."

Release Management

Related to the setting of individual priorities, the product owner is also responsible for release management, deciding how many features need to be included in a product before it can be released. This is critical with new products, because you do not want to launch something that will not resonate with your target customers.

In our example of Cayman Design, the product owner determined that a web site displaying data for New York City was sufficient for an initial release. Once the product is in production, new features can be released as soon as they are available. For example, we could add cities to increase the number of customers that we can attract; this is referred to as "increasing the addressable market." As soon as the data for Boston is imported and tested, then Boston can be released into production.

However, other features might be more complex, requiring several sprints to complete. These features would need to wait for a formal release, as opposed to being pushed to production after each sprint or iteration. If we look at the weather calendars that Cayman Design wants to offer, there are a number of component pieces that must all be delivered in a single release for the feature to work correctly. For example, one sprint may be dedicated to inventory management—making sure that the calendars are available and can be shipped in a timely fashion when an order is received. A second sprint may be dedicated to payment processing—ensuring that credit card authorizations are handled appropriately and that a process is in place for credit card declines. Yet a third sprint could be dedicated to e-mail confirmations of orders received and order shipment information. The work done in these three sprints could be held in a testing environment until all are available, and they would be pushed to production together—as part of a single release.

It is the responsibility of the product owner to determine what constitutes a release and then manage the feature set within that release.

Who Is the Product Owner?

Given these responsibilities for understanding the marketplace, authoring and prioritizing the requirements, ensuring adequate completion, and managing the releases, who are the best people to fill this critical role? The most important consideration when selecting a product owner is to make sure that the person has an eye on the marketplace and the needs of customers and prospects. It is critical that the product owner know WHAT the team needs to build, so he or she must have easy access to feedback and market drivers.

The person who plays the role of product owner can vary depending on the organization. For example, the product owner may be a product manager, if the company has a formal product management organization. Otherwise, there are several other ways to fill this role. First, you can have business analysts (BAs) serve as product owner, and these BAs can be in either IT or other organizations. People in account management who are responsible for engaging with current customers can be a fit too. If the development work being undertaken is more operational in nature, then someone with operational expertise can fulfill this function. As long as care is taken to create a solid feedback loop, then the product owner can come from many areas of the company.

Product Ownership—Breadth

Another nuance of the product owner role is the breadth of his or her ownership. Does one product owner manage multiple products? Or is one product so big that it requires multiple product owners? Both of these situations are common in the workplace where teams are thin and expectations are high.

To examine the first instance, what are the advantages and disadvantages of having one product owner responsible for multiple products? The biggest risk factor is time and attention. Can the product owner devote adequate time to every product that he or she is responsible for? Does this person have the necessary depth of understanding to truly collaborate with IT on the best solutions? It is a risk, but certainly one that can be overcome.

In the instance where the product is large enough to have multiple product owners, there is a chance that the priorities will not align. Related to the previous reference of business value, if one product owner wants to expand to new cities to attract new users but another product owner places top priority on improving the processing speed, then you can run into conflicts. However, one of the core tenets of Agile is collaboration, which includes collaboration between product owners. Product owners need to be in communication with each other to clearly articulate the best plan for all groups—knowing that at any given time, one group's needs will take precedence over another's.

Even if you have a single product owner for every product, that does not mean that things are easy. Between systems there are interactions, and to create a new feature or make a modification, the product owner may need to consider dependencies.

Using our Cayman Design example, the product owner has decided to place the highest business value on driving incremental revenue. Thus, the weather application that Cayman Design has offered will have an additional feature allowing their end users to purchase weather calendars that provide statistical information for the next 12 months based on historical data and trends. To sell these calendars, the front-end web interface needs to be designed to take order information from a consumer; the order is then sent to a back-end order management application where the data is stored and the product purchase is fulfilled.

From an Agile perspective, there may be one product owner for the front-end web application and another for the back-end order management system. To be able to sell these calendars, enhancements will need to be made in both systems. The two product owners will have to collaborate to make sure that the timing of the enhancements is aligned. It does not necessarily mean that the changes to the two systems have to happen at the exact same time, but it does mean that they need to be coordinated, tested, and launched in concert.

Scrum Master

The second of the three defined roles in Scrum is the Scrum master, which is a new and very different position for many organizations. The Scrum master is responsible for leading the development team and working through any issues that arise during a sprint. The specific responsibilities can vary based on the size and experience of the team, as well as the size and complexity of the work effort. There are some consistent personality traits that lead to a successful Scrum master. For example, the Scrum master must be willing to make decisions and actively work throughout the organization to remove impediments or roadblocks for the team. Being Scrum master is not right for everyone: Some people are not comfortable with the visibility associated with the role or taking the initiative necessary to succeed (Schwaber and Beedle 2002, p. 32).

Removing Impediments

Removing impediments is one key role that the Scrum master plays. An impediment is anything that gets in the way of the developers getting their work done. A number of tasks are easier to do when not interrupted, such as studying for a test, building a model airplane, painting a room, or writing code. When we get into a rhythm, we can get a tremendous amount of work done because our minds can focus on the task at hand. What happens when we are interrupted by the telephone or someone asking a question or a noisy neighbor? Any of these things can break our rhythm, and getting started again after an interruption is not as simple as sitting back down and picking up where we left off. "When subjects reengage in a sequence of tasks following an interruption, there is an increased response time, or 'restart cost'" (Dreher and Berman 2002, p. 14595). This "restart cost" can be significant and can result in lost productivity. These interruptions are one type of impediment. It is the Scrum master's job to remove as many impediments as possible.

Here are a few other examples:

1. The team in the next aisle plays music while they are working, and they play it so loud that it causes you to lose your concentration. Rather than try to work through it or create a scene by shouting that they need to knock it off, the developer can let the Scrum master know of this impediment, and the Scrum master can coordinate with the other team to find a workable solution; it might be the investment of headphones, or setting a specific time when playing loud music is acceptable.
2. The product owner that you work with does not always provide complete information, and you have questions. But he or she is in meetings all the time, so you spend hours trying to find the person to get your questions answered. This is another perfect item to give to the Scrum master as an impediment: The Scrum master can find a solution that might involve daily meetings with the product owner, setting specific times when the product owner is available, or working out a system via instant message or text message for quick direction. Whatever the appropriate solution, the Scrum master is responsible for clearing the impediment so the developer can write code.
3. Members of the organization stop by your desk to ask questions because you are the subject matter expert (SME) on a particular item; this happens frequently in the workplace and can be a true productivity killer. The people doing the interrupting have valid reasons for doing so—there is a customer waiting on an answer, another team cannot proceed because they need additional information, an executive needs input for something he or she is working on—but the act of stopping what you are doing and shifting to the topic of the question makes it challenging to reengage once the question is answered. The Scrum master can serve as a blocker for this type of activity, by either answering the majority of the questions or creating a predefined timeframe when answering questions will not be disruptive.

There is significant value in having a team member who can remove these types of roadblocks so that developers can spend the majority of their time writing code. The ability to tackle these issues requires determination and stubbornness (Schwaber and Beedle 2002, p. 32), so selecting the right person for the role is important.

Communicator and Liaison

With any project, there are many questions about how something should be done or what exactly is meant in a certain requirement; the Scrum master is the coordination link to getting all of the necessary answers. This may involve attending a number of meetings or seeking out specific people. The Scrum master is also responsible for conveying information back to the team. If something material changes on a project, such as the proposed delivery date, the Scrum master may be the first to hear this news, and he or she is responsible for ensuring that the team is kept fully informed. Agile strives for "no surprises," and the Scrum master can assist with this goal by keeping the team apprised of all information.

Adherence to Scrum Best Practices

The Scrum master is also responsible for making sure that the team is adhering to the principles of Scrum. For example, if you have a particularly quiet teammate and another member who is fairly dominant, it is the Scrum master's job to make sure all voices are heard. That might mean asking specific questions to the quiet team member and paying close attention to the answers. It might also mean delicately informing the dominant team member to stop talking and let everyone participate. This might sound like a small responsibility, but effective team management can be the difference between the success and failure of a project.

Another example is adherence to the meeting schedule, which is explained in detail in Chapter 8, "Tracking and Reporting." One of the meetings that is part of the Scrum process is the Sprint retrospective. This meeting takes place at the end of each sprint, and it is a time for the team to reflect on what went well in the last sprint and what needs improving in the next sprint. This is a meeting that can be dismissed as unnecessary, but it is actually vitally important to the Agile process. It is the Scrum master's job to make sure that the team does not cut corners that diminish the effectiveness of Agile.

The Scrum master also needs to hold the team accountable for honoring their commitments. If the team is not completing testing or documentation, the Scrum master needs to work with the team to improve their performance and address any root causes that might have led to the lapse.

The Scrum Master Role

Like the product owner, the Scrum master's role can vary from company to company and team to team. Here are several variations.

Full-Time or Part-Time

There is debate over whether the Scrum master should assume this role full-time. If you have a large team, many new members, a complex project, a weak product owner, or other similar factors, it might be wise to have the Scrum master dedicated full-time to a single team, therefore assuming no other responsibilities. Conversely, if your team is small or experienced and working on something well defined, then you might decide that the Scrum master could be a working member of the team, meaning that he or she assumes the Scrum master duties in addition to writing code that contributes to the project. Another approach is to have a single Scrum master preside over more than one team.

Jeff Sutherland (2010), a signer of the Manifesto, recommends full-time assignments, but sees opportunities for flexibility for smaller teams, where the Scrum master is also a working member of the team. Mike Cohn, a well-known author and expert on Scrum, would prefer that a Scrum master serve in only that role, but if there is bandwidth for additional responsibilities, the Scrum master should lead more than one team (Cohn 2010, p. 124).

Permanent or Rotating

Another variation is determining if the Scrum master is assigned on a permanent or long-term basis, or if you can rotate the Scrum master responsibilities among the team members. As with the full-time vs. part-time decision, permanent vs. rotating depends on a number of factors.

If you have a natural leader who enjoys playing the role of Scrum master, then the continuity and consistency of that assignment can be quite beneficial. However, if you have an experienced team who are disciplined about their adherence to Agile practices, then rotating the Scrum master duties might provide a nice variety for the team.

In most instances, though, the Scrum master is a challenging and significant role that deserves respect (Cohn 2010, p. 122). Therefore, organizations in the early stages of adopting Agile should not explore part-time or rotating Scrum masters until they have matured their Agile practices sufficiently.

Who Should Be the Scrum Master?

When a new team is formed, determining who should be the Scrum master is a big decision, and there are several likely areas to search for talent.

- **Technical Lead or Lead Developer**
  A common choice for a Scrum master is the person on the team who has demonstrated a capacity for decision making by being the lead developer or the technical lead. These people are usually very proficient at the application and are adept at solving complex problems, so they naturally rise as potential leaders. Whether they are a good fit for the Scrum master role depends on their personality and preferences. First, they must be willing to coach and collaborate with team members versus making

decisions and dictating to the team. Also, they must be comfortable with the visibility of the role, because it often requires more interactions with management and other departments.

- **Project Manager**
  Some project managers are a natural fit to morph into Scrum masters, but that is certainly not always the case. The project manager's role in a Waterfall environment is typically that of accountability and enforcement. The project manager would likely have a detailed project plan clearly outlining due dates and task owners. That person's job is to make sure that everyone completes their tasks on time and as expected; this is very different from the role of Scrum master, who needs to serve as a coach and a collaborator (Hunton, 2012). When an unexpected problem arises, some project managers approach it by completing risk matrixes and reassigning tasks and establishing a new timeline, while escalating the occurrence to upper management. The Scrum master would take an entirely different approach: collaborating with both the team and the product owner on what they learned and how it could affect the product. By working collaboratively, the Scrum master would seek a new solution and would actively participate in brainstorming and creative problem solving.

  Some project managers can easily make the shift from the command and control practices often associated with Waterfall projects to being collaborative in an Agile environment, but it certainly is not always possible.

- **IT/Functional Manager**
  Another often debated subject is whether the Scrum master can or should be the IT manager. Again, this depends entirely on the makeup of the organization. As we demonstrated in Chapter 2, "Organizational Culture Considerations with Agile," moving from a Waterfall environment to Agile can have serious implications to the organization and culture. If your organization has been in Waterfall for quite some time, then you might have IT managers who are accustomed to making all of the decisions. They might be more comfortable assigning tasks and managing the Scrum team as individual employees, rather than a team; if this is the case, then the IT manager should absolutely *not* be the Scrum master. The team will never find its own rhythm if they are being managed in a Waterfall manner. In fact, on many Scrum teams, the managers are not allowed to attend the Scrum meetings, or if they do, they are not allowed to speak.

  Conversely, if your team is new or you are working in more of a start-up environment, then it is perfectly acceptable to have the IT manager double as the Scrum master. This makes particular sense if you are constrained in your resources.

Who makes the best Scrum master? As with most things in Agile, the answer is—it depends. Good Scrum masters can be developers, quality assurance (QA) folks, or BAs. In fact, the Scrum master does not even need to be in the IT organization. There have been successful models where the Scrum master is an analyst from account management or a customer service organization. The important thing when choosing your Scrum master is that the person should be able to remove impediments, minimize interruptions, lead the team, and enforce the principles of Agile.

Product Owner + Scrum Master

For an Agile implementation to maximize its effectiveness, the product owner and the Scrum master both need to be enthusiastic advocates for their respective roles. Both need to be strong communicators who are committed to the success of the product and the team, focusing on collaboration and finding creative and workable solutions to the problems that naturally arise.

Review 1 At this point, the reader should be able to answer Review Questions 1–5.

The Team

The final defined role within Scrum is the Scrum team, full of talented people who will ultimately deliver on the project. Like product owners and Scrum masters, there is great variability in how the teams are formed and who is included. Before we dive into the optimal team makeup in size and membership, let's cover the key foundational considerations for an effective Scrum team. It is imperative that a Scrum team operate with trust, transparency, and teamwork.

Working Agreement

One way that trust and teamwork are established and enforced is through the creation of a working agreement: This is a document or set of expectations that define how the Scrum team is going to work together. The working agreement is the first point of collaboration for a new Scrum team as they define their relationships. It is more than just rules of engagement for team behavior; the working agreement ultimately reflects the values and commitment of the team (Derby 2011).

Working Agreement Topics

Chris Sterling presented a list of potential working agreement topics in his blog, "Creating a Team Working Agreement" (2008).

> With Scrum Teams I have found the following topics are a good starter list to start the creation of a Working Agreement:
>
> - Time and location of Daily Scrum
> - Testing strategy (unit, functional, integration, performance, stress, etc. . .)
> - Build and infrastructure plans (shared responsibilities)
> - Team norms (be on time, respect estimates, help when needed, etc. . .)
> - How to address bugs/fires during Sprint
> - Product Owner availability (phone, office hours, attendance in Daily Scrum)
> - Capacity plan for initial Sprint(s)

Exercise

Create a working agreement with a group of people that you work with. Discuss what matters to you as a team and how you can increase your effectiveness through teamwork. Document and post your agreement, and check back every week or two to see how you are doing. Are most people honoring the agreement? If not, why not? After several weeks, discuss whether the working agreement has brought the group closer together. What has been positive and negative about the experience?

Fist of Five

"Fist of five" is another important concept to understand when discussing Scrum teams and the desire for trust, transparency, and teamwork. Here is how it works: Whenever a team comes to a decision point where they are discussing several options and there is no ideal solution, they may vote on the best available option. A team member will propose a direction forward and the team will demonstrate their acceptance by holding up their hands with the number of fingers that corresponds with their level of support.

- 5 fingers = I am all in. I completely agree.
- 4 fingers = I buy into the option and I will support it.
- 3 fingers = I have some reservations, but I can support the decision and move forward.
- 2 fingers = I have reservations, and I cannot support this decision without further discussion and clarification.
- 1 finger = I cannot support this decision. I completely disagree.

The fist of five allows all team members to show their level of support so there can be no "quiet dissenters" or people who say nothing in the meeting and then sabotage the decision afterward. To use a classroom example, if you work on a group project, you may need to decide which language you are going to write an assignment in for a software development class. Your team decides to use Java, and as you are coding, you run into some troubles. The team member who acts as the dissenter might say "I always thought we should have used .NET, but nobody listens to me." Fist of five deals with this type of situation at the time the decision is made. The team will decide on Java and everyone on the team will vote. As long as everyone shows 3, 4, or 5 fingers, the team is free to proceed. If anyone shows a 1 or a 2, the team needs to stop and discuss the issue further. The team should not move forward until every team member is at a 3 or higher. Another common problem that fist of five solves is the team dynamic with introverts and extroverts. There are people who are naturally quieter in their demeanor and do not want to interrupt others or jump into a heated debate; fist of five allows those people to have their voice heard in a very nonconfrontational manner. By simply holding up a "2," that person now has the opportunity to express concerns or ask critical questions.

Self-Organizing

The working agreement and fist of five reinforce one of the critical points of Agile and Scrum—that the team must be self-organizing. What does this mean? Not only does the team get to decide how they will work together, but they also are empowered to define and evolve their roles within the team.

Michael James (2010) describes the value of self-organizing teams quite well in the Scrum Reference Card:

> Self-organizing teams can radically outperform larger, traditionally managed teams. Family-sized groups naturally self-organize when the right conditions are met:
>
> - Members are committed to clear, short-term goals
> - Members can gauge the group's progress
> - Members can observe each other's contribution
> - Members feel safe to give each other unvarnished feedback

Another critical difference between Waterfall and Agile is the handling of task assignments on self-organizing teams. Once the sprint has been groomed (described in detail in Chapter 6), the team members can select the tasks that they want to work on. This ownership of task assignment is a huge departure from Waterfall, where the manager often told each developer what he or she was expected to accomplish. The ability for each team member to pick assignments leads to significant lifts in job satisfaction. It also invites the opportunity for cross-training, because less experienced people could request tasks that they would like to learn, and they can be mentored by the more experienced members of the team. This is all positive, but it is worth pointing out that all of the work still needs to get done, so although the team is self-organizing, they cannot neglect certain less desirable tasks, such as documentation. How the team chooses to assign documentation, though, is within their control.

Team Size

The best practice is for a team of five to nine people. The reason for this recommendation is easy to understand: Anything fewer than five means you lose an element of collaboration and the ability to assign tasks to different people based on the requirements of the sprint, but more than nine means you can have too much collaboration with a variety of opinions and personalities that must be managed as a cohesive unit. If you have a product that requires a large team, it might be worth breaking it into two teams; this adds complexity, but can certainly be managed.

Cross-Functional

The team needs to be cross-functional so that the requirements can be designed, coded, and tested within a single sprint. Therefore, each team should be composed of people with these skills so they can develop working software without the involvement of ancillary resources. This is particularly important when it comes to testing. Scrum strives for working software at the end of each sprint, and this requires that the code be tested thoroughly so that it could be deployed, if that was the release plan. Having full-time, dedicated testing (QA) people on each team can facilitate this goal.

Consistency in Membership

The team should be as static as possible, meaning that team membership should not change frequently, and it should never change during a sprint. The reason for this is the desired consistency and teamwork that Agile strives to create. If a developer works with the same group of people for a period of time, they get to know one another and can establish trust. Creating an environment of trust is absolutely critical in Agile, because it is *the team* that commits to the deliverables in the sprint. If team members don't trust each other, then how can they commit to delivering a feature when they are not certain that everyone can or will live up to their responsibilities? Ideally, you want to create a team where mutual respect, teamwork, and trust are present and evident. When team membership changes regularly, it is difficult to get trust established, and the team's rhythm is out of sync.

Full-Time Membership

Also, where possible, the members need to be assigned to only one team. There are instances where this is not possible so the teams have to adjust, but the best practice is full-time membership. Imagine if you do not have enough QA (testing) resources, so you decide to share a QA resource across two teams. Even if that worker is dedicated and experienced, the time may come when the testing for one team runs into a problem and that QA resource has to spend more time than expected resolving the issues. The other team is then short-changed of their QA resource, which may force them to miss their deliverables. Obviously, if using a shared resource is the only option available, then it can be managed, but it is not ideal.

However, there are some resources that would not have enough work if they were assigned to a single Scrum team full-time; examples are the database administrator (DBA) and the user interface (UI) designer. Often, a DBA resource may be required for only a few hours during a sprint, and as long as the team has access to a resource when needed, there is no need for the DBA to join the team full-time.

Chickens and Pigs

The concept of "chickens" and "pigs" within Scrum comes from the comic strip shown in Figure 4.1.

Figure 4.1 *Chickens and pigs comic strip*

Source: Used with permission from Michael Vizdos.

The point of this cartoon is that some people in the Scrum process have a higher level of commitment (pigs) than others (chickens) based on the nature of their work. For example, developers are pigs: "Team members commit to a goal and do the work that is required to meet it. They are called pigs, because they, like the pigs in the joke, are committed to the project" (Beedle and Schwaber 2002, p. 42). This commitment cannot be taken lightly. It is a promise, and the developers know that if something goes wrong, they might have to work long hours in order to deliver on that commitment. They are, in effect, putting their reputations on the line every time they make a commitment. The more promises that are kept, the more the team's reputation in the organization goes up; but if several promises are missed, then the team is held in lower regard. Hence, the developers are pigs because their level of commitment is absolute. Chickens, on the other hand, are definitely interested in the project and want to see it succeed, but their reputations or careers (or proverbial "necks") are not on the line. The best way to describe these terms is through an example.

Product owners are great to look at because sometimes they are chickens and sometimes they are pigs. First, the team gets together with the product owner to determine the priorities for the next features that will be worked on. The product owner has to be knowledgeable about the feature request and the business value that it will bring to the company. He or she must be able to articulate exactly the reasons for advocating for one feature over another with information (not opinions) and must be ready to answer clarifying questions for the team. In this discussion, the product owner is clearly a pig: He or she is heavily invested in and committed to the outcome.

The next step is for the Scrum team to discuss coding options and different ways they can design the solution that the product owner is advocating. They could get into a heated debate, for example, over the technology design. When the Scrum team is getting into the details of the coding options, the product owner turns into a chicken: Although this person's input may be interesting, it is not the product owner's decision on the technology. That belongs to the team writing the code, and they are the pigs.

As is discussed in Chapter 8, there are even meetings where chickens are not allowed to speak. Although the naming convention is a bit silly, it works well in practice because you could literally stop a meeting and ask, "Are you a chicken or a pig?" and everyone will know the distinction you are making. It can move the conversation along with greater productivity than if every person in the room carried the same amount of influence.

Practical Examples of the Scrum Roles

Within any position or role, there are people and personalities who will excel and those who will struggle or may even fail. The following section walks through examples of both the strong and the weak.

Product Owner

There are many examples of good and bad product owners in the workplace. These are challenging jobs with a number of conflicting inputs regarding prioritization, so it takes a strong personality with a collaborative work behavior to be successful.

Let's look at Keith, who was assigned as the product owner to an application that had several high-profile and demanding clients. Keith researched all of the necessary competitive and market information so he could ascertain the best prioritization for the development work that needed to be done. An account manager who handles one of the high-profile clients did not like Keith's prioritization because something the client wanted was not at the top of the list. Keith was very deliberate in his analysis, and he believed that the requested feature would not be adopted by others in the marketplace—it would really apply just to this one client, almost as if it was custom code; therefore, he put other features that he believed would drive more business value ahead of the requested client feature. But that did not satisfy the account manager, because she thought her client's request was vitally important. So she pleaded with Keith again and again: She called him and sent him e-mails and held meetings and pestered Keith relentlessly to try to get him to change the prioritization. Finally, in a moment of frustration, Keith said, "Fine. You go talk to the IT manager of the development team. If she thinks they can get it done, then so be it."

Keith was having a bad day, and in that moment was a very bad product owner. The product owner sets the priority for the work of the IT team based on knowledge and research of the marketplace and what will drive the highest business value. Further, the product owner must collaborate with all of the constituents to "sell" the prioritization. He or she must gather input from a number of sources, including account management. It was Keith's decision—and his alone—as to whether the client request would be prioritized high on the list; by deferring to the IT manager, he was shirking his responsibilities. He should have either convinced the account manager that his backlog was prioritized correctly by articulating the business value of the high-priority items, or, if he could not do that, then he should have reprioritized the backlog to move up the client's task, based on the information learned from the account manager. Being a product owner is a difficult balancing act, but the role is critical and must be performed well for Scrum to be effective.

By contrast, Kelly is a great product owner. She actually moved her desk to sit with the Scrum team so she could be immediately available to answer questions. Kelly spent a portion of her time with the account managers, salespeople, and actual customers so she could stay on top of how customers were using the product and what problems they were having. She also learned from the salespeople what objections they were hearing from prospective clients. She was able to distill all of that feedback into the user stories that she created. She understood which features would drive the most business value so she could effectively prioritize. Kelly also listened to her Scrum team and understood enough about the technology to contribute to the discussion around various choices that could solve a particular problem. The best product owners have enough technical expertise to be able to follow a technical conversation and contribute salient points to the discussion. They do not have to be developers by any means, but they should demonstrate a technical aptitude.

Scrum Master

Let's look at examples of good and bad Scrum masters. Everyone has their strengths and for some personalities, it is a natural fit.

Consider Steve. He was brought in from another team to be the Scrum master of a team that was really struggling. Steve started by getting to know all of the developers on his team. He met with each person individually to learn his or her impressions of the problems. Then Steve began actively advocating for the team. When decisions were not being made in a timely fashion, Steve escalated the issue so his team could get the answers they needed to write the best code. When the team had a disagreement, Steve jumped right in and facilitated a healthy but heated discussion about how to solve the problem. When required to make decisions, Steve gathered the best information available at the time, consulted with people internal and external to the team to check his facts, and then chose a path, informed all parties, and stood behind his decision when it was questioned. His leadership allowed the team to focus on the code they were designing, writing, and testing so that they could meet their commitments and feel a real sense of accomplishment. Steve is a great Scrum master.

Steve's team sits very near Ray's team, who is not sharing in their success. Ray is the Scrum master, and he has a rather timid personality. When conflicts on Ray's team arise, he watches nervously and encourages everyone to be nice but he does not help them resolve the problems. He acts more like a disengaged referee. Ray's team has two very strong, dominant personalities and two very introverted and quiet people. Ray does not like confrontation, so when the two strong personalities dominate the conversation, he allows it to happen. Therefore, the more timid people do not say anything and just go along because they do not want to rock the boat. This is very unfortunate, because the two quiet developers are quite knowledgeable about the system, and they have noticed flaws in the design of the code. The strong personalities do not seem to understand or care about the risks, which jeopardizes the entire effort. Because Ray allows this dominance on the team, he is part of the problem instead of being part of the solution. For a Scrum master, avoiding confrontation is not healthy or helpful. Confrontation does not have to be negative; it can be respectful and lead to the best deliverable. Ray is not an effective Scrum master, and he is jeopardizing the success of his team.

Team

Now let's consider a good team and a bad team and what aspects make them so.

The green team has a team member, Joe, who is very smart, so much so that the rest of the team has trouble keeping up with him when he gets going on an idea. Joe is almost always right in his direction but he processes information in his brain so quickly that when he talks, it is a bit like gibberish to the rest of the team because he does not clearly state how he got from problem to solution. On some teams, this type of savant could be extremely frustrating because when Joe talks, the team rarely understands what he is saying. But the green team is highly effective, and they recognize and value the intelligence and ideas of their super-smart colleague. They brainstormed the right way to allow Joe to communicate his ideas and thought patterns. They painted all of the walls in the area with white board paint, which allows you to write on the walls and then erase when you are done. They encouraged Joe to write down his train of thought in solving a particular problem. This allows the rest of the team to slowly digest what he is conveying, and they have a written record to access when they are trying to recall a specific detail. The green team rallied together and found a solution that would allow everyone to actively contribute and drive toward the best possible solution.

The blue team, on the other hand, is not optimized. They have a member, John, who is equally talented but far more disruptive. John is negative and not a team player. He is dismissive of every idea that is not his own. John is very intelligent and knows the system very well, so his behavior is tolerated even though he is so negative. The sense is that the team could not do without him because of his expertise, but his presence has created a tense and unproductive work environment. His team members are reluctant to confront him because he is so aggressive in his negative demeanor. The issue of John's attitude has been raised with both the Scrum master and the IT manager, but neither are willing to address the problem because they fear losing his expertise on the system. As a result, this team operates in a constant state of fear. They do not know how John will react in any situation, so they all retreat and wait for his reaction before they express their own opinions. The team is failing to meet any of its deliverables because no one can commit to certain tasks when John is behaving like a bully and driving all of the discussions. This is an ineffective team who would be far better off if John was removed. They might suffer a bit from the lost expertise, but they would gain far more by being allowed to brainstorm and work together.

What is interesting is that all of these examples come from a single company. Within any Agile implementation, there are both things that go well and areas for improvement. Every team, every Scrum master, and every product owner should always be aware of opportunities to learn, improve, and be more effective.

Review 2 At this point, the reader should be able to answer Review Questions 6–10.

Extended Team Members

Within Scrum, there are the three core roles that we have just discussed: product owner, Scrum master, and the team. Beyond that, a number of necessary contributors make up the extended team.

Project Sponsor

Most large efforts need a project sponsor to advocate for the project. What distinguishes project sponsors from the other roles is that they have the authority to allocate funds and people to projects. They are true decision makers and can back up their commitment with actual resources. The person in this role is often an executive who is advocating for this effort and is responsible for the strategic implications.

Stakeholders

Another critical role in the Agile and Scrum process is the stakeholders. These are people who are either directly or indirectly affected by the project. Internal stakeholders are inside the company, and could range from users of the system to the CEO, depending on the size and scope of the project. External stakeholders are outside the company, and again could range from users of the system to shareholders of stock in the company. Therefore, a single project can have multiple stakeholders, and this audience is critically important to keep informed on the project's progress and to consult with for key decisions.

For example, one obvious stakeholder is the leader of the sales organization. How the product is developed, the features that are included, the timing of the release, and the scalability of the application are important data points for sales to know and potentially influence. It is the product owner's responsibility to gather input from sales to consider in the prioritization of features and release management.

Other examples of stakeholders could include the leaders of the following types of organizations:

- The operations team, who will be responsible for on-boarding (or turning on) new customers
- The customer service representatives (CSRs), who must support end users who call in with questions
- The technical help desk, because they will take technical questions from internal and possibly external users
- The finance or billing organization, which is tasked with billing customers and thus booking the revenue

There can be many others, and virtually every organization within a company may have some stake in an upcoming project, depending on the size and scope of the effort. Stakeholders are critical because their impressions, whether they are correct or incorrect, of how a project is proceeding can influence funding, timelines, team resources, etc. It is essential to recognize and appreciate the role of the stakeholders.

Project Manager

Within Scrum, many advocate that a project manager is no longer needed because that person's core responsibilities have been absorbed by the roles within Scrum (Cohn 2010, p. 139). To examine this further, let's outline the traditional tasks of a project manager and discuss who might own them within Scrum.

- The project manager must **plan for and track** all aspects of the product release. Within a highly evolved Scrum team, the Scrum master would own all of these activities.

- Project managers are responsible for **securing the approval and the funding** for the project and providing all of the necessary paperwork and tracking mechanisms against that approval. In an Agile organization, the product owner would ensure that all funding was in place to accomplish their vision for the product.
- The project manager also manages **project risks** and issues. Within any given project, there will always be unforeseen items that come up, and it is the project manager's role to document issues as they arise. Risk planning is important and can make a big difference to a project. If the Scrum team is high functioning, they will anticipate and mitigate risks.
- The project manager is tasked with **communicating status**. This is a large and important role, because transparency is critical within Agile practices. Communication regarding the team and the sprint progress would belong to the Scrum master; communication with stakeholders on product features and release management would be the responsibility of the product owner.

Although it is true that all of these functions could (and perhaps should) be managed within the existing Scrum roles, most organizations have not yet reached this level of maturity with their Agile practices, so there is still a place for the project manager role.

Roles in Other Methodologies

Now that the roles within Scrum are well understood, it is easier to compare and contrast the roles in the other methodologies.

Project Sponsor

As previously mentioned, this role is critical because it possesses the authority and budget to actually approve a project. In Crystal, FDD, Lean, and Scrum, this person is referred to as the sponsor, sometimes as the **executive sponsor** or **project sponsor**. In DSDM, the term **project champion** may be used.

Requirements Gatherer

This role is the person who gathers the requirements, understands the needs of the customer/end user, communicates the business value, and sets the detailed vision of what the product needs to be.

As already described in detail, the **product owner** fills this role in Scrum. The name encompasses the essence of this particular function—this person "owns" the product. Lean software development also defines this as the product owner.

Within XP, this role is referred to as the **customer** because he or she represents the needs and priorities of the ultimate end user (Chromatic 2003, p. 59). Those in this role are responsible for understanding what end users really need, how much they value it, and what they will pay.

In feature-driven development (FDD), the role of requirements gatherer is split between two titles: the **chief programmer,** who is responsible for prioritizing the work to be done, and the **domain experts,** who know the application in great detail and can articulate the business needs to the developers (Palmer 2013).

In DSDM, this responsibility is also divided between several roles. The **visionary** understands the long-term direction and the ultimate goal for the product. The **ambassador user** acts as an ambassador for the end users and makes sure their needs and priorities are considered. The **advisory user** will be more focused on the usability and workflow details for the product (Wikipedia 2013).

In other methodologies, the requirements gatherer is not a specifically defined role but rather is included in the collaborative discussions regarding the project. For example, within Crystal, the end users (customers) interface with both the user interface (UI) designers and the business analysts, so both would be responsible for collecting, documenting, and prioritizing the project goals and requirements.

Project Manager

As mentioned, there is some debate over this role within Scrum, but other methodologies still define and see value in naming someone to serve as the project manager. Within Crystal and DSDM, for example, the role follows this definition and is called the **project manager**; in the XP world, this role is the same, but it is called the **tracker**. In FDD and Lean software development, the project manager role is expanded to include caring for the team and ensuring that their environment is optimized (Chedalawada 2010). The functions surrounding team dynamics and efficacy belong to the Scrum master in Scrum, as previously described.

Team Coach

Although FDD and Lean include maximizing dynamics within the project manager role and Scrum assigns these responsibilities to the Scrum master, several other methodologies have a specific role for the coach.

Within XP, this type of function is split between two roles, the **coach** and the **big boss**, but one person may cover both. The coach is viewed as the mentor to the team; he or she has earned the team's respect and leads by example (Chromatic 2003, p. 64). The big boss is responsible for holding the team accountable and ensuring that they do what they say they are going to do (Beck 2000, p. 84).

Within DSDM, the role is split between the **team leader** and the **coach**. The specific responsibilities of the team leader include working with the team on the immediate deliverables—the day-to-day activities, timeliness of deliverables, and full team participation (Caine 2013); the coach is focused on ensuring that the team understands and embraces the principles of Agile.

Crystal does not specifically define this type of role.

What makes this team coach role unique within Agile is that it does not correlate to any management responsibilities. The coach, or Scrum master, does not make decisions about hiring and firing and does not own the preparation of annual reviews or appraisals of the team members' performance. Instead, the coach's role is to make sure that everyone on the team is actively participating, has what they need to do the job (information, tools, support, knowledge, etc.), and is fully engaged in the end deliverable. The inclusion of this type of role has proven quite impactful because it encourages the people doing the work, in this case the developers and testers, to have a voice in their work environment and the product deliverable. This type of active engagement is a big departure from the Waterfall world, where managers simply told developers what to work on.

Architect or Technical Lead

Many of the Agile methodologies have a technical lead or architect who is responsible for making technical decisions about how the product or feature should be deployed. Feature-driven development calls this the **chief architect,** and those in the role are responsible for the overall architecture of the application or environment and ensuring that individual features do not compromise the integrity of the system (Palmer 2013). In DSDM, this role is referred to as the **technical coordinator**; in Crystal, it is the **architect**; and in Lean software development, it is the **technical owner**. Scrum does not specifically name this position; typically a member of the team is viewed as the technical lead, but the team participates actively in all technology discussions.

Large organizations may need several roles, as required by the technical complexity of the environment, such as an **enterprise architect** or an **application owner.**

Enterprise architect is a role in IT with the task of making sure that all of the projects will stitch together in an architecture that can be maintained. The person in this role worries about integration, scalability, response times, enterprise hardware strategies, and enterprise-wide disaster recovery.

An application owner may be required if multiple development teams are working on a single application. They have the same responsibilities as the enterprise architect but for a specific application. This role has to make sure that application testing and the code integration are tightly monitored.

Development Team

The development team is sometimes viewed as a single entity, as it is in XP, Scrum, and Lean software development, although within the team there are members with specific expertise. Every team will have developers, and most also include testers. Within Agile, product or features are intended to be designed, coded, and tested by the team, so including all of those functions is standard.

However, other roles may or may not be included. An example is the **user experience designers** [UX designers, sometimes referred to as user interface (UI) designers or usability professionals]. This role will be essential on teams where mapping the end user experience is central to the success of the product or feature. These people may be assigned to a team full-time, but more often they float between several development teams because their expertise is somewhat rare and must be shared across the organization. In the Crystal methodology, the **UX designer** is a specifically defined role that is always part of the team. Crystal also specifically recognizes a **programmer** and a **tester**. Within DSDM, there are named functions for a **solution developer** and a **solution tester**.

Feature-driven development has perhaps the most interesting split of the development team by introducing the concept of "classes." This is best described in contrast to XP and Scrum.

XP, like Scrum, includes a practice called collective ownership—the idea that any developer can update any artifact, including source code, as required. FDD takes a different approach, in that it assigns classes to individual developers, so if a feature requires changes to several classes, then the owners of those classes must work together as a feature team to implement it (Ambler 2013). Therefore, within FDD, there are **class owners** in the development teams.

Documentation and Training

Some Agile teams may include people responsible for documentation; the amount of documentation required in the Agile methodologies varies depending on the nature of the project and the tools in place to organically capture documentation (such as user stories). There may be a need for a technical writer—referred to as a **scribe** in DSDM—to document the application. In addition, an organization may need a training professional to prepare end user documentation or actually deliver end user training. Typically these roles are considered part of the extended team within Agile.

Agile Coach

Large organizations with several Agile teams may want to employ the assistance of an **Agile coach**, either as a full-time employee or as a consultant. The Agile coach oversees the company's Agile implementations and makes sure that each team is operating at maximum efficiency. This can be a critical role in ensuring consistency among numerous self-organizing teams. Although you do not want to remove the autonomy of individual teams, it is worthwhile to have someone with cultural oversight to ensure that Agile principles are being consistently and appropriately applied throughout the organization. The Agile coach can also help with training and providing feedback when issues arise.

Kanban

You may have noticed that the roles within Kanban have not been specifically mentioned; this is deliberate. Within Kanban, there are no prescribed roles, and Kanban cautions against role creation simply for the sake of process (Kniberg and Skarin 2010, p. 11). Kanban is described in detail in Chapter 8, and the focus is on process improvements and removing bottlenecks so role specification is less important.

> **Review 3** At this point, the reader should be able to answer Review Questions 11–15.

Practical Examples of Roles

The best way to understand the roles and how they interact is to walk through a handful of examples and dig into issues that could arise. To achieve this, we look at three scenarios using the Scrum methodology:

- A start-up company with limited resources and one Scrum team
- A mid-sized company with multiple teams but who are working mostly on stand-alone applications
- A large multinational company with multiple Scrum teams working on a single application

Start-Up

This is a small organization with only a handful of people, all "wearing multiple hats" or playing several roles. In our pretend company, we have a sales leader with two salespeople, a business analyst, an IT manager, four developers, and one tester (QA). We are going to enhance our product, so the roles might look like this:

- sales leader = project sponsor/key stakeholder
- business analyst = product owner
- IT manager = Scrum master, enterprise architect, application owner
- four developers and one tester = Scrum team

The project sponsor sets the overall objective, scope, and budget for the effort. The product owner gathers the requirements, interviews prospects, goes on sales calls to learn more, and prioritizes the items that will add the most business value to the top of the backlog. The product owner also works with the Scrum master (who in this case is also the IT manager) to manage the timelines and risks and reports status to the key stakeholder. The Scrum master organizes the team, removes impediments, reduces interferences, and clarifies issues with the product owner. The enterprise architect (who in this case is the same person with the Scrum master responsibilities) ensures that this development effort will fit in with the larger ecosystem and ensures that all of the necessary hardware and environments (development, QA, and production, as examples) are all in place. The team consists of the developers and the QA tester. The team's membership is fixed (there are no other people), and the tester is responsible for testing both this code release and the integration to existing code.

This is an example where a few people are playing multiple roles, but it can and does work for a number of smaller organizations. As the company grows, additional head count can be added to augment the team and spread the roles to more people.

Mid-Sized Company

Next we have an organization with six Scrum teams that are all working on different applications. In our example, we focus on one team and their development effort on a front-end e-commerce application.

- sales leader = project sponsor/key stakeholder
- account management leader = stakeholder with an emphasis on existing customers and feature enhancements that they desire

- product manager = product owner
- IT manager = IT manager
- Scrum master = Scrum master
- Agile coach = Agile coach
- enterprise architect = enterprise architect
- six developers and two QA = Scrum team

In this example, the product owner meets with the sales leader and the account management leader to determine the size, scope, timing, and funding for this development effort. The product owner begins to write requirements/user stories with input from many across the organization.

The IT manager assigns members to the Scrum team and ensures that the team is fully staffed. The IT manager will handle all personnel issues, such as performance management (appraisals/reviews) and any hiring decisions.

The Scrum master assembles the team, and he or she works closely with the product owner to make sure that all requirements/user stories are understood and prioritized. The Scrum master and product owner also coordinate to track the project progress and any identified risks and report back to the stakeholders on a regular basis.

The Agile coach meets with the Scrum master and the team both to ensure that members have what they need and are adequately trained and to answer questions. The Agile coach may also share best practices or lessons learned from other Scrum teams within the company, since he or she has a broader view of the activities.

The Scrum team designs and develops code to meet the business requirements identified by the product owner.

The QA testers test the code as it is developed and ensure that each sprint culminates with code that is ready to be deployed, according the release plan as defined by the product owner.

The release date is met, error-free code is deployed, sales has what is needed to drive revenue, and everyone is happy.

Large Multinational Company

In this example, we have an organization with six Scrum teams all working on one customer relationship management (CRM) application that will be put into production in 12 months.

- VP of customer support = project sponsor/key stakeholder
- chief information officer (CIO), chief financial officer (CFO), head of sales = stakeholders

- director of product management, sometimes called the chief product owner (Cohn 2010, p. 328) = lead product owner overseeing efforts of all six teams
- product manager = product owner per team
- IT manager = IT manager, possibly over more than one team
- Scrum master = Scrum master per team
- Agile coach = Agile coach
- enterprise architect = enterprise architect
- application owner = application owner
- various subject matter experts (SMEs) to assist with workflow decisions
- six Scrum teams

In this example, the VP of customer support, working closely with the application owner, defines the work streams and the high-level milestones and assigns work streams to teams. The stakeholders all review and agree on the work stream breakdown and the milestones.

The enterprise architect crafts a plan for how all of the component pieces will fit together from an infrastructure perspective before any major code is written. The resulting architecture will influence all of the teams and their direction. The application owner will ensure that the milestones and activities of the individual teams work in concert toward a united goal of a single CRM system.

Each of the six teams will have a product owner who will be responsible for writing user stories/requirements for their respective team. The director of product management/chief product owner oversees the activities of all six product owners, making sure each understands the priorities of the product backlog and how the components will fit together for a cohesive end user experience. Each team will have a Scrum master who will ensure that their team is working effectively and will remove any impediments that come up along the way.

Because of the size of this project and the complexity of multiple teams, it is a good idea to have an Agile coach onboard who can float from team to team and optimize their effectiveness as well as work with the product owners, Scrum masters, and the stakeholders to confirm that everyone continues to work toward a common goal. The coach would also ensure that risks, delays, and business problems are all addressed in a timely manner using the collaborative framework of Agile. As workflows for the CRM system are defined, coded, and tested, it is likely that a number of SMEs will play a role, because they are best suited to identify issues and considerations.

The biggest challenge in a project like this is the communication and the integration of the multiple teams. Many such projects fail because one or more teams hit significant hurdles that they are unable to overcome and they cannot deliver their code; this then affects the successful teams because they cannot integrate their complete pieces into the overall system, so the whole project falls into a state of disarray. The oversight by the chief product owner, application owner, enterprise architect, and the Agile coach is one of the best practices to ensure that all six teams complete their work so that the whole can be created by the sum of its parts.

Conclusion

Through this chapter, we learned the key roles as they exist in the Scrum methodology and used that as a backdrop to all of the other methodologies. We learned the responsibilities of a product owner and the traits and challenges that affect success. The role of Scrum master is interesting and unlike any role that existed before Agile, with an emphasis on ensuring team effectiveness. The team is empowered and self-organizing and positioned to make significant contributions. The extended team members play critical roles in the success of the effort. We looked at practical examples of how these roles interact in a variety of situations, which helps to increase understanding and appreciation of Agile roles.

Summary

- Scrum, the most widely adopted Agile methodology, has three defined roles—product owner, Scrum master, and the team.
- The product owner is responsible for setting the product vision, defining release management, setting priorities based on business value, accepting the sprint results as complete, incorporating stakeholder feedback, and supporting the team. In short, the product owner defines the "what."
- The Scrum master is responsible for making sure that the team has the best environment possible to complete their work. This includes removing impediments, minimizing interruptions, ensuring team cohesiveness, and enforcing the principles of Agile.
- The Scrum team is a self-managing group of cross-functional resources who commit to delivering working software in every sprint. The team

makes the technical and design decisions to execute on the user stories presented by the product owner. The team determines "how" the work will get done.

- Working agreements are the set of rules and/or values that govern the team's interactions. Each Scrum team establishes their own working agreement and uses it to reinforce team norms and relationships.
- "Fist of five" is a voting mechanism with Agile that facilitates discussion and decision making. As long as each participant is a 3 or higher, the decision is made and the team can move forward.
- "Chickens" and "pigs" are terms that come from a famous Agile cartoon: Pigs are deeply committed to the work (i.e., developers), and chickens are interested and supportive (i.e., stakeholders.)
- The project sponsor or champion is a critical role because it possesses both the budget and the authority to approve a project and make it happen.
- Scrum does not have a specific role for a project manager but does value the skills and deliverables by managing them within the team. Other methodologies, such as Crystal, FDD, and Lean software development, continue to utilize this role; XP does as well, though it is called a tracker.
- Stakeholders can be both internal (executives, users of the system) and external (customers or company shareholders), and they must be kept informed of project progress and deliverables. Their impressions, whether correct or not, can influence a project's funding and potential success.
- The role of product owner in Scrum and Lean software development includes gathering and prioritizing requirements. In XP, this is called the customer, and FDD and DSDM have multiple roles that fulfill the function: In FDD, it is the chief programmer and the domain experts, and in DSDM, it is the visionary, ambassador user, and advisory user. Crystal advocates for collaboration between the customer and the designer with no specific role.
- Team coach is a role that is handled several ways. Lean and FDD put the responsibility of team effectiveness on the project manager, and Scrum advocates for a Scrum master. DSDM has two roles that share this task—the team lead and the coach. XP has both a coach and a big boss, though one person can play both roles.
- An architect or tech lead is not a specific role in Scrum because the responsibilities belong to the team. FDD has a chief architect, Crystal has an architect, DSDM has a technical coordinator, and Lean software development has a technical owner.

- Documentation is still required in Agile, and the depth of documentation should be dictated by the value it delivers. Only one methodology, DSDM, specifically gives the documentation author a title: "scribe."
- Many companies will utilize an Agile coach to ensure a cohesive implementation of the Agile principles across multiple self-organizing teams.
- Kanban does not name specific roles because it is focused primarily on process improvements and removing bottlenecks.

Review 4 At this point, the reader should be able to answer Review Questions 16–20.

Interview with Roman Pichler

Roman Pichler is a leading Agile and Lean product management expert, and the founder of Pichler Consulting. Roman's expertise includes Agile market research, product planning, and product strategy; Agile product roadmaps; and Agile product definition including personas, user stories, scenarios, and user interface design. Roman is the author of four books on Agile and Scrum, including *Agile Product Management with Scrum.*

Roman's involvement with Agile started in 1999. He coached his first Agile project in 2001 and began working with Scrum in 2004. Roman has more than ten years' experience in helping companies transition to Agile. This includes rolling out Scrum in several companies, and teaching and coaching executives, product managers, product owners, development managers, project managers, and teams. He is the founder of the London Scrum User Group, an active contributor to the Scrum Alliance and the London product management community, and a regular speaker at international conferences. Roman was named *one of the 20 most influential Agile people* in April 2012. To learn more about Roman, you can visit www.romanpichler.com.

Kristin and Sondra: What is your definition of the product owner role?

Roman: The product owner is the person who owns the product on behalf of the company. The individual is responsible for the success of the product and has to be empowered to make the necessary decisions.

In practice, the application of the role varies. It is influenced by several factors including the market, the product life-cycle stage, and the organization. For instance, working as a product owner of a brand-new mobile app developed by a small team in a small to mid-size company will differ from looking after an existing healthcare product, which is developed by several teams in a large enterprise.

I find that the product owner role is particularly valuable in the early life-cycle stages when the product is developed and introduced to the market. In these stages, the product owner resembles an "intrapreneur," an entrepreneur within the enterprise.

Kristin and Sondra: How do you define the success of the product?

Roman: Broadly speaking, a successful product does a great job for its users and customers, and it benefits the organization developing it. Examples of the latter include entering a new market or market segment, meeting a revenue target, and strengthening the brand.

A great way to determine the product success is to carry out some customer discovery or problem validation work, including business modeling. Tools like the Business Model Canvas and Lean Canvas help determine what success means for a specific product.

Kristin and Sondra: What are the core responsibilities of the product owner?

Roman: The simple answer is: Whatever it takes to achieve product success in a healthy, sustainable manner! Here are some duties that I regard as important:

- Have a vision of where to take your product.
- Understand the product's business model, including its value proposition and the desired business benefits.
- Carry out product roadmap planning—particularly when you work with an existing product.
- Collaborate closely with the development team and the Scrum master.
- Describe the desired user experience and the product features, and capture them in the product backlog.
- Determine what needs to be done next, and select the right sprint goal.
- Select the appropriate research/validation technique to expose the product increment to the right people, including customers, users, and internal stakeholders.

- Analyze the feedback/data gathered, derive the right insights, and action them. This often results in updating the product backlog.
- Look after the budget, understand the progress made, and manage the delivery/launch date.
- Coordinate the product launch activities.

Techniques such as user observations, problem interviews, competitor analysis, business modeling, product roadmapping, personas, user stories, scenarios, design sketches, product presentations, user tests, metrics and analytics, and release planning help the product owner carry out the duties well.

Kristin and Sondra: Any closing thoughts?

Roman: Working as a product owner is a multifaceted job that requires different skills. But it provides the opportunity to create something new, to develop new products and features that hopefully benefit the users and the organization. It's a great job, in my mind!

Interview with Lyssa Adkins

Lyssa Adkins's book, *Coaching Agile Teams*, has set a new high-water mark for the practice of Agile coaching. Since 2004, Lyssa has taught Scrum and Agile coaching to well over a thousand students, coached many Agile teams, and served as master coach to scores of apprentice coaches. In both one-on-one settings and small groups, she enjoys a front-row seat as remarkable Agile coaches emerge and go on to entice the very best from the teams and organizations they coach. Before Agile, she had than more 15 years of expertise leading project teams and groups of project managers.

She believes that Agile is more than an alternative project management methodology, and she is passionate about deepening the roles in Agile—specifically Agile coach and Agile manager—to help Agile move into its fullest expression.

She holds numerous certifications, including: Certified Scrum Coach (CSC), Certified Scrum Trainer (CST), Project Management Professional (PMP), Six Sigma Green Belt (SSGB), and Organization and Relationship Systems Certified Coach (ORSCC). She is also a trained Co-Active Coach and Leader. For more on Lyssa, please visit http://www.agilecoachinginstitute.com.

Kristin and Sondra: What are the most important skills for a Scrum master?

Lyssa: Above all, the Scrum master's primary purpose is to help the team move toward high performance, producing products they are proud of and that fulfill the intended purpose in the world.

Perhaps surprisingly, then, technical or industry knowledge is not a key characteristic for success as a Scrum master. In fact, too much familiarity with the subject matter can actually be a detriment because it can keep the Scrum master "in the weeds." With Agile methods, team members are the ones "in the weeds," and rightly so. They are the knowledgeable insiders about the subject matter, the product, and the best ways to build things. This liberates the Scrum master to focus at the process level, considering questions such as: How is the team doing with the Agile process? What is the level of quality of their conversations? What is their ability to work with conflict as a positive force? Are they producing innovative and purposeful products? This is a completely different role, and one that requires a toolbox of skills more than any specific knowledge.

Working at this level, key skills for the Scrum master are facilitation, teaching, mentoring, and professional coaching. These skills allow them to work with team dynamics at the whole-team level as well as with individuals who often experience change and the resistance that comes along for the ride. Of course, deep knowledge of Agile practices and Agile values is key, as well. Ah! Finally! Here is the Scrum master's knowledge area and the subject matter expertise they bring to the team. Notice, though, that it is only one area of many.

Kristin and Sondra: How does a Scrum master develop over time?

Lyssa: Although Scrum often comes into an organization through its software development function, it doesn't stay there. It moves out into the organization, first requiring businesspeople to take up their role as the drivers of the product, then moves even further to challenge the organization's processes, structures, and leadership culture. That can become quite a tall order for a Scrum master!

To meet the ever-increasing challenges in an organization, Scrum masters develop from working with one team to working with an entire enterprise. Along the way, they acquire more skills and models for working with people at all levels. They also undertake a significant amount of self-development to increase their personal "leaderfulness," a key attribute for working with executives.

At the entry level, a Scrum master works with one team, being their on-the-ground Scrum guide and team development coach. They focus on helping the team use Scrum well. They also work to help the team remove the impediments directly blocking in the team's path. As the Scrum master gains experience with Scrum and working with team dynamics, they can grow into an Agile coach.

Kristin and Sondra: If you are just starting to adopt Agile, who are the best internal employees to tap for the Scrum master role?

Lyssa: The best people to tap for the Scrum master role are ones who find other people interesting and who find team dynamics absolutely fascinating. A person's previous role or domain knowledge is not a strong indicator of how they will flourish, or merely survive, in the Scrum master role. It's easy to learn Scrum and hard to help people use it well. To do so requires a love for helping people develop themselves while they are developing great products.

References and Further Reading

Adkins, Lyssa (2010). *Coaching Agile teams: A companion for ScrumMasters, Agile coaches, and project managers in transition*. Boston: Addison-Wesley.

Ambler, Scott. (2013). Feature driven development (FDD) and Agile modeling. http://www.agilemodeling.com/essays/fdd.htm.

Beck, Kent. (2000). *Extreme Programming explained*. Boston: Addison-Wesley.

Caine, Matthew. (2011). DSDM Atern roles and responsibilities—overview. http://www.mcpa.biz/2011/10/dsdm-atern-roles-and-responsibilities-an-overview.

Chedalawada, Alan. (2010). Standard work and the Lean enterprise. http://www.leanssc.org/files/201004/powerpoint/4.21%205pm%20Chedalawada%20StandardWorkAndTheLeanEnterprise.pdf.

Chromatic. (2003). *Extreme Programming pocket guide*. Newton, MA: O'Reilly Media.

Cohn, Mike. (2004). *User stories applied: For Agile software development*. Boston: Addison-Wesley. Kindle edition.

Cohn, Mike. (2010). *Succeeding with Agile: Software development using Scrum*. Boston: Addison-Wesley.

Cohn, Mike. (2013). Product owner. http://www.mountaingoatsoftware.com/scrum/product-owner.

Derby, Esther. (2011). Working agreements. http://www.estherderby.com/2011/04/norms-values-working-agreements-simple-rules.html.

Derby, Esther, and Larsen, Diana. (2006). *Agile retrospectives: Making good teams great*. Raleigh, NC: Pragmatic Bookshelf.

Dreher, J. C., and Berman, K. F. (2002). Fractionating the neural substrate of cognitive control processes. *Proceedings of the National Academy of Sciences*, *99*(22), 14595–14600.

Hunton, Steve. (2012). A ScrumMaster is not a project manager by another name. Blog entry, August. http://www.scrumalliance.org/articles/436-a-scrum-master-is-not-a-project-manager-by-another-name.

James, Michael. (2010). *The Scrum reference card*. http://www.scrumreferencecard.com.

Kniberg, Henrik, and Skarin, Mattias. (2010). *Kanban and Scrum—Making the most of both*. Raleigh, NC: lulu.com.

Palmer, Stephen R. (2013). FDD: People. http://www.step-10.com/SoftwareProcess/FeatureDrivenDevelopment/FDDPeople.html.

Pichler, Roman. (2010a). *Agile product management with Scrum: Creating products that customers love*. Boston: Addison-Wesley.

Pichler, Roman. (2010b). The product owner role: Product owner on one page. http://www.romanpichler.com/blog/roles/one-page-product-owner.

Poppendieck, Mary, and Poppendieck, Tom. (2003). *Lean software development: An Agile toolkit*. Boston: Addison-Wesley.

Richards, Keith. (2007). *Agile project management: Running PRINCE2 projects with DSDM Atern*. London: TSO (The Stationary Office).

Schwaber, Ken, and Beedle, Mike. (2002). *Agile software development with Scrum*. Upper Saddle River, NJ: Prentice Hall.

Sterling, Chris. (2008). Creating a team working agreement. Blog entry, May 2. http://www.gettingagile.com/2008/05/02/creating-a-team-working-agreement.

Sutherland, Jeff. (2010). Scrum handbook. http://jeffsutherland.com/scrumhandbook.pdf.

VersionOne. (2013) "8th annual state of Agile survey." http://www.versionone.com/pdf/2013-state-of-agile-survey.pdf.

Wikipedia (2013). Dynamic System Development Method. http://en.wikipedia.org/wiki/DSDM.

Review Questions

Review 1

1. What are examples of increasing business value?
2. What are the considerations when one product has multiple product owners?
3. What is the product owner's responsibility in reviewing the sprint results?
4. Who are the likely candidates to serve as Scrum master?
5. In what circumstances is it a bad idea to have the IT manager be the Scrum master?

Review 2

6. What is a "working agreement"?
7. How can "fist of five" help in the decision-making process?
8. How large should a Scrum team be? Why does it matter?
9. What are some of the benefits of self-organizing teams?
10. Who is a "pig," and what is meant by this distinction?

Review 3

11. What are the distinguishing characteristics of a project sponsor?
12. What is a project manager called in Extreme Programming (XP)?

13. Which methodology has more roles, Kanban or DSDM?
14. What would be the role of an Agile coach?
15. Provide several examples of stakeholders.

Review 4

16. Who is responsible for writing and prioritizing the requirements/user stories?
17. What should be the driving factor in prioritization?
18. What is the most widely used methodology?
19. What are examples of impediments?
20. Within Scrum, who is responsible for testing?

Chapter 5

The New Way to Collect and Document Requirements

Learning Objectives

- Recognize the differences between Agile and Waterfall with regard to requirements gathering and documentation
- Understand the format used within Scrum for user stories, including epics and acceptance criteria
- Explore several examples of how user stories are broken down from epics to child user stories and how acceptance criteria add important details to the story
- Learn how the other methodologies differ from Scrum in their terminology and practices
- Examine how requirements can be enhanced by using personas or engaging user experience (UX) designers to better understand potential system users
- Understand how user stories and Agile development efforts map into a marketplace driven by consumer demands and customer-specific development requests
- Value the importance of communication and transparency when it comes to requirement specifications and priorities
- Explore Lean software development and the Lean start-up concepts and how they influence the product development process

This chapter focuses on the front end of the Agile process, where customer and market feedback are incorporated into meaningful requirements. It addresses terms and ideas such as user stories, epics, acceptance criteria, understanding and measuring business value, prioritization, roadmaps, and Lean software development.

Old Form of Requirements Gathering

A big difference between the Waterfall methodology and Agile is the way that requirements are collected and shared. In Waterfall, all requirements need to be collected in their entirety before they are passed to IT for evaluation. Waterfall is a linear process where one stage must end before the next stage can begin; therefore, all requirements must be known and documented up front and completely. As you can imagine, this is nearly impossible because the marketplace is dynamic and things are constantly evolving. The result is frustration between product people and developers, because the developers never think that they are getting everything they need, and the product people are frustrated because there is no way for them to have thought through every possible detail. The other problem with the old method of exchanging requirements is the lack of dialogue. Product people work for months gathering and documenting requirements, which are sent to IT with little communication and no collaboration. IT does not have the opportunity to ask questions or offer suggestions relative to requirements, and so they do not have the chance to improve the quality by overlaying their expertise. Finally, the Waterfall method fails to keep up with the needs of the business because it is difficult to incorporate changes in requirements. The Agile framework is built to embrace change.

Agile Requirements in Scrum

As we have seen with the Agile values and principles, Agile operates in a completely different and innovative way compared to Waterfall. Instead of documenting all of the ins and outs of a complex system, Agile calls for simple instructions for a simple feature, and details are added as it is discussed. Requirements are focused on meeting the needs of the user/customer, delivering tangible business value, and inviting collaboration.

To best explain this concept, we start with Scrum and dive into how requirements are gathered—or elicited—and documented. Once that foundation is presented, we layer on the other methodologies and their unique traits.

In Scrum, the requirements are called *user stories*. A user story, by definition, must be small enough that it can be designed, coded, and tested within the sprint or iteration. Since the length of a sprint or iteration is short—two to four weeks—that forces our user stories to be simple and concise.

What exactly is a user story?

- **What:** A user story is a description of the requested feature (or component of a feature) that is short and simple.
- **Who:** A user story incorporates the perspective of the person who will use or benefit from the requested feature.
- **Why:** A user story incorporates the "value" of the feature so the team can understand what is driving this particular request.
- **When:** The user story will not actually specify a time frame, but there is a concept of time based on the prioritization of the user story: Those that are more time sensitive, or that drive more business value, are prioritized to the top of the list.

User Story Format

The user story format is very precise and allows us to collect valuable information in a user-friendly sentence structure. Here is the basic format:

As a <type of user>, I want <some goal>, so that <some reason>.

These data points are all significant and helpful; each allows the product owner to express an element about the request, and it invites dialogue and collaboration with the developers.

- As a <type of user> = why is this significant? It is important for developers to understand the perspective of the user who will be taking advantage of the code. You might design a feature far differently if you know that the end user is highly sophisticated versus one who is technically challenged.
- I want <some goal> = this part of the user story expresses what the user is trying to accomplish: I want to be able to log in. I want to be able to reset my password. I want to be able to run a report. Understanding the feature request is critical to delivering the right thing.
- So that <some reason> = this is perhaps the most critical part of the user story format. Understanding why the user wants to accomplish something can be very enlightening to the goal just described.

For example, a request came in to Cayman Design that *a web site administrator for our weather application wants to be able to run reports every 15 minutes*. The developers would then try to figure out how to load new data and create a script to produce reports with very quick turnaround. But when the reason is added (so that) . . . *so the web site administrator would have the chance to see when the application is approaching a threshold that will slow down the system*. Now the developers have more information, and they might suggest a different way to solve that need, such as setting a threshold alarm that proactively sends notification if volumes get within a certain level of tolerance. Because what the user wants is a way to be notified of a possible problem, they do not really want reports every 15 minutes; they just did not see another way to solve the problem.

Let's look at another example:

> As a concerned and retired grandmother, I want to receive weather alerts for areas where my children and grandchildren live so I know when I need to worry and call them to make sure they are safe.

This is a pretty good user story. You know the Who = an older woman. Does this matter? Absolutely. You can assume that the user might not be as familiar with technology options so she needs a simplified user interface. She might even have failing eyesight, so perhaps she needs bigger buttons and a bigger font. It might even influence your color choice. The What = grandma wants to receive alerts about possible weather events in specific parts of the country; that makes sense and is easy to understand. The Why is also very important: She wants the alerts so she knows when to worry (and not) and so she can reach out to her family when she thinks they might be in danger. Is that relevant? Absolutely. Because knowing that she wants to know when to worry, the product owner and the team can deprioritize any messaging about stable, uneventful weather patterns. This user story is specifically looking for dangerous weather events—tornadoes, hurricanes, flooding, blizzards—that are occurring in particular locations in the country.

The Who, the What, and the Why create a powerful combination so that the team has much more to go on than the traditional way of documenting requirements. Another valuable aspect about the user story format is that it invites conversation or negotiation: Let's talk about grandma, and discuss the best way to solve her problem. It is no longer a situation where the product owner has to know everything and provide irrefutable documentation of a desired feature. Now the team and the product owner are going to work together to find the best way to meet the needs expressed in the story.

Roman Pichler, an Agile expert on the role of the product owner, states it this way:

> A user story is not a specification, but a communication and collaboration tool. Stories should not be handed off to the development team but be complemented by a conversation (2010a).

When it comes to writing good user stories, an acronym was first mentioned in 2003 by Bill Wake, and it still is used today when measuring user story effectiveness.

Product owners need to INVEST in a good user story.

- **Independent**—The user story must be able to stand alone. It must be a feature or a component of a feature that can be tested and implemented as a unique element. To the extent possible, user stories should not be dependent on other activities. Ideally, they are written so that they can be delivered in any order (Cohn 2004, loc. 646).
- **Negotiable**—As mentioned, a user story should invite collaboration and discussion about the best way to solve the business problem that is presented. The team, the Scrum master, and the product owner must be open to conversation about available options.
- **Valuable**—The reason why we do anything in Agile is to drive business value, and the more business value being delivered, the higher the priority of the story. If the story does not add business value, the team should not work on it.
- **Estimatable**—Is story too big or too vague? It must be clear enough that the developers and testers can reasonably estimate the complexity and length of time to deliver.
- **Small**—The story should be small enough to be completed within a single sprint or iteration.
- **Testable**—It is enough of a feature, and it is written in such a way that it can be tested to make sure it works as expected.

Epics

Most user stories do not start as user stories; they start as "epics." An epic is simply a user story that is too big to be designed, coded, and tested within a single sprint. Most requirements start out as epics because we have an idea that we start to describe in the first user story. As we collaborate with the team and users, we realize that the feature has many different facets. As they say, "the devil is in the details," and as we discuss those details, the epic will break down into numerous child stories. There is typically a parent–child relationship, with a single epic spawning many child stories. This is not a bad thing: You have to start with the big idea, or even a small one, before you can discover all of the detailed decisions that it will take to deliver on that idea.

Mike Cohn introduced the concept of a "product backlog iceberg" (see Figure 5.1) when it comes to epics, and the iceberg suggests that stories need to be broken down into great detail only as you get closer to pulling them into a sprint (Cohn 2010, p. 244).

If a user story, or feature, will not be addressed for three to six months, then it is perfectly fine for that story to sit in the backlog as an epic. As time passes, and the opportunity to work on that story gets closer, the product owner and the Scrum master need to start breaking down that epic into the child user stories. By the time you get to the Sprint planning meeting, as described in Chapter 6, "Grooming and Planning," no story should still be an epic.

The best way to understand epics is to look at an example.

"As a host, I want to make a Thanksgiving dinner, so that my guests think I'm a good cook." This is a pretty good user story. You know the Who (the

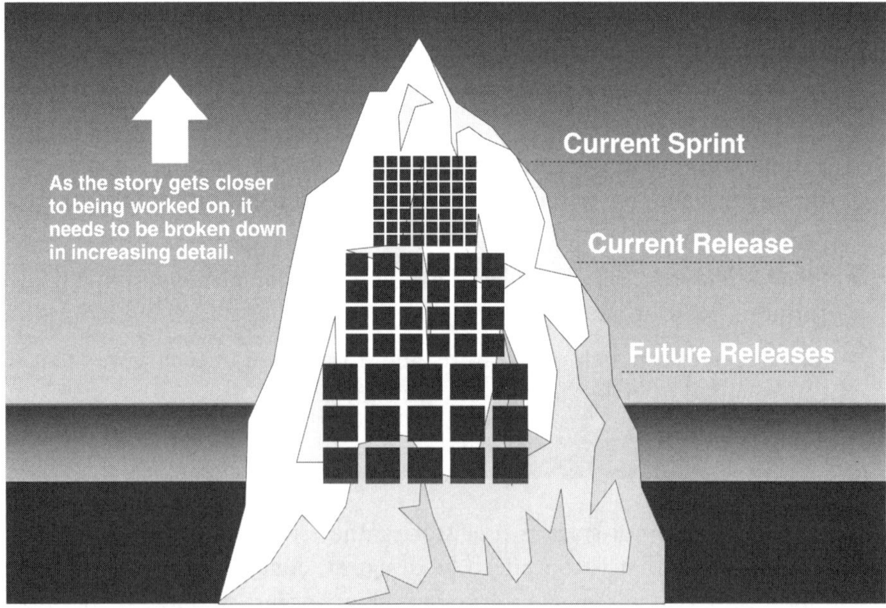

Figure 5.1 *Product backlog iceberg*

host or hostess), the desired What (make a Thanksgiving dinner), and the Why (want to be seen as a good cook). Thanksgiving is a US holiday that takes place on the fourth Thursday in November. If it is March, then having a Thanksgiving story in epic form is perfectly fine; it will take a while before we will actively work on it, so there is no business driver to force us to break that epic user story down into child user stories just yet. But as October arrives, we should start looking at the epic and breaking it down. Here are just a few examples of child stories that might come from our Thanksgiving epic.

"As a host, I want to bake a pie, so that my guests have dessert." This is a good child user story. Of course, the host needs to do some baking so that the guests will think he or she is a good cook. This user story is much smaller than hosting the entire dinner and can probably be executed on in a single sprint. If the team decided that they wanted to make the crust first and then make the pie filling and finally bake the pie—then those could be three more child stories, if we thought we needed to be that precise.

Here is another user story related to our Thanksgiving meal epic: "As a host, I want to send invitations for Thanksgiving dinner, so that my guests know where and when the dinner will be held." This is an interesting child story because it has nothing to do with cooking or baking, but it is absolutely essential to fulfilling the Thanksgiving epic. You will recall that the user in the epic story is a host. One cannot be a host without having guests, so this child user story gets to the heart of the matter. Now, there will be guests in attendance, so our user is truly acting as a host. Again, this story might split into even more child stories if we wanted to differentiate between writing the invitations, addressing the invitations, mailing the invitations, etc.

As our final example, this could be another child user story: "As a host, I want to set my table, so that my guests have a place to eat dinner." Again, this user story has nothing to do with cooking or baking, but is essential to hosting a successful dinner party. The guests must have utensils and plates in order to think the host is a good cook, which is the stated goal of the epic user story.

Having the right tools to track parent epic stories and their associated child user stories is quite helpful. Systems are in place that will allow you to enter a story and then write the child stories underneath the parent story; this sort of tracking is particularly useful when you are trying to see how different elements fit together. If you can look up a child story in the system and map it back to its parent epic, it can be very helpful in understanding how the feature works.

Acceptance Criteria

Acceptance criteria are the tests that the product owner will use to grade the successful development of the user story. The best way to explain acceptance criteria is again with an example. If your professor says, "You have a paper due next Friday about the impact of prayer in medical healing," then you know when the assignment is due and the topic. However, if the professor says, "You have a paper due next Friday about the impact of prayer in medical healing and it needs to be 10 pages, double-spaced, and you need to cite three references, including one from a medical journal," then you will probably feel much more comfortable about the assignment because you know at least some of the criteria you will be graded on. Acceptance criteria work in the same way: They give the product owner the opportunity to specify how he or she will "grade" the success of the sprint/user story and, like all things in Agile, it invites collaboration and dialogue. Going back to our Thanksgiving example, we can see how acceptance criteria can work.

"As a host, I want to bake a pie, so that my guests have dessert." The acceptance criteria might be as follows:

- Verify that the pie is round.
- Verify that the crust is on the outside of the pie.
- Verify that the filling is on the inside of the pie.
- Verify that a toothpick inserted in the middle comes out clean.

This gives the development team much more information about the product owner's vision of the user story. Again, it should invite conversation. What if the developers know of a new, better way to make pies, but their shape needs to be square? The team can bring this up to the product owner, who might say that the shape is actually quite important and it needs to be round. Or the product owner might say that round is the only shape he or she knew about, so entertaining a new, better option is a great idea. This is the type of collaboration and negotiation that would have been extremely difficult with the Waterfall methodology.

Another example is "As a host, I want to set my table, so that my guests have a place to eat dinner."

- Verify that each place has a dinner plate in the middle.
- Verify that each place has a dinner and salad fork to the left.
- Verify that each place has a knife and spoon to the right.
- Verify that each place as has a water glass above the knife.
- Verify that each setting has a napkin folded on top of the plate.

Let's consider another type of negotiation that might take place with this set of acceptance criteria. Perhaps the development team knows that adding a salad fork to the user story is going to add a significant amount of work, maybe even to the point of having to remove other elements from the user story to fit it in. The product owner, the Scrum master, and the team can have an objective conversation about the importance of the salad fork. The product owner might say, based on the market trends and competitive information, that having a salad fork is crucial to launching an effective product to the marketplace, and therefore, it must be included, so perhaps as a trade-off, we can remove the requirement of the napkin. Or the product owner might say that the salad fork was a "nice to have," not a "need to have," so we will remove it from the acceptance criteria. Just like everything in Agile, the point is not that you will have blissful interactions with no unanswered questions and no difficult trade-offs; the point of Agile is that we will discuss the trade-offs early and often so we make the best decisions for the product/feature given what we know at the time. Collaboration is the key, and product owners and developers are committed to working together to build the best possible product.

Referring to his recommendations for effective user stories, Roman Pichler says the following about acceptance criteria: "Acceptance criteria complement the story's narrative: They allow you to describe the conditions that have to be fulfilled so that the story is done" (Pichler 2010b).

User Story Writing Best Practices

Not every product owner is necessarily going to know how to write good user stories, but this is a skill that will grow with time and experience. The best way to improve the quality of user stories is collaboration. The product owner, working with the Scrum team, can continuously improve the quality of the stories over time.

What follows are several discussion points regarding user story writing.

Agree on the Depth of Technical Detail in the User Story

Agile has a firm distinction of the line between what the product owner owns and what the Scrum team owns. The product owner is responsible for ensuring that the company builds the right product (the What); the Scrum team is responsible for ensuring that the product is built correctly, or the right way (the How). The reality is that different teams will adopt different lines of delineation depending on what works best for them. For example, a product owner who is particularly technical may include some design ideas in the user story. Like every other aspect of a good user story, the design ideas should be negotiable with the Scrum team, so the product owner should never dictate the design of a solution. Conversely, if the application is well known by the development team, then the user stories might be a bit more vague in their description, leaving a good deal of latitude for the developers to implement and elaborate on during the sprint. Here are some sample user stories for Cayman Design.

- As a busy executive, I want to be able to save favorites on my mobile weather application so I can choose from a finite drop-down list to easily locate the weather in the destination I am traveling to. *In this example, the favorites do not have to be available via a drop-down list, and perhaps one could view that as being too descriptive in the "How." As long as it is negotiable and sparks collaboration, that additional detail is not problematic.*
- As a traveler using the weather application, I want the application to auto-fill based on the first few characters that I type—for example, BOS would bring up Boston as an option—so I can quickly find what I am looking for without typing all of the keys. *In this example, the development team might need more around the "What." How many keys are typed before we offer suggestions? Do we care about capitalization? Do we default to US destinations? However, if we have done something similar elsewhere in the application, then this level of detail could be sufficient.*

Ensure That Epics Are Appropriately Broken Down

As we have discussed, almost all user stories start out as epics, and must be broken down into smaller user stories that can be implemented in a single sprint. The product owner needs to be detail oriented enough to see the value in breaking down the user story/epic without feeling as if he or she is too far in the weeds. Individual user stories can sometimes make it seem as though things are moving too slowly when the product owner wants to pick up speed. It takes discipline and collaboration to make sure that the appropriate level of detail is being considered and passed on to the Scrum teams. For example, our preceding user story may be an epic. Let's look at how this could be broken down.

- EPIC: As a busy executive, I want to be able to save favorites on my mobile weather application so I can choose from a finite drop-down list to easily locate the weather in the destination I am traveling to.
- CHILD 1: As a busy executive, I want to be able to save a search location to my list of favorites from my mobile device so I can reuse that search on future visits.

- CHILD 2: As a busy executive, I want to be able to name my saved searches from my mobile device so I know how to access each saved search in the future.
- CHILD 3: As a busy executive, I want the name of my saved searches to default to the city name, unless I choose to manually override it, so that I can streamline saving my searches.
- CHILD 4: As a busy executive, I want my "saved favorites" option on the user interface to be presented on a mobile device near the "search location" so I have the option of starting a new search or using a saved one, and can minimize my keystrokes within the weather application.

As you can see, breaking down epics can describe a number of elements that might not have been clear in the initial user story. For example, we are going to have to take great care in the user interface to make sure that it is easy to save locations, recall saved locations, and accept/reject the default location name. These aspects may not have been considered with the original epic story and will certainly invite additional conversation about how best to achieve the desired business value.

Adding Acceptance Criteria

Acceptance criteria are a great way to ensure that a story is understood and to invite negotiation with the team about the business value that we are trying to create. Let's look again at our child user story and add acceptance criteria.

- **Child User Story:** As a busy executive, I want the name of my saved searches to default to the city name, unless I choose to manually override it, so that I can streamline saving my searches.
- **Acceptance Criteria:** Verify that the correct city name is auto-populated when the search found the location by *City/State* and the Save option is chosen from a mobile device.
- **Acceptance Criteria:** Verify that the correct city name is auto-populated when the search found the location by the *ZIP code* and the Save option is chosen from a mobile device.
- **Acceptance Criteria:** Verify that the default location name is saved to the database.
- **Acceptance Criteria:** Verify that the default location name is populated as a saved location in future visits.

- **Acceptance Criteria:** Verify that the location name can be manually overwritten if the default location name is not desired.
- **Acceptance Criteria:** Verify that the overwritten location name is at least two characters long, alphanumeric.

Again, it is clear from the acceptance criteria that there is a lot to think about for this relatively simple user story. One point that became apparent in the final acceptance criteria is that we have to define the length and parameters for a saved location name. We need to ensure that the definition is acceptable to the database and any downstream systems that may need to save or display that information. Plus, we probably now need a new user story about what error messages will be displayed if the user enters something that does not meet the criteria. For example, if a user just types "A" as the saved location name, we will need an error message that says the location name must be at least two characters; this error handling is an entirely new user story with new acceptance criteria. It represents one of the most valuable things about acceptance criteria—they often create new user stories. This is a great asset because it shows how the team is working together to define more and more of the product up front through thoughtful dialogue, instead of someone just making an uninformed assumption.

Exercise

1. Create three child user stories from the following epic user story. "As a business traveler, I want to be alerted if weather is likely to delay my flight."
2. Choose one of the child user stories that you just created and write three acceptance criteria for it.

Additions and Considerations from the Other Methodologies

Reviewing requirements and user stories in Scrum helps us to understand how other methodologies compare in their descriptions.

Extreme Programming

Extreme Programming (XP), like Scrum, calls the requirements "user stories"; they are ideally written by the customers or those representing the customers in terms of what they want the system to do for them (Wells 1999).

In addition, XP also values the importance of user stories for estimation, because the purpose of the stories is to understand the scope of what is requested so we can accurately estimate implementation time (Khramtchenko 2004, p. 6).

Dynamic Systems Development Method

Dynamic Systems Development Method (DSDM) shares many of these same concepts with regard to requirements and also specifically calls out the need to focus on the critical functionality first. DSDM weighs the importance of the requirements using the MoSCoW rules, which are as follows:

- **Must have:** All features classified in this group must be implemented, and if they are not delivered, the system would simply not work.
- **Should have:** Features of this priority are important but can be omitted if time or resources constraints appear.
- **Could have:** These features enhance the system with greater functionality, but the timeliness of their delivery is not critical.
- **Want to have:** These features serve only a limited group of users and do not drive the same amount of business value as the preceding items.

Alistair Cockburn takes a very user-centric approach to requirements and all aspects of the **Crystal Family methodology**. In an August 2010 blog, he stated, "We need to learn what the **Interests** are of the key stakeholders, what the **Needs** are of the users, and also what the **Styles** of those key users are. By Styles, I mean the users' operating styles, the way they might include the product into their life."

The usability of products and features is core to the Crystal principles, so the requirements should be very mindful of uses and ease of use.

Feature-driven development (FDD) is closely aligned with Scrum because it defines a user story as a feature that is a small, client-valued function that can be implemented in a short period of time (Goyal 2008, p. 8).

As already described, a user story in Scrum follows this format: *As a <type of user>, I want <goal> so that <reason>*. For example, "As a web site customer, I want the sum of my purchases displayed so that I know how much this is costing me." FDD uses a convention of: *<Action> the <Result> by/for/of/to <object>* so the same scenario might read: "Calculate the total of a sale," where calculate = action, total = result, and sale = object.

Lean software development and the Lean start-up take an innovative approach to requirements gathering and management, so a section later in the chapter is devoted to Lean.

Review 1 At this point, the reader should be able to answer Review Questions 1–5.

Enhancing Requirements

There are a number of ways to enhance the requirements gathering effort with additional information or practices, depending on the nature of the product. We discuss personas, usability, and business value as examples.

Incorporation of Personas

Another element that can enhance the effectiveness of user stories is to incorporate personas. A persona is defined as "a user-archetype, a fictional representation of target users you can use to help guide decisions about product, features, navigation, (and) visual design" (Grosjean 2009).

Personas were introduced in software development in 1999 in Alan Cooper's book, *The Inmates Are Running the Asylum*. Cooper created these fictitious people to act as users of the system so they could contemplate the user interaction when brainstorming design options.

Some of Cooper's specific guidance on personas is as follows:

- You want a finite number of personas, so your goal is to narrow down the people you are designing the system for.
- A primary persona is someone who must be satisfied but who cannot be satisfied by a user interface that is designed for another persona.
- You want to know what the persona's goals are so that you can see what your system needs to do, and not do.
- If you identify more than three primary personas, your scope is likely too large.
- Sometimes you want to identify negative personas, people that you are not designing for.

Let's explore a few example personas using our Cayman Design's weather application. Our grandmother who wants weather alerts could be one persona; we will name her Patricia. She is female, more than 70 years of age, retired, and living in Florida. Patricia has three children and eight grandchildren. Her children live in Charlotte, NC (hurricane and flooding risk), Topeka, KS (tornado risk) and Phoenix, AZ (heat and wildfire risk). She owns a laptop, plays solitaire, and uses e-mail extensively; thus she is slightly ahead of her peers in terms of technology adoption.

A second user persona for our weather application is a busy executive, Sam, who lives in New York City and travels extensively for his job. He is 45 years old, holds an MBA from Harvard, and is currently the CFO at a financial institution. He is married with two children, and he travels about 60% of the time. Sam feels pressed for time and is very adept with technological tools. We will focus our mobile applications and travel status alerts on Sam's persona.

It is easy to see how developing specific personas can reinforce the needs of the user and allow for a more detailed discussion about the features and priorities that will matter most to them.

Although personas are used by the product owner in the creation of more effective user stories, they can be equally important to the Scrum team because it helps the developers and testers to connect with the end users more intimately and resist the urge to create software targeted at the generic masses (Spagnuolo 2013).

Human–Computer Interaction (HCI) and Usability

Another way to add depth to the user stories is to incorporate usability. For this, we turn to usability experts such as those with experience in **human–computer interaction** (HCI), which is the study of people and their interactions with computers.

The idea behind HCI and usability is that wireframes or prototypes can be developed "on paper," or in systems that involve minimal development; the concepts are discussed in more detail in Chapter 9, "Agile beyond IT." These wireframes are then shown to the product owner and even to the end users so they can react to the workflow and the usability before anything is written in the code; this gives the product owner and the team feedback to improve the stories and the design so the development team starts with something that has already passed a usability screening. Companies that have engaged with an HCI or usability expert are typically pleased with the investment because expensive development resources are not used until the workflows are vetted. There is, however, a note of caution when it comes to incorporating usability designers with Agile because often their work involves months of analysis, so it could restrict the ability of the team to be iterative and collaborative if the entire workflow is preestablished.

Can user experience designers fit within fast-moving Agile teams? Of course. Ideally, we would like the user experience designer to be part of the Scrum or Agile team and to be available to answer questions or clarify items on the features currently being developed. We also want our user experience designers to be one or two sprints ahead of the team, thinking about the upcoming features and how their usability can be considered and tested (Cohn 2010, p. 152).

Another approach that aids in the integration of user experience designers into a Scrum team is to have the developers start on the tasks that are heavy on development and light on user interface work while the user interface designers are investigating, creating, and verifying designs for future sprints (Miller 2005, p. 7).

Like all things in Agile, usability can be incorporated into the flow of the team, provided care is taken to collaborate and learn from the iterations and experiences.

Business Value

The point of all user stories, both epics and child stories that have been broken down, is to deliver business value. It is the very reason that we write software and deploy code—to increase the business value of the application. As discussed earlier, business value can take many forms:

- Increased revenue
- Expansion of addressable market (i.e., with this new feature, more people will be interested in buying it)
- Decreased cost
- Increased customer satisfaction
- Increased processing speed
- Increased stability of the application
- Improved usability
- And more . . .

We should always test our user stories to make sure they are delivering business value, and if they are not, they should be either removed from the backlog or deprioritized to ensure that higher-value features are worked on first.

Here is an example of a user story whose business value is suspect. The Cayman Design team is working on the weather application having the ability to look up locations by city/state, by zip code, and by point of interest; there is a user story in the backlog to add the ability to look up by longitude and latitude coordinates. There is no identified business need for this feature, but it would be really cool to add it, and the developers think it would be relatively easy. The product owner needs to evaluate the business value of this request. Will it increase revenue? No. Will it expand the addressable market? No. Will it decrease costs?

No. And so on. Once it is determined that this request/user story will add no business value—despite how cool or easy it is—it should be either removed or deprioritized to let other features that will drive business value be completed first.

This example might be obvious, but it can be harder to discern the low-value user stories when you are trying to define a product. One of the easiest traps to fall into is "the 1% case." There will always be an instance where one customer might need a feature given a specific set of circumstances, but 99% of the customers/users will never have this need. The prudent product owner is always vigilant about this and makes sure that the team does not work on something for the 1% at the expense of the needs of the 99%. This can be particularly tricky when working with seasoned IT professionals who have had to build for the 1% before, and who can be quite forceful in suggesting that the 1% MUST be considered. It is incumbent then on the product owner to do the research so they have a data-driven response showing how much more important it is to drive business value and to address the needs of the 99%.

From User Stories to Deliverables

User stories are a building block to larger development efforts, and a strong Agile team needs to clearly understand how the pieces fit together to deliver maximum value to the marketplace.

Release Management

Release management is another critical aspect of Agile. Because the user stories and the features they support are so small—small enough to be coded, designed, and tested within a single sprint—they are often not enough to release to the marketplace. It is quite common to need several sprints' worth of code to have a meaningful enough product/feature to release. Many companies also choose to group their enhancements together into quarterly or biannual releases. An important role for the product owner is to determine the right amount for a release. If you are launching a new product, you may take many months' worth of sprints before you release the first version; on the other hand, if you have a mature product that is quite reliable, then you might release code at the end of every sprint so the application is continuously being enhanced. There are a number of factors to consider when doing release management, such as the following:

- Is this feature complete enough to meet the needs of the marketplace?
- Do we need to release less frequently because releases can be disruptive to our customers?

- How long is our build process? If it takes two weeks to run all of the processes necessary to release code, then you certainly do not want to do it after every sprint.
- Release management, also described in Chapter 4, "Describing the Different Roles," is an important effort that can differentiate the product in the marketplace and provide the Agile teams with helpful information about how the epics and stories fit into a larger picture. Release management is also a critical element of the Lean efforts that are described later in the chapter.

Managing Features—Marketing/Sales versus Development

One of the challenges with an Agile implementation is matching the need to be iterative with the need to respond to the marketplace with feature set expectations and delivery dates. Existing customers may demand commitment dates, and they want to know what features will be included in each release. This undoubtedly presents challenges, especially as you learn more about the complexity of what you are trying to accomplish.

One way to manage is to decide on a small number of features that will be included in a product launch. At Cayman Design, we accomplished this by coming up with two features that would be included in the first launch—two features and two features only; they were big efforts that would immediately deliver value to current customers and prospects. By knowing the promised features, the marketing team had the information that they needed to prepare collateral materials and product presentations. The sales team was able to start drumming up support in advance of the product launch with absolute confidence of what would be delivered.

Does this give our product owners and Scrum teams enough flexibility to be Agile and to learn as things evolve? Yes, it does.

The secret is that the features are not defined in great detail. The features, as envisioned, would be very rich. As time goes on and new challenges emerge, such as lost resources or unexpectedly complex integrations, the team adjusts the scope by reducing the components that would be included with the committed features. For example, if we started with 100 unique components per feature, we might launch with only 30. This method of managing the product launch can be quite effective: It gives the definition required by marketing and sales while maintaining the flexibility product owners and Scrum teams require to respond to changing variables.

Here are the elements of successfully managing marketing, sales, and customer expectations within Agile:

- Define the features that you are willing to commit to. We suggest no more than three. You want the features to be compelling and broadly defined so you have wiggle room within the scope.
- Unleash sales and marketing to hit the marketplace with the committed features and timeline.
- Between the Scrum team and the product owner, manage expectations and scope for each feature. As complexities or challenges come up, narrow the scope of the committed feature.
- Deliver on time. Once the product is launched, beef up the deployed features with future code releases to add back any removed (actually delayed) scope.

This process will not work for every situation or every product launch, but it can help in many situations.

Customer-Specific Code

Another complexity with Agile is managing existing customer expectations when they want specific development that they are willing to pay for. This process challenges the Agile principles of iterative development because it is typically time-bound, and scope must be defined and agreed upon before starting the project. These projects tend to be more Waterfall in nature, but there are several Agile techniques that can be employed to improve the experience over Waterfall. First, express the requirements in the user story format; this change alone will lead to more effective requirements discussions and will invite collaboration with the customer. Second, make sure the customer knows that development will progress in a series of sprints, and provide some transparency on what will be included within each sprint. It may be wise to invite the customer to the Sprint review (demo), described in Chapter 8, "Tracking and Reporting," where the code is demonstrated to the product owner. The customer could then see the progress and may want to make changes to their requirements. If changes are requested, the customer management team may need to execute a scope change to the contract, so the product owner and Scrum team will need to be extremely careful about incorporating customer feedback. Finally, the Agile practice outlined here, where the company commits to specific features but retains flexibility

Table 5.1 *Dos and Don'ts of Customer-Specific Code*

Do	Don't
Commit to features.	Adjust the scope without the involvement of the account management team.
Document the requirements in user story format.	Commit to a date that is "optimistic" given current resources and conditions. Make sure that dates can be reasonably met.
Be transparent about development progressing in a series of sprints.	Agree to user stories or requirements that are vague in nature or could easily be misinterpreted.
Consider inviting the customer to the Sprint demonstrations/reviews.	

in the breadth of the scope, will enable the Scrum team and product owner to manage customer requirements in an iterative fashion.

To summarize how to handle customer-specific (and paid for) code requests, Table 5.1 presents some dos and don'ts.

Although certain aspects of customer-specific code requests do not fit in an Agile framework, there are ways to manage things effectively by being collaborative and transparent with the customer.

Review 2 At this point, the reader should be able to answer Review Questions 6–10.

Communication

Having solid requirements and a clear action plan with the team is only a piece of the requirements effort. Effective Agile implementations are strong on transparency, which means that key stakeholders, both internal and external, are well informed on the activities under way and their impacts to the organization.

Sharing the Vision

Another thing that is important within Agile is to ensure that the team, the product owner, the stakeholders, and other roles defined in Chapter 4 understand the vision and what will be included in the release. This job usually falls to the product owner, and it can really help with complex or large projects. A best practice to consider is hosting a meeting for everyone who may be affected by this effort at the start of the project. If this is a new product, many product owners lead a kick-off meeting, but even existing products that are undergoing enhancements might benefit from a team meeting to ensure a common understanding of the goals and the business value that the team is trying to deliver.

Here is a good example of why this is important. Cayman Design is creating a new product that will involve numerous sprints, probably six months' worth, before the first launch. There is a lot of code to be written and decisions to be made before the product will take its final shape. The team may want to dive right in and start writing code, but taking a moment to share the vision can help with expectations and avoid rework later down the line. For example, reporting is one of the last things that most product launches consider because it comes at the end of the process. Once in the marketplace, the product has to be selected, ordered, delivered, and used before reporting comes into play. However, the decisions that are made about what data to store, in what format, and for how long will dramatically affect Cayman Design's ability to create reports. Sharing the vision with the reporting team early on can prove to be quite beneficial. The reporting team might notice a key piece of data that they will need to have, and if they can alert the developers before the code is written, it is much easier than trying to add a new data element after the code has already been designed, written, and tested.

Sharing the vision also forces the product owner to have a vision. This may sound like an obvious statement, but sometimes people are moving so fast, from project to project, from action item to action item, that they do not stop to take a breath and review the big picture. Stephen Covey captures the essence of this concept when he compares managers to leaders:

> You can quickly grasp the important difference between leadership and management if you envision a group of producers cutting their way through the jungle with machetes. They're the producers, the problem solvers. . . . The *leader* is the one who climbs the tallest tree, surveys the entire situation, and yells, "Wrong jungle!"
>
> As individuals, groups, and businesses, we're often so busy cutting through the undergrowth we don't even realize we're in the wrong jungle. (Covey 1989, p. 101)

In Agile, we want our product owners to demonstrate true leadership over their product, to know if the Scrum team is coding in the right jungle. By having a presentation or meeting about the desired deliverable, the product owner has the opportunity to stop and think about what he or she is trying to achieve;

articulating this vision might help the product owner find gaps or potential problems in his or her thought process. And by sharing it with others, the product owner benefits from the wisdom of the group, who will ask provocative questions and drive further clarifications.

Roadmaps—Internal and External

Product management will often produce a written document called a "roadmap." Some companies produce versions that are available for external clients, but others publish only internal roadmaps, for employees, that go into a deeper level of detail. Still other companies create both.

External Roadmaps

An external roadmap basically declares what new products or features you are going to bring to the market by a specified date. These documents are usually produced only for existing customers or late-stage prospects because they include information that can be used inappropriately by the competition. It is unusual to find a roadmap posted on the company's web site for public viewing. Different companies have very different ways of managing external roadmaps: Some go into great detail, and some are more precise on the date, perhaps even regarding a specific delivery date. Most external roadmaps, however, list broad explanations of what is coming in future quarters or six-month intervals.

Some Agile purists have a hard time with the concept of roadmaps because Agile is supposed to be iterative and constantly changing to respond to the needs of the marketplace. Although this is true, most companies and their customers expect a degree of transparency and commitment about what is to come. Cayman Design is a company selling directly to consumers (business to consumer, or B-to-C), so a published roadmap may be less important than for a company serving other businesses (business to business, or B-to-B). Because B-to-B customers might be building their own software to interconnect, they need to be able to anticipate the features and dates so they can align their own roadmap with the company's deliverables. Figure 5.2 presents an example of an external roadmap.

Internal Roadmaps

Internal roadmaps can be a bit easier because they do not represent a "commitment" to existing clients. They can be as simple as a different view of the product backlog, including features and delivery dates so that internal parties can plan their action items accordingly. When working with IT, the product owner

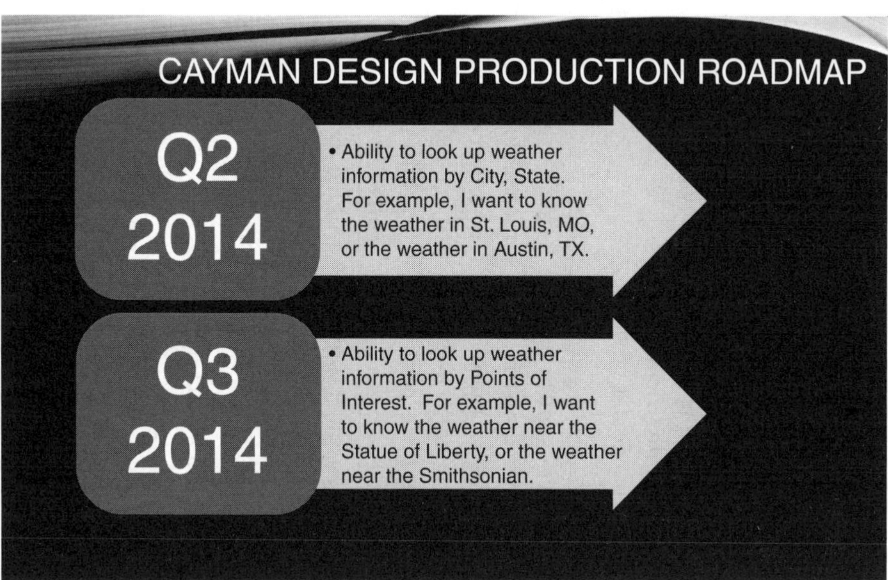

Figure 5.2 *Example external roadmap*

> **Review 3** At this point, the reader should be able to answer Review Questions 11–15.

is likely to use the product backlog for all of their conversations, collaboration, and priority management. However, others in the organization, such as sales, marketing, and possibly operations, do not need to know the details of each user story—they may be more satisfied with understanding the epics so that they can prepare their teams for what is coming. Table 5.2 presents an example of an internal roadmap.

Both internal and external roadmaps require a clear owner of who is responsible for information updates, the frequency of updates, and communication strategy. Typically product owners or product managers own the roadmaps and update them weekly, monthly, quarterly, or as needed, depending on the nature of the core business. Communication can vary from e-mail notification of an update, to a formal meeting, to simply making the updated information available on a shared collaboration site. Roadmaps are not a requirement for Agile, and as mentioned, some purists do not like them, but they are typically part of the reality for an organization, so determining what to include and how to produce roadmaps is a worthwhile discussion.

Table 5.2 *Example Internal Roadmap*

Title	Description	Date	Dependencies	Target Market	Changes
Look up by City/ State	Set the location for the weather information based on the city and state entered into the interface.	Q2 2014	State table to convert 2-digit abbreviations to state names and vice versa	Consumers who are traveling or have family/friends in a particular city/state	No changes from previous roadmap
Look up by Points of Interest	Input a point of interest and have it map to a location that can then present the weather information to the end user.	Q3 2014	Interfacing to a third-party program that contains points of interest with their locations identified	Consumers who are traveling for sight-seeing and want to know the weather in their location.	This has been moved down in priority because of dependency on the third-party software.
UI 1—Increase the font size on the search box	Increase the font size to Arial 12.	Q3 2014	None	Existing customers and attracting new users	Added to roadmap
UI 2—Reorder display of weather information for each location	Reorder the display to (1) Current temp (2) Hi/ Low temps for today (3) Percent chance of precipitation.	Q4 2014	None	Existing customers and attracting new users	Added to roadmap

Lean Product Development and the Minimum Viable Product (MVP)

A final related topic as we close this chapter on the new ways to gather requirements and release management is to explore Lean software development. The concept of Lean is adapted from manufacturing, where engineers at Toyota envisioned a new way to manage the supply chain of automobile production by empowering frontline workers in decision making, shrinking the size of batch production, reducing inventory to a just-in-time model, and accelerating cycle times (Ries 2011, p. 18).

Many aspects of Lean can be applied outside of manufacturing. Two brilliant Agile minds, Mary and Tom Poppendieck, were the first to adapt the principles in their book, *Lean Software Development: An Agile Toolkit* (2003). Their approach was targeted at the software development cycle, and they came up with seven core principles that compose their toolkit (Poppendieck and Poppendieck 2003, p. xvi):

1. **Eliminate waste.** Waste is anything that does not add value to a product, value as perceived by the customer.
2. **Amplify learning.** Development is an exercise in discovery.
3. **Decide as late as possible.** Delaying decisions is valuable because better decisions can be made when they are based on fact, not speculation.
4. **Deliver as fast as possible.** Design, implement, feedback, improve: The shorter these cycles are, the more can be learned. Speed assures that customers get what they need now, not what they needed yesterday.
5. **Empower the team.** Top-notch execution lies in getting the details right, and no one understands the details better than the people who actually do the work.
6. **Build integrity in.** Software with integrity has a coherent architecture, scores high on usability and fitness for purpose, and is maintainable, adaptable, and extensible.
7. **See the whole.** The interdependencies between systems and processes must be optimized as a whole, or else the customer experience becomes fragmented and suboptimized.

A slightly different adaptation of the "Lean" movement came from Eric Ries with his groundbreaking book, *The Lean Startup*, which has created an entire movement, not unlike Agile. Ries explains why some start-ups or entrepreneurs fail while a small percentage actually succeed. One explanation is that markets are changing so quickly that product development cycles, even when using Agile, are having a hard time keeping up. Ries suggests that product owners define the minimum viable product, or MVP, with the minimum features required to address a need in the marketplace; they launch with that very thin product offering, see how the market responds, and then course-correct in future launches. It is a radically different way to look at product development because the goal is not to launch a fully functional product; it is to be quick to market with something that solves a piece of the business problem and expand from there. The reason why Lean product development is getting so much attention and traction is that many companies have spent years developing something that the market either does not want or will not pay for; this gets the product in front of the paying public with the minimum effort possible. Based on how the product is received and what features deliver the most value (and hence the highest ROI, return on investment), the product owner and development team can quickly reprioritize the backlog to respond to real market feedback to continue to add business value and drive revenue.

The value of Lean is incorporating a continuous feedback loop from actual customers, which is more reliable and honest than internal feedback, so the teams can continuously learn and work on the most important things with a minimal amount of waste. It is easy to see how these engineering and manufacturing principles make so much sense in the world of software development. It is absolutely critical that the product owner envision a product that is needed in the marketplace. After all, Peter Drucker has been quoted as saying, "There is surely nothing quite so useless as doing with great efficiency what should not be done at all" (Goodreads 2013).

To illustrate the idea of the minimum viable product, let's look at Cayman Design and our weather application. We made the decision, as detailed in Chapter 4, that we would launch our weather application with only data for New York City. Some might consider this a risky move since we have a limited target audience; we could have waited until data for Boston, Dallas, and San Francisco was included as well and would likely have had more traffic and certainly more users. By choosing the MVP with only New York City data, we were able to get our product out in the marketplace sooner, and we could immediately start gathering real feedback from real users. By investigating the site analytics, we can learn where our New York users are spending most of their time and where they are getting hung up in the application; using Agile, we can then quickly incorporate that feedback into subsequent releases of the software. Thus, when we expand to Boston and other cities, we are doing so with actual user-driven improvements.

Product owners and others responsible for gathering customer feedback will see the value of Lean software development and the minimum viable product, but they may need to fight the internal organizational inertia to build a robust, feature-rich product. The concept of starting small and gathering input to influence future deliverables is usually understood and supported; the actual activity of releasing something to the marketplace that is limited in its features and addressable audience is often harder to embrace.

Conclusion

This chapter outlined the importance of user requirements and how Agile approaches this effort very differently from Waterfall. The very format that is used to capture requirements is different, as are the collaboration and negotiation with various stakeholders and technical experts to achieve the best possible solution in the shortest amount of time. Adding elements such as acceptance criteria, personas, business value, and the minimum viable product forces Agile teams to think differently about how to best meet the needs of the marketplace. This new way of thinking leads us to better products and more satisfied customers, which is a winning combination.

Summary

- In the Waterfall methodology, user requirements should be completed before engaging with development teams. This linear model does not suit the evolving needs of today's dynamic marketplace.
- In Agile, a user story, by definition, must be small enough to be designed, coded, and tested in single sprint, or iteration.
- The user story format is *As a <type of user>, I want <some goal>, so that <some reason>*. Each element is important for helping to clarify exactly what we are trying to accomplish with our software.
- We want to INVEST in good user stories, meaning that they are Independent, Negotiable, Valuable, Estimatable, Small, and Testable.
- Epics are user stories that are too large to be completed in a single sprint. Most user stories start as epics, and there is no need to break them down into smaller user stories until the team is getting close to working on them.

- Acceptance criteria are the details added to a story representing how a story will be "graded" or deemed complete by the users. Acceptance criteria often lead to healthy conversations about trade-offs between development teams and product people.
- DSDM employs a prioritization method called MoSCoW, where stories are depicted as Must Haves, Should Haves, Could Haves, and Wants.
- The Crystal Family methodologies focus heavily on the user experience and understanding exactly how end users will interact with the software.
- Feature-driven development has a similar user story format to Scrum: *<Action> the <Result> by/for/of/to <object>*.
- A persona is a fictitious character that represents a key user of the system. Personas are named and detailed to assist in the requirements clarification and prioritization process.
- User experience designers and HCI experts contribute to strong requirements by mapping and testing the workflows and usability considerations before development begins.
- Release management is the activity of grouping features and enhancements together into a compelling release to the marketplace.
- Customer-specific code is a challenge in Agile development practices, but it can be incorporated with a few clear interactions.
- All product development efforts should be guided by a vision for the product that is clearly articulated and understood throughout the organization.
- Roadmaps (both internal and external) are communication devices that bring transparency to Agile development efforts.
- Lean software development and the minimum viable product (MVP) of Lean product development are great adaptations of Agile principles in a competitive marketplace where real user feedback is essential.

Review 4 At this point, the reader should be able to answer Review Questions 16–20.

Interview with Ellen Gottesdiener and Mary Gorman

Ellen Gottesdiener, founder of and principal with EBG Consulting, is an internationally recognized facilitator, coach, trainer, and speaker. Her first book, *Requirements by Collaboration: Workshops for Defining Needs* (Addison-Wesley, 2002), describes how to use multiple models to elicit requirements. She has established herself as an expert in Agile product and project management practices, product envisioning and roadmapping, business analysis and requirements, retrospectives, and collaboration. Her most recent book, *Discover to Deliver: Agile Product Planning and Analysis* (EBG Consulting, 2014), coauthored with Mary Gorman, provides the essential planning and analysis practices you need to deliver high-value products.

Mary Gorman, vice president of Quality and Delivery with EBG Consulting and coauthor of *Discover to Deliver* with Ellen Gottesdiener, is an expert business analyst, facilitator, coach, and trainer. She has deep expertise in business systems, product development, and Agile analysis. Mary has been a driving force for Agile within the International Institute for Business Analysis (IIBA) by spearheading the IIBA® Business Analysis Body of Knowledge® and the IIBA® certification exam. She is a CBAP™ (Certified Business Analysis Professional™) and Certified Scrum Master. Mary's experience allows her to work with global clients, speak at industry conferences, and continue to write on requirements topics for the Agile and business analysis community.

Kristin and Sondra: What is different about Agile requirements?

Ellen and Mary: With Agile, it's a different mind-set. You don't think of requirements as a static set of statements to be implemented. Rather, you expect and enable your product to evolve in functionality and value as you continually discover and deliver high-value product options.

During planning, you think of requirements as not-yet-validated options for achieving a certain value by solving a problem or taking advantage of an opportunity. After delivery, you validate whether or not the built option provided the anticipated value. In Agile, the goal is to assess value constantly, adapt as conditions change, and deliver value quickly and often.

Kristin and Sondra: How do you measure business value as it relates to story prioritization?

Ellen and Mary: The product's business value—what the sponsoring party will gain or possibly lose—is both tangible and intangible. Tangible value comes from meeting business goals and objectives and is often measured in revenues and costs. The product's intangible value may be more difficult to identify and measure. It might include the product's desirability or how the product affects the company's reputation.

Your product—whether it's an application, a service, or a system, and whether it's commercial or internal software—must deliver both tangible and intangible value to be successful. When prioritizing stories for the next planning horizon, you elevate those that will deliver value.

Kristin and Sondra: How do Agile teams gather requirements?

Ellen and Mary: We prefer to use the word "elicit" rather than "collect" or "gather." "Elicit" connotes that we draw out, deduct, derive, infer, provoke, and evoke requirements during discovery. This is important and challenging work! Elicitation goes hand in glove with analysis. As we elicit, we analyze, which may lead to further elicitation for clarity and elaboration of requirements.

Another distinction is our definition of "team." The team needs to include stakeholders from three realms: business, technology, and customer. They work together as product partners to envision and deliver the product.

Elicitation and analysis work best when teams use techniques that engage, involve, interest, challenge, and excite the product partners as they conduct what we call "structured conversations" to explore, evaluate, and confirm product options. Such conversations are structured around a framework we call the 7 Product Dimensions. These are the seven categories of product options: requirements regarding the users, the interfaces, the actions, the data, the controls (constraints), the environment, and the quality attributes of the product.

Note that the 7 Product Dimensions include nonfunctional as well as functional options. Collectively, they provide a holistic view of the product.

As they work, team members keep in mind that requirements come in varying levels of granularity, depending on the planning horizon you're working in—that is, the time period you want your plans to cover. We divide the planning horizons into three: the Big-View (as long as two years), the Pre-View (the next product release, typically a few months), and the Now-View (the next iteration, typically a few weeks). You can think of these levels as

Wants (Big-View), Needs (Pre-View), and Requirements (Now-View). In this scheme, the requirements are small, carefully sliced, and highly granular.

Kristin and Sondra: What are the most important aspects of a good user story?

Ellen and Mary: We've found stories to be useful conversation starters. We use the structured conversation to explore and evaluate a story across the 7 Product Dimensions. For example, the partners learn who the user is, which interfaces are needed, what the detailed actions are, which data is created, read, updated, and/or deleted, which controls must be enforced, what the user's environment is like (where they will actually interact with the product), and what quality attributes are needed (availability, performance, security, etc.). The conversation isn't complete until the story is "confirmed." The partners define concrete examples and unambiguous acceptance criteria to ensure that their expectations of the story are the same.

To recap, a user story needs to address all 7 Product Dimensions. The structured conversation is a framework for exploring, evaluating, and confirming the partners' understanding of the story.

Kristin and Sondra: What are the best tips for managing scope creep?

Ellen and Mary: Here are our top five tips:

- Develop a vision for the product, and define the goals and objectives you anticipate the product will deliver.
- Identify and collaborate with the stakeholders (customer, business, and technology partners) early and often throughout discovery and delivery.
- Ground your scope decisions in the product's vision, goals, and objectives, as well as the partners' value considerations.
- Use lightweight, organic models to analyze all 7 Product Dimensions.
- Get real! Use concrete examples to explore and confirm the product.

Kristin and Sondra: What is the most important coaching advice that you give to teams?

Ellen and Mary: Be transparent—identify and socialize the product's ends (vision, goals, objectives) along with the partners' value considerations. Be collaborative and creative—use a variety of techniques to engage the partners and visualize the product's requirements. Be open, clear, and consistent when making product decisions.

References and Further Reading

Adkins, Lyssa. (2010). *Coaching Agile teams: A companion for ScrumMasters, Agile coaches, and project managers in transition*. Boston: Addison-Wesley.

Ambler, Scott. Personas. http://www.agilemodeling.com/artifacts/personas.htm.

Coad, Peter, De Luca, Jeff, and Lefebvre, Eric. (1999). *Java modeling in color with UML: Enterprise components and process*. Upper Saddle River, NJ: Prentice Hall.

Cobb, Charles G. (2013). *Managed Agile development: Making Agile work for your business*. Parker, CO: Outskirts Press.

Cockburn, Alistair. (2006). *Agile software development: The cooperative game* (2nd ed.). Boston: Addison-Wesley.

Cockburn, Alistair. (2010). Requirements are sins. Blog entry, August 20. http://alistair.cockburn.us/Requirements+are+SINs.

Cohn, Mike. (2004). *User stories applied: For Agile software development*. Boston: Addison-Wesley. Kindle edition.

Cohn, Mike. (2008). User stories for your product backlog. http://www.mountaingoatsoftware.com/uploads/presentations/User-Stories-Product-Backlog-Scrum-Gathering-Chicago-2008.pdf.

Cohn, Mike. (2010). *Succeeding with Agile: Software development using Scrum*. Boston: Addison-Wesley.

Cooper, Alan. (1999). *The inmates are running the asylum: Why high-tech products drive us crazy and how to restore the sanity*. Indianapolis, IN: Sams Publishing.

Covey, Stephen R. (1989). *The 7 habits of highly effective people*. New York: Free Press Simon and Schuster.

DSDM. (2011). Dynamic Systems Development Method. http://dsdmofagilemethodology.wikidot.com.

Goodreads. (2013). http://www.goodreads.com/author/quotes/12008.

Gottesdiener, Ellen, and Gorman, Mary. (2012). *Discover to deliver: Agile product planning and analysis*. Sudbury, MA: EBG Consulting.

Goyal, Sadhna. (2008). Major seminar on feature driven development Agile techniques for project management and software engineering WS 2007/08. Munich: Technical University of Munich. http://csis.pace.edu/~marchese/CS616/Agile/FDD/fdd.pdf.

Goyal, Sadhna. (2010). *Influence of bugs on a software project: Effect of time of bug discovery on the duration and budget of a software project.* Saarbrücken, Germany: VDM Verlag Dr. Müller.

Grosjean, Jean Claude. (2009). Personas in Agile development: YES we can! Blog entry, December 2. http://www.agile-ux.com/2009/12/02/personas-in-agile-development-yes-we-can.

Khramtchenko, Serguei. (2004). Comparing eXtreme Programming and feature driven development in academic and regulated environments. Final paper for CSCIE-275: Software Architecture and Engineering, Harvard University, May 17. http://www.featuredrivendevelopment.com/files/FDD_vs_XP.pdf.

Marchesi, Michele, Succi, Giancarlo, Wells, Don, Williams, Laurie, and Wells, James Donovan. (2002). *Extreme Programming perspectives.* Upper Saddle River, NJ: Pearson Education.

Miller, Lynn. (2005). Case study of customer input for a successful product. Alias, Proceedings of Agile conference, Toronto, Canada. http://agileproductdesign.com/useful_papers/miller_customer_input_in_agile_projects.pdf.

Pichler, Roman. (2010a). *Agile product management with Scrum: Creating products that customers love.* Boston: Addison-Wesley.

Pichler, Roman. (2010b). 10 tips for writing good user stories. Blog entry, October 7. http://www.romanpichler.com/blog/user-stories/writing-good-user-stories.

Pichler, Roman. (2012). A template for writing great personas. Blog entry, May 3. http://www.romanpichler.com/blog/agile-product-innovation/persona-template-for-agile-product-management.

Poppendieck, Mary, and Poppendieck, Tom. (2003). *Lean software development: An Agile toolkit.* Boston: Addison-Wesley.

Ries, Eric. (2011). *The Lean startup: How today's entrepreneurs use continuous innovation to create radically successful businesses.* New York: Crown.

Spagnuolo, Chris. (2013). Know your users—create personas. Blog entry, January 8. http://agile.dzone.com/articles/know-your-users-create.

Wake, Bill. (2003). INVEST in good stories, and SMART tasks. http://xp123.com/articles/invest-in-good-stories-and-smart-tasks.

Wells, Don. (1999). User stories. http://www.extremeprogramming.org/rules/userstories.html.

Wells, Don, and Williams, Laurie. (2002). Extreme Programming and Agile methods—XP/Agile. Universe 2002: Second XP Universe and First Agile Universe Conference, Chicago, August 4–7 (Lecture Notes in Computer Science). Berlin: Springer.

Review Questions

Review 1

1. What is the user story format in Scrum?
2. Name three of the six elements of a user story represented in the acronym INVEST.
3. What is an epic?
4. What are the MoSCoW rules in DSDM?
5. What is Crystal software development very interested in with regard to requirements?

Review 2

6. What is the value of personas?
7. Can user experience designers participate on a Scrum team? Why or why not?
8. What are three examples of business value?
9. What is *release management*?
10. For customer-specific code, how should the team incorporate customer feedback and potential changes to the scope of the project?

Review 3

11. Who should articulate the product vision to the organization?
12. Are external roadmaps typically accessible by the public (everyone)? Why or why not?
13. What are the differences in terms of audience, details, and committed dates between internal roadmaps and external roadmaps?
14. Who owns the roadmap creation, updates, and communication?
15. How does the transparency afforded by Agile help the organization?

Review 4

16. What does MVP stand for, and what does it represent?
17. Why does the Lean software development advocate for making decisions as late as possible?
18. What could real user feedback tell you about your product that internal conversations would not reveal?
19. Should user stories be complete and thorough before discussions begin with the development teams? Why or why not?
20. Why is the Agile way of gathering requirements such an improvement over the Waterfall methodology?

Chapter 6

Grooming and Planning

Learning Objectives

- Understand the elements of a product backlog and what traits lead to the strongest deliverables
- Dive into prioritization and learn different methods for understanding what is the most important feature or item to work on
- Explore estimation and the different practices and measures that are used today
- Understand story points and planning poker as ways to discern the level of effort and complexity of the user stories/requirements
- Learn the other inputs that affect the planning process, such as team velocity, definition of "done," technical debt, and bugs/defects
- Evaluate Sprint planning and the XP planning game to learn how commitments are made and work is planned
- See how maintenance work can be incorporated into Agile teams
- Review the triple constraints model and how it is handled within the Agile framework

As the development process progresses, the requirements/user stories are groomed into functional input for the development teams. The priority of the user stories and the estimates of their size are important factors when the development team is considering their commitment to the work. This chapter presents a variety of strategies for grooming the stories. Once the grooming is complete, the sprint planning begins, incorporating the velocity of the team, the definition of "done," the amount of technical debt, and more. Finally, we explore the theory of triple constraints (scope versus time versus resources) and how the management of these can affect the development process.

Product Backlog (Scrum and XP)

The full list of desired features, or user stories, are captured in what Scrum and XP call a "backlog." The highest-priority stories reside at the top of the backlog and are in the lowest level of detail. As mentioned in Chapter 5, "A New Way to Collect and Document Requirements," stories that are deeper in the backlog, meaning they will not be worked on for some time, will likely be in epic form, which is perfectly acceptable.

Backlogs vary in their depth, breadth, and quality. Jeff Sutherland (2011), one of the signers of the Agile Manifesto, pleads for technical excellence in the quality of the product backlog, citing it as one of the areas of improvement for Agile teams.

Mike Cohn provides sound guidance on how to improve backlog quality using the acronym DEEP, which stands for Detailed appropriately, Estimated, Emergent, and Prioritized (Cohn 2010, p. 253).

Detailed appropriately means that the highest-priority stories contain sufficient detail for the development teams to deliver them: Questions are answered, and the necessary clarifications are included in the story description. Acceptance criteria, as described in Chapter 5, are a component of the essential detail for the story.

Estimated means that the team understands the stories and believes there is adequate information to estimate the level of effort or amount of time required to deliver the story. We explore estimating thoroughly in this chapter.

Emergent refers to the backlog's constant evolution: As new information is learned about the marketplace, a competitor, or a technological advancement, the backlog is modified, reprioritized, or clarified.

Prioritized means exactly that—the user stories are in priority order, with the highest-priority items that will deliver the most business value at the top of the backlog for immediate development. We also cover the prioritization process in this chapter.

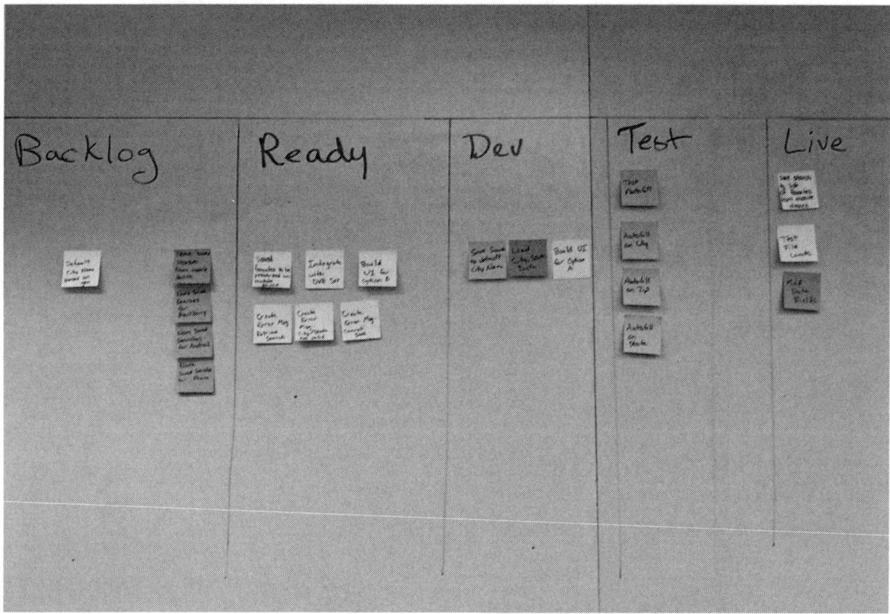

Figure 6.1 *Backlog in stickies*

Where the product backlog is housed will vary from company to company. Some firms, typically with smaller teams that are all colocated, may have a physical backlog with sticky notes hanging on the wall in priority order (see Figure 6.1). As collaboration between the business, product owner, and development team affects the priority, the sticky notes are simply rearranged.

Some companies, particularly those with virtual or remote team members, will opt to house their product backlog in a tool such as Jira Agile (see Figure 6.2), Rally, or numerous other online options.

Feature-Driven Development (FDD)

Feature-driven development (FDD) takes a different approach to the concept of requirements. As you may recall from Chapter 4, "Describing the Different Roles," FDD breaks down the development team differently and does not adopt the idea of collective development, where a single team is working together in the code to deliver a feature. FDD works with the concept of "classes" that must be integrated to deliver the full feature set. To manage requirements, FDD breaks the features down into a hierarchy of three levels. The highest level is the problem domain or the subject area, which is then broken down into the business activities, and then the individual features are assigned to a

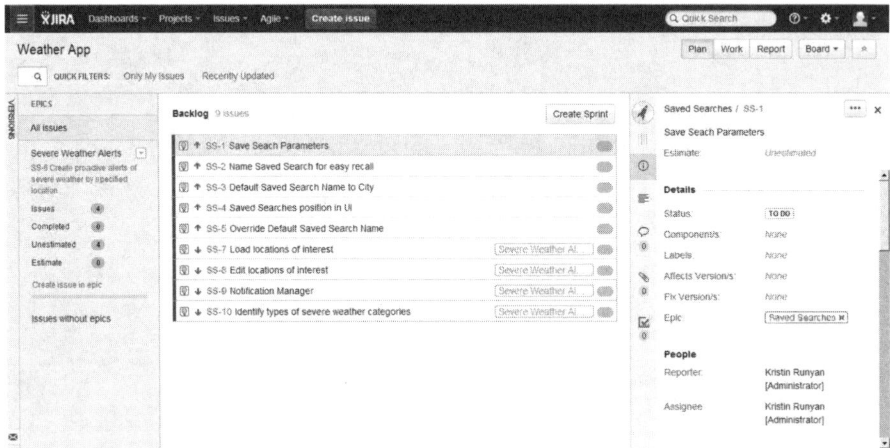

Figure 6.2 *Backlog in Jira Agile tool*

Source: Used with permission from Atlassian (Jira Agile).

business activity. This is a more model-driven approach, referred to as the "plan by feature" process, and allows FDD to support large projects and teams (De Luca 2003).

Prioritization of Stories

As the P in the DEEP acronym, product backlog requirements/stories must be prioritized. There are a number of tools and methods to assist with this activity.

Prioritization Based on Value

We first discussed the concept of prioritization based on business value in Chapter 4. Targets such as increased revenue, decreased costs, and improved customer service can be the high-level objectives, but now we dive a bit deeper into the value equation. There is more to the concept of value beyond just the benefits that we have previously discussed; there can also be negative impacts associated with failing to take action. If your competitors have a distinct advantage over you, then there are real penalties for not offering a competitive feature set. Let's consider Cayman Design and our weather application. If our weather app offers weather only in the United States but many of our executive business travelers (like the Sam persona from Chapter 5) are traveling to the UK and

Mexico and our competitor offers those locations, we may risk losing customers like Sam if we do not respond with a comparable feature set. Sometimes value is driven by proactively going after new markets and new opportunities. Other times, value is derived from a more defensive or reactive posture when we are simply matching the features of our competitors.

Value must also be supported by a positive return on investment (ROI), so the cost to deliver a desired feature must be considered. If there is no way to recoup your investment because the cost of delivering the feature is so high, then the value deteriorates and the feature should be deprioritized. For example, data format for weather information in Iceland is not compatible with our application and would require a significant amount of code to convert it to a usable format. The cost of the data conversion compared with the revenue potential for adding Iceland data reveals that this would not be a wise undertaking and would cost far more than it is worth. Therefore, a user story requesting Iceland data should be removed from the backlog with the explanation for the decision.

Lastly, there is a consideration of the risks associated with the feature development: If this feature might jeopardize the stability of the application, then its value is diminished. You can see that value is not a simple equation and that many factors—revenue, cost, risk, and penalties—must be considered.

Value Stream Mapping

Value stream mapping is another concept transferred from Lean manufacturing to software development. The mapping exercise is designed to remove waste from the product development cycle. The mapping begins and ends with customer activity, and the entire process is viewed from the customer's perspective; this allows organizations to find breakpoints or bottlenecks in their process, where the customer experience is less than optimal. Sometimes this happens because the organizational processes get in the way. For example, have you ever talked to a customer service representative about a billing question and then wanted to change your mailing address, only to be told that the person you are talking to cannot handle that additional transaction? This happens when a company has developed organizational silos without regard to the customer impacts of those silos. The concept of value stream mapping is to flow all of the transactions from the eyes of the consumers to ensure that their experience is seamless and optimized.

Because Lean emphasizes eliminating waste and delivering the most value in the least amount of time, mapping the value stream from the customer's perspective can help with prioritization activities to ensure we are satisfying a meaningful customer need in a way that adds value to the organization.

MoSCoW

Another method of prioritization that we introduced in Chapter 5 is the MoSCoW method favored by Dynamic Systems Development Method (DSDM 2011). Under this method, the "must haves" would clearly take priority over the "should haves," and so on. Here again are the elements of MoSCoW:

- **Must have:** All features classified in this group must be implemented, and if they are not delivered, the system would simply not work.
- **Should have:** Features of this priority are important but can be omitted if time or resources constraints appear.
- **Could have:** These features enhance the system with greater functionality, but the timeliness of their delivery is not critical.
- **Want to have:** These features serve only a limited group of users and do not drive the same amount of business value as the preceding items.

Using Cayman Design as our example, we want to produce our weather-related calendars for purchase to create a new revenue stream. For this product, we have certain priorities with respect to the payment processing portion.

- **Must have:** Ability to accept MasterCard and Visa
- **Should have:** Add American Express and Discover
- **Could have:** Add ACH payments for transactions directly through banking institutions
- **Want to have:** Add gift cards

As you can see, if we cannot accept MasterCard and Visa, then our offering is not viable; therefore, that requirement is a "must have." Adding American Express and Discover is important to our success, so they should be added as quickly as time allows; hence they fall into the "should have" category. Accepting ACH payments will broaden the appeal of our product but it does not have to be delivered early in the project, so that is a "could have." Adding gift cards will serve only a limited audience, so that would fall into the "want to have" category.

Kano Model

The Kano model was introduced in 1984 by Noriaki Kano and was created to help companies learn how to build better products to "delight" the customers.

The model assists with the prioritization process because it breaks down features into three categories. The first is **basic needs,** which are sometimes referred to as satisfiers/dissatisfiers. These are the features that must be there for the product to work, in the eyes of the customer: The functionality is expected, and if it is not included, it causes great dissatisfaction. After a consumer's basic needs are met, then there are **performance needs,** which add necessary functionality to enhance the user experience. The final category, which results in true product differentiation, consists of features that **delight** or excite users, and they are an unexpected bonus from the consumer's viewpoint. The challenge when it comes to prioritization is to focus on enough of the basic needs, performance needs, and delighters to deliver a compelling product to the marketplace. If you have a product with only delighters but no basic needs, then you might have something really innovative that does not work. Conversely, if you have something that satisfies every basic need but does not delight, then customers may not be compelled to buy it because it does not offer anything special or different from the competition.

Another aspect of the Kano model that is critical to understand is the evolution of the feature categorization: Over time, delighters will become performance needs, and performance needs will become basic needs. To illustrate this concept, think of the first iPad that you experienced. It had a number of features that delighted: The touchscreen with the swiping capabilities was awe inspiring when first encountered, but now if we see a tablet that is not a touchscreen, it is completely dissatisfying. The delighters have become basic needs as the competition has evolved and the technology has advanced. Therefore, companies must continue to prioritize delighter features if they want to remain innovative.

Review 1 At this point, the reader should be able to answer Review Questions 1–5.

Estimating

In addition to effective prioritization, grooming and planning sessions require sound estimates for how long the work is likely to take. There are a number of different ways to come up with the estimates, just as there are many different ways to prioritize the feature requests.

Level of Effort (LOE) or T-Shirt Sizing

Perhaps the least precise but easiest method of estimating goes by one of the following names: "T-shirt size," "level of effort" (LOE), or "small, medium, large." The last title is the most descriptive because the development team just estimates each story as small, medium, or large; teams may add extra-small and extra-large, depending on what they have decided as their measure. The advantages of this approach are that it is very simple and can be done quickly; the disadvantages include a lack of precision and an inability to add up several stories into a meaningful measure. For example, it is hard to say "our team can work on two smalls and one medium at a time." For these reasons, teams often use this form of estimating early in the process and refine it later.

Ideal Time (Days or Hours)

In this form of estimating, the developer determines the amount of time that a task would take under ideal circumstances—meaning no interruptions, no meetings, and no phone calls—and that is set as the ideal time. This is an easier metric for developers to assign than actual clock time because it is difficult for them to factor in all of the possible interruptions that might occur. Each organization will have some factor that is applied to convert ideal time to clock time; a ratio of 2 to 1 is fairly common, meaning that within every hour, 40 minutes are spent on concentrated work, with the other 20 minutes consumed by interruptions or breaks (Jones 2007, p. 141).

Ideal time is a useful metric because it is relatively easy for a developer to estimate, provided that the requirements/user stories are well defined and thorough.

Hours

"Hours" are simply the number of hours that the development team estimates will be required to complete the user story. This is an accurate way to measure because there is only one definition for an hour—60 minutes—so there is no room for misinterpretation. The disadvantage to using hours at this stage is that the team might be lacking information to make such a precise estimate. Because hours are so defined, there is a greater risk of executives and stakeholders placing inappropriate expectations on the team to deliver exactly in the estimated time frame.

Story Points

In Scrum, many teams use the concept of "story points," which are an arbitrary measure that allows the teams to understand the size of the effort without the potentially binding expectations that come with hours.

Fibonacci Sequence

When estimating in story points, many teams use the Fibonacci sequence, a mathematical tool defined in the thirteenth century for rational approximations. The sequence is the sum of the prior two numbers: 1, 2, 3, 5, 8, 13, 21; as you can see, 1 + 2 = 3, 2 + 3 = 5, 3 + 5 = 8, and so on. The Fibonacci sequence is helpful for Agile estimating because as the points get higher, the degree of uncertainty is increasing. For the purposes of Agile estimating, the sequence has been modified to account for the needs of software development. Some teams have added a ½ for the user stories that are so small in effort they really do not need estimating. Also, many teams replace the 21 with 20 and add 40 and 100; the idea is that if a story is estimated at greater than 13 story points, there is a good chance that it is still an epic and needs to be broken down. The difference between a 20, 40, or 100 is just a sense for the size of the epic.

There are a couple of other considerations on either side of the spectrum. First, some teams add a 0 (zero) to their Fibonacci sequence, but one might question why a story with zero points or no level of effort is even in the mix. Some teams use this as a placeholder to remind them of an activity that another team must complete; a dependency (Cohn 2005, p. 53). For example, this task requires no effort on the part of Scrum team A but needs to be delivered by Scrum team B before Scrum team A can complete its work; therefore, it sits in Scrum team A's backlog with zero points.

Some teams add 200, 500, and/or infinity (∞). The reason for these additions is that people (typically management or stakeholders) are used to comparing things as though they relate, which is not always the case. For example, the team estimates an activity at 100 points because it is an epic and they do not have enough information to make a more precise assessment. As that feature is better understood and broken down, it is eventually delivered in five months. Some members of the management team might now equate a 100-point story with a five-month delivery cycle, which is not true at all. The next 100-point story—which is equally epic and lacking in information—may take twice as long to deliver, so there is no relative comparison. To eliminate the opportunity to compare, some teams have started using infinity to represent "not enough information."

One additional thing to keep in mind is that unlike hours, which have a fixed and commonly understood definition, story points are more abstract and negotiable. One team may assign 3 points to a story where that same story on another team would have been a 2 or a 5. As long as everyone on the team agrees to the size of a story point, then all of the estimating will be coherent.

The easiest way for a team to get started using story points is through relative sizing; this involves identifying a task that everyone is familiar with and assigning a point value to it. Let's say that adding a field to the database happens frequently, so everyone is aware of the effort and time required. The team assigns that activity as 5 story points, and then every subsequent story is compared to that one. Is this activity bigger or smaller than adding a field to the database? If it is bigger, then it could be an 8 or a 13; if it is smaller, it could be a 2 or a 3. Starting with something relative provides a benchmark for new teams. It is also worth noting that the testing activities should be included in the story point estimation. If an action is easy to develop but challenging to test, then it should receive a higher estimate because designing, coding, and testing are all part of completing a story.

Team Participation

How does an Agile team actually execute on the estimation process? In all instances, we are looking for participation from the developers and testers because we want to benefit from the wisdom of self-organizing teams. Outlined next are several strategies that teams have used to come to consensus on estimation.

Planning Poker

Having the development team participate in the activity of estimating can have distinct advantages over asking a single developer to size a feature. If the team is using story points, as just outlined, one of the fun and effective ways to increase engagement is through a game called "planning poker." Each team member is given a set of number cards with the modified Fibonacci sequence—1, 2, 3, 5, 8, 13, 20, 40, 100. Sometimes teams use a regular deck of cards, using aces for 1 and the face cards for the larger numbers. After the product owner and the team have discussed the user story in detail and everyone believes they have an adequate understanding, the Scrum master or coach will call for each team member to lay down the card representing the number of story points that he or she assigns to this user story. Many Scrum masters ask all team members to "throw" at the same time so that no one can be influenced by their teammates.

In addition to an estimated size, we are looking to see if there is a discrepancy. If a user story is discussed and one team member throws a 2 but another throws a 13, then there is a difference that needs to be discussed. It does not mean that one person is right and the other is wrong; this actually identifies a lack of common understanding as it relates to the user story. Just like all of the other opportunities within Agile for collaboration and discussion, this discrepancy should be explored. Why did the developer who threw the 13 think that this task was so big? Is there a point of interconnection that the other developer (who threw the 2) was not thinking of? Did they just understand the request differently? Or has the low estimator done something like this before, so he or she is very confident in that assessment? Again, the value is in the dialogue, so everyone can come to a common understanding of the request and what it will take to fulfill it. The result could be that the team agrees on a 2 or a 13 or on a number in between. The point of the exercise is to facilitate collaboration and negotiation so the team is clear on the desired feature and confident in their ability to deliver.

If you have a distributed team so not all team members are in one location, there are tools such as http://www.planningpoker.com/ that allow you to have the same poker game over the Internet.

Wide-Band Delphi

The Delphi method takes the same approach as planning poker but addresses the estimating in a more structured and formal way. A facilitator calls a meeting of the experts and a feature request is discussed. Each expert participant then completes an anonymous estimation form and submits it to the facilitator. The facilitator compiles the responses and redistributes them to the experts—continuing to maintain the anonymity of the respondents. Based on the new inputs, the expert team discusses the feature request again, clarifies any incorrect assumptions, gains a better understanding of the feature, and submits new estimation forms to the facilitator. This process is repeated until the estimations are an agreed-upon value. Although there is more effort to the Delphi method, it may produce more accurate results because of the anonymity of the respondents, which prevents a strong personality from swaying the group. The disadvantages are that it is time-consuming, and the experts are not required to reveal their biases to the group (Wu 1997, sec. 2).

Crystal Family

The Crystal Family software methodology calls for three distinct phases of estimates. Early on, in the **proposal** stage, the developers review the initial requirements and work breakdown to provide an estimate of the work. The project then moves into the **exploration** phase, where many more details are gathered and as a result of the new information, the estimates are refined. Finally, the team moves into the **planning** meeting, where each element is broken down into a discrete task and assigned to a developer. The developer has the opportunity to update the estimate at that time (Cockburn 2004).

We discuss more about planning meetings later in the chapter.

Extreme Programming (XP)

Within XP, it is critical that the developers are the ones making the estimates and no one else; they are also the only ones who can make changes to estimates. The goal is to instill a degree of responsibility or ownership of the estimates to the developers. The XP process also provides a feedback loop for the actual time required, so developers can continue to improve their estimates over time (Beck 2000).

Lean

Within Lean, since the concept of reducing waste is so important, it favors waiting until the feature is nearly ready to be worked on before completing an estimation. If you have a full feature list that contains requests with the associated details and estimates that are so far down in the queue that it is highly unlikely they will ever be completed, you run the risk of creating inaccurate expectations, and you are increasing the amount of waste in the process. "Investing time estimating projects that will never get done is also a waste" (Poppendieck and Poppendieck 2006, p. 57).

Scrum: Product Backlog Grooming

The activities of prioritization and estimation often take place in a session called *product backlog grooming*. This is typically a meeting between the product owner and the Scrum master/coach and may include the entire development team. The grooming session is also used to clarify and improve on the user stories; this could include identifying and breaking down requirements that are too big (epics), improving poorly written stories, and adding acceptance criteria. Once the participants have a clear understanding of the features/stories, they can discuss the prioritization of those stories and add the estimates.

The goal of the grooming session is to leave the meeting with good, solid user stories that are prioritized, discussed, well understood, negotiated, and agreed upon so that the next few action items (described next) can take place to ensure a successful sprint.

The product owner is responsible for leading the grooming session. Good product owners value the dialogue between the participants and recognize the benefits of the diverse backgrounds and perspectives of the group (Rubin 2012).

Additional Inputs

Once the backlog grooming is complete and the team understands the highest-priority user stories in sufficient detail, the next meeting or ceremony in the

Scrum methodology is Sprint planning. Before we can effectively execute on that meeting, several additional data points must be collected and understood.

Team Velocity

Within Agile, as teams spend time together and work through a few sprints, they start to get a sense for their "velocity": This is the amount of work that the team can usually deliver within the time frame of a sprint or iteration and can be used as a predictor for future iterations. Story points are the most common units of measure for velocity, though hours could be used if the team was estimating in hours. It would be challenging to calculate velocity for a team estimating in t-shirt sizes (or small/medium/large) because the estimates cannot be mathematically summed.

When a team first comes together, it is difficult to estimate their velocity because they have not yet experienced an iteration as a team. The first few iterations are usually more guesswork than precision, and that is fine because it provides the opportunity to inspect and adapt. Once the team is established and finds their rhythm, velocity is a great tool to use when establishing their commitment for future iterations.

Nevertheless, a few factors can disrupt velocity. If the team members are not dedicated to the team full-time, for example, it is hard to predict their availability to work on the next iteration; their other responsibilities could consume 20% or 50% or 80% of their available time, so it is difficult to count on their contributions. Similarly, if the team members change frequently, it is difficult for the team to find their rhythm—if Bill is part of the team and then removed and then put back on the team, it is hard for the other team members to depend on his deliverables.

Another negative impact on velocity is modifying the length of the sprint: If the team works on a two-week sprint, then a one-week sprint, then a two-week sprint again, it becomes difficult to gauge their capacity over a specified time period. Ideally, you want a team to work together for several iterations of consistent duration; then you will have the data you need to calculate the team's velocity for planning purposes.

Personnel considerations for things such as vacation and training are yet another dynamic that will affect velocity. If a team will have two members on vacation for half of their iteration, then clearly they should not commit to the same level of work as if everyone were present. Although this might sound obvious, when a team experiences a dip in velocity, it tends to raise questions: Why was team A progressing at a velocity of 30 points per sprint for four iterations and then suddenly dropped to 20 points for the most recent sprint? Rather than raising alarms that something is amiss on the team, the best place to start is to simply look at team member availability.

Other elements that affect velocity could be external to the team, such as the stability of the infrastructure. If the development team is continually called upon to fix production problems, then they will have less time to spend writing new code. As we discussed in Chapter 2, "Organizational Culture Considerations with Agile," if the executive team and/or stakeholders are not committed to the sacredness of the sprint and repeatedly introduce new changes, then calculating the team's velocity can be very challenging.

There is no defined number of sprints that must be completed in order to calculate velocity; it is an ongoing, evolving measurement to be used as an input for the planning process.

Velocity should *not* be used as a management metric because it is based on story points, which are an arbitrary unit of measure defined by each individual team; teams with a higher velocity may not be more productive than others with lower velocity. In fact, management needs to be careful to avoid using velocity as an indicator of performance or productivity because it could lead to unhealthy behaviors on the team (Rubin 2012, p. 137). There are a few different ways to calculate velocity over time. Some teams simply average their totals for all of the sprints/iterations that they have worked on. Other teams, particularly those that are new to Scrum and are improving in their abilities, will use the concept of "yesterday's weather," therefore using only the last two to three sprints as indicators of their future capacity.

Exercise

Here are the velocities of two teams:

	Team 1—Completed Points	Team 2—Completed Points
Sprint 1	15	5
Sprint 2	20	11
Sprint 3	18	6
Sprint 4	14	12
Sprint 5	16	14
Sprint 6	24	20
Sprint 7	19	24
Team Velocity	?	?

Calculate the velocity of team 1 using averages for all data points. Calculate the velocity of team 2 using "yesterday's weather" by including only the last two sprints. Which team has higher productivity? What are some of the reasons that velocity on team 1 might drop to 10 on the next sprint?

Extreme Programming also has the concept of velocity for planning purposes, but it allows for two types of planning: You can either set a date and determine how many stories can be implemented by that date, or define a specific scope and determine how long it will take to finish a defined set of stories. Either way, the team's velocity is used to make the projections (Wells 1999).

Because Lean encompasses some of the manufacturing ideology, the developers are working with a pull scheduling system, where they "pull" in the right amount of work that can be completed in the time frame allowed. Once the team establishes their velocity, they will pull in only the amount of work that they can reasonably complete (Poppendieck and Poppendieck 2006, p. 70).

Definition of "Done"

Within several of the Agile methodologies, including Scrum, there is an element called the **definition of "done."** This is a meaningful conversation that the development teams, product owner, and stakeholders need to have to ensure a common understanding of completion. When different people have a different definition of done, expectations will not be met and dissatisfaction can result. If this is difficult to conceptualize, just think of someone offering to clean up the break room. To that person, that might mean simply throwing away the trash, but someone else might define it as throwing out the trash, washing the dishes, wiping down the tables, and sweeping the floor. If the second person comes to inspect the work after the first person is "done," he or she is going to have quite a different perspective regarding the completeness of the work.

The same is true on development teams. Does your team include code reviews in your definition of done? Does your product owner think that the team is going to update the release notes before a sprint is considered completed? These are important conversations to have to ensure that everyone is on the same page. Every new team should dedicate time to discussing and agreeing on their definition of done, which may or may not include elements such as code that is checked in and integrated and has automated tests (Cohn 2010, p. 259). When the definition of done is clear and well understood, then we ensure that the conclusion of every sprint will meet everyone's expectations.

Extreme Programming handles the definition of done slightly differently: When a task is completed, it is crossed off of the board. To ensure that done means done, in XP, only the customer (not the developer) can cross off a task (Beck and Fowler 2001, p. 81); from Chapter 4 you will remember that the customer in XP is equivalent to the product owner in Scrum.

Incorporation of Technical Debt

One of the discussion points with regard to the product backlog is the inclusion of technical debt. With Agile, teams are moving very quickly, and sometimes to achieve the sprint goal within the time frame allotted, the team, either knowingly or unknowingly, creates technical debt.

There are many definitions of technical debt; in fact whole books have been written on this subject alone (see References and Further Reading for details), so we use a basic description here, for illustrative purposes. Technical debt was first discussed on the C2.com wiki page, and the definition created by Ward Cunningham is commonly used today: "Technical Debt includes those internal things that you choose not to do now, but which will impede future development if left undone. This includes deferred refactoring" (Cunningham 2012). Chapter 7, "Testing, Quality, and Integration," provides much more information on refactoring.

There are two basic kinds of debt—unintended and intentional. Unintended technical debt is simply the consequences of the team's learning curve. Perhaps they designed something poorly or did not test thoroughly enough, or the business was not 100% certain about the business requirements. No matter what the root cause, this type of debt is unintentional—no one meant to write bad code or be sloppy—and it happens as part of the continuous learning process that is essential to Agile.

Intentional technical debt is incurred as trade-offs are made in the development process. We may choose to incur technical debt for short-term, tactical reasons or long-term, strategic ones. Let's consider some examples. Because our weather application for Cayman Design is going to be available with only information for the New York area in its first iteration, we are going to code the database lookups in a way that is quicker to deliver the initial release but will not be scalable once the data for the entire country is loaded. We decide that this is the best path, knowing that it will create technical debt, because it is the fastest way to release the initial version. It will allow us to research and learn more about the optimal database design once we better understand how users will interact with the application. Another example might be that Cayman Design is a cash-strapped start-up and can afford only certain hardware until we get revenue coming in, so we must code to those constraints. Again, we realize and accept that this creates technical debt that will have to be cleaned up once we are a thriving, profitable organization.

When we are ready to tackle technical debt, should it be included in the backlog of prioritized stories? Although there is some debate on this topic, most experts agree that it should. The technical teams may have to argue their case to the product owner to prioritize the efforts appropriately, and a good product owner should listen and understand the impact of allowing the debt to fester.

Bugs

Bugs, also referred to as defects, are different from technical debt in that they are usually errors in the writing or implementation of the code that are impeding the performance or usability of the application. In many companies, bugs are handled outside of the feature release (sprint) process because of their immediacy. Within organizations where bug fixes are resource intensive and can wait for the development cycle, bugs should also be included in the backlog and prioritized accordingly.

Review 2 At this point, the reader should be able to answer Review Questions 6–10.

Scrum: Sprint Planning

In Scrum, once we have the necessary inputs, we are ready for the Sprint planning meeting. In this meeting, we are going to decide exactly what we are going to work on during the sprint and we are going to plan for it—hence the name: Sprint planning.

Inputs

There are a number of inputs to the Sprint planning meeting, such as the following:

- Groomed and prioritized backlog
- Estimates for the highest-priority stories
- The velocity of the team
- Definition of done
- The schedule of the sprint—are there vacation days or a company holiday that will affect the amount of work we can commit to?
- Other inputs—are team members getting new monitors, is there an All-Hands meeting that everyone is required to attend?

Planning Session

The Sprint planning meeting has two distinct objectives. First, we want to make sure that everyone on the team has a complete understanding of the user stories. Team members may not all have attended the backlog grooming session, so it is important that everyone have the opportunity to ask questions and gain a clear understanding of the top-priority stories. The second objective is to allow the team to break the work down into individual tasks and determine who will own each piece of work. Let's walk through this process step-by-step.

1. Once we understand the user stories, the team will decide how many stories can be committed to during this sprint. This is the sprint goal.
2. The team then breaks the user stories down into individual tasks.
3. Each team member selects the tasks that he or she is willing to own and complete.
4. The team member then estimates—in hours—how long it will take to complete each task.

Important things are happening in this small list that need to be discussed in greater detail. With item #2, user stories are broken down into tasks. Some teams skip this step and a single developer is responsible for the entire user story delivery. More frequently, each story will contain several distinct pieces—for example, there is an update to the user interface, a new database field, an update required for the API to add the new field, and so on. Each of those individual tasks can be owned by different developers depending on their level of expertise. Furthermore, in item #3, team members select the tasks that they will own, which creates an opportunity to cross-train or develop new skills, as we have discussed in previous chapters. One developer, for example, may be the expert on inventory but another may be interested in learning inventory; the second developer could pick up inventory tasks during the Sprint planning meeting. Then when they get to step #4, the team might add some time to their estimates of how long it will take to complete the inventory tasks because the second developer is less experienced and will need more time.

Another important outcome of the Sprint planning meeting is that story points are converted to actual hours and the hours are attributed to the tasks, not the stories. The thought is that story points are appropriate for stories in backlog grooming and hours are appropriate for tasks in Sprint planning because the level of detail is increasing and therefore the confidence in estimating is greater and can be more precise. For the teams that estimate in hours to begin with, this step is still important, because the original estimates may need to be modified now that the team knows more and the developer who will be doing the work is known.

Output

There are two primary outputs from the Sprint planning meeting. First is the Sprint goal, the user stories that are committed to for this sprint. Second is the Sprint backlog, which is the list of tasks and owners. The Sprint backlog is the team's "to do" list for the sprint.

Chickens and Pigs

The Sprint planning meeting also demonstrates the role assignment for chickens and pigs, which was introduced in Chapter 4. In the first half of the Sprint planning meeting, when the user stories are being described and discussed, the product owner is absolutely a pig: He or she is deeply invested in the conversation and is committed to the positive outcome of the meeting. When the meeting shifts to the developers breaking down the stories into tasks and selecting their tasks, the product owner's role shifts to that of a chicken: He or she is interested in the outcome of the conversation but the level of commitment has been reduced, since he or she will not be doing the actual work (coding and testing.)

Extreme Programming: XP Planning Game

XP has a ritual similar to the Scrum backlog grooming session and the Sprint planning meeting: the planning game. The planning game also consists of two parts: release planning, which is most similar to backlog grooming, and iteration planning, which is most similar to Sprint planning. Each meeting has three distinct phases—exploration, commitment, and steering. Table 6.1 compares the two aspects of the planning game side by side.

It is important to note the participants in the different parts of the planning game. "Because customers have the most information about value—they're most qualified to say what is important—they *prioritize*. Because programmers have the most information about costs—they're most qualified to say how long it will take to implement a story—they *estimate*. Neither group creates the plan unilaterally. Instead, both groups come together, each with their areas of expertise, and play the planning game" (Shore 2010).

Table 6.1 *The XP Planning Game*

	Release Planning	Iteration Planning
Description	Determine what requirements will be included in the upcoming release(s) and the planned delivery dates.	Outline the specific tasks and commitment by the members of the development team.
Participants	Customers and developers	Developers only
Exploration phase	Customer provides highest-priority feature requests (user stories).	Requirements are converted to individual tasks.
Commitment phase	Team determines what functionality will be included and commits to due dates.	Tasks are assigned and estimates are refined. Deliverable is committed to.
Steering phase	Plan is reviewed and can be adjusted, if needed, to add or remove stories.	Tasks are performed and deliverable is compared to original feature request for completeness.

Maintenance of Legacy Code

In many organizations, the Agile teams are tasked with not only writing new code but also handling the maintenance of the legacy code base that is in production. Planning the amount of work that a team can commit to in an iteration may depend on the likelihood of maintenance work. Here are three examples of ways that teams have dealt with this issue.

Build Time into the Sprint

Perhaps the most common way that teams deal with unpredictable bugs and maintenance issues is to reserve some time for them within the sprint. For example, the team can handle 40 story points per sprint, but they commit to only 35 points so they will have some time available for the bugs that need immediate action. Bugs may account for more than the allotted 5 points in some sprints and less in others, but on the whole, the team learns their rhythm and builds in enough reserves to handle whatever may come up.

Assign a Team Resource to Maintenance

Rather than have every developer allocate time for maintenance work, some teams dedicate a resource to the unexpected. For example, if a team has five developers and two QA resources, one of the developers does not take tasks during sprint planning so he or she has no committed work as part of the sprint. This member participates in all of the meetings and in team activities and brainstorming, but his or her role is to work all of the unplanned activities that arise during the sprint, thus allowing the rest of the team to stay 100% focused on their sprint commitments.

Split into Two Teams

If you have a large team, another option is to split into two teams, one to handle the new development or enhancements and one to handle the bugs and maintenance. If the enhancement team uses Scrum, it is likely that the maintenance team will fare better with Kanban since their workflow is less predictable; Kanban is described in detail in Chapter 8, "Tracking and Reporting." One consideration in this approach is rotating team members between the two teams so that everyone has the opportunity to grow and contribute. Cayman Design makes a practice of transferring two developers from the enhancement team to the maintenance team after each sizable release; that way the enhancement developers that have moved can teach the maintenance developers about the new features while they are working side by side. The two developers that move from the maintenance team to the enhancement team bring a keener insight into the issues that the users are running into in production so they can actually educate the enhancement team as well.

Triple Constraints

There is a long-held principle within the project management discipline that projects are made up of three variables: schedule/time, cost/resources, and scope/quality (see Figure 6.3). The theory is that you cannot adjust one without affecting the other two. If you shorten the schedule and say that a release is due one month earlier than planned, then you will also need to add resources or reduce the scope in order to meet the new desired date. Likewise, if you remove resources from a project, you will need to either extend the time frame to push out the delivery date or reduce the scope. Finally, if you add to the scope, then you will need to either extend the time frame or add resources. This model

Figure 6.3 *Triple constraints*

certainly helps with project management because it clearly depicts the trade-offs that must be made when a significant variable changes.

Agile looks at the theory of triple constraints slightly differently. First, there is a school of thought that scope and quality are, in fact, two very different things: A team could deliver the prescribed scope at lesser quality, or it could maintain acceptable quality standards with a reduced scope. As Wells (1999) explains, "The base philosophy of release planning is that a project may be quantified by four variables; scope, resources, time, and quality. Scope is how much is to be done. Resources are how many people are available. Time is when the project or release will be done. And quality is how good the software will be and how well tested it will be. No one can control all [four] variables. When you change one, you inadvertently cause another to change in response."

It is important to understand the concept of the triple constraints when engaged in planning and grooming, because one must grasp that changing one variable will impact other variables and appropriate adjustments will be needed.

Another way to look at this in an Agile environment is to suggest that resources and time are fixed. The team size is five to nine people, so that cannot change. The date is fixed by the duration of the sprint, in many cases two weeks. Therefore, scope must be flexible to be able to be designed, coded, and tested within the confines of the sprint. By managing the size and priority of the stories in the backlog, you are effectively managing the scope while the time and resources are fixed.

Kanban

You may have noticed the absence of Kanban in this chapter, and that is deliberate. Kanban follows a different practice when it comes to planning and executing on an Agile work effort, which we tackle in Chapter 8. We call it out here, however, so that readers are aware that Kanban is an important methodology worthy of detailed discussion.

Review 3 At this point, the reader should be able to answer Review Questions 11–15.

Conclusion

Grooming and planning are critical activities within the Agile practice because they incorporate the values and principles that we aspire to regarding self-organizing teams, face-to-face collaboration, sustainable work environments, and frequent delivery of working software. If teams do not spend adequate time with backlog grooming and focus on ensuring that user stories/requirements are detailed appropriately, prioritized, and estimated, it is extremely difficult for the developers and testers to execute on their work. Likewise, if the sprint planning efforts are sloppy or undervalued, then the importance of delivering on the committed work is marginalized and teams will not excel. Agile provides a structured framework to facilitate important conversations about difficult work; through this framework, teams can elevate their performance and deliver real business value to customers and the organization.

Summary

- Agile teams need to groom the work and spend time and energy in planning cycles to ensure successful delivery of working software.
- The product backlog, which houses all of the requirements/user stories, should be DEEP—Detailed Appropriately, Estimated, Emergent, and Prioritized.
- Feature-driven development uses a technique called "plan by feature" to ensure that developers understand the feature categorization and priority.
- Prioritization by business value is common, and it is more than just proactive measures such as increased revenue or improved customer service.

Sometimes priority is driven by reacting to the competition, evaluating the cost of an effort, and understanding the risk that a new feature might introduce to the technical environment.

- Value stream mapping is a useful exercise taken from the Lean principles, where an entire interaction is viewed through the eyes of the consumer to identify bottlenecks and inconsistencies.
- Using the DSDM method of prioritization called MoSCoW, we identify the **M**ust haves, **S**hould haves, **C**ould haves, and **W**ants.
- The Kano model emphasizes that to be successful, products must fulfill basic needs and enhancement needs and delight end users. Over time, delighters can become basic needs, so ongoing innovation is important.
- Estimation can be done in t-shirt size, ideal time, hours, or story points, with story points being the most common in Agile. Estimations should always include testing.
- Most teams use the Fibonacci sequence for story points, which is a mathematical series where the first two numbers sum to the third: 1, 2, 3, 5, 8, 13, and so on. For most Agile teams, any story larger than 13 points is too big to fit in a single iteration.
- Planning poker is a game/tool used in Agile to estimate the size of efforts where team members play a card corresponding to their estimate. Differences are discussed and reconciled to ensure teams have a common understanding of the effort required to complete the story.
- Wide-band Delphi is a similar but much more formal and structured sizing exercise, in which estimates are submitted to a facilitator anonymously and discussed until reconciled.
- Product backlog grooming is a Scrum event where the team collaborates on the user stories. In this meeting, the product owner is a "pig" and clarifies the requirements.
- Other inputs to the product backlog grooming include the velocity of the team, the definition of "done," and the incorporation of technical debt and bugs.
- Technical debt can be either intentional or unintended, and if not appropriately addressed, can jeopardize the long-term viability of the system.
- The Sprint planning meeting is another Scrum ceremony where the top user stories are committed to for the iteration, and the team breaks down stories into individual tasks.

- Tasks are *selected* by the team members, not assigned, which is a large shift from Waterfall practices and leads to higher developer engagement.
- Extreme Programming hosts a similar meeting called the planning game, where the "customer" sets the priority and the developers estimate the size of the effort.
- Many organizations must consider incorporating maintenance work on the platform and balancing it against the product development enhancements within an iteration.
- The triple constraint of time, resources, and scope is expanded in Agile to include quality, and teams must understand the trade-offs when adjustments are made to projects.

Review 4 At this point, the reader should be able to answer Review Questions 16–20.

Interview with Mike Cohn

Mike Cohn ran his first Scrum project in 1995 and has been a vocal proponent of Scrum ever since. As an author and Scrum Alliance Certified Scrum Trainer, he had brought Agile and Scrum into the mainstream. His books include *Agile Estimating and Planning, User Stories Applied for Agile Software Development*, and *Succeeding with Agile Software Development Using Scrum,* as well as several books on Java and C++ database programming. Mike is a founding member of both the Agile Alliance and Scrum Alliance, Inc., where he currently serves as chairman of the board of directors. Through his leadership at Mountain Goat Software, a process and project management consultancy and training firm, he uses his 20-plus years of experience in a variety of environments to help companies adopt and improve their use of Agile processes and techniques in order to build extremely high-performance development organizations. He has worked with companies of all sizes including Bioware, Capital One, Electronic Arts, Google, High Moon Studios, Intuit, JDA Software, LexisNexis, Lockheed Martin, Microsoft, Nielsen Media Research, Pearson, Phillips Electronics, Sabre, Siemens, Sun Microsystems, Texas Instruments, Turner Broadcasting, Ultimate Software, and Yahoo!. He has also served as a technology executive in organizations of various sizes, from start-ups to Fortune 40 companies.

Kristin and Sondra: Backlog grooming—who should attend? How do you maximize the value of the meeting? Can it ever be fun?

Mike: Product backlog grooming is not yet an official Scrum meeting. It's just something that many teams have discovered is a valuable thing that can lead to a more productive sprint planning meeting. As such, there's no consensus on who attends. My view is that a subset of the team is adequate. Although I'm generally a big believer of whole-team involvement, that isn't really practical for this meeting. Product backlog grooming usually happens two to three days before the end of a sprint. There is almost always someone on the team who is frantically busy two or three days before the end of a sprint. If we make that person attend another meeting, we could risk delivery of whatever product backlog item the person is working on.

Maximizing the value of a product backlog grooming meeting probably comes down to the same few things for any meeting: Keep it as short as possible, show up prepared, and encourage everyone to participate.

I have a hard time thinking of any meeting as truly fun, but I do think that when working with the right teammates, meetings can be viewed as welcome breaks from the more intense work of the team. Good teams can establish a rhythm where teams alternate from very intense mental work either alone or in pairs punctuated with occasional meetings. The meetings can have as much of a social tone as anything else and be a case for some joking around with teammates and just a bit of mental break before diving back into the more mentally intense solo or paired work.

Kristin and Sondra: What are the most common mistakes in a sprint planning meeting?

Mike: The most common mistake in sprint planning is misunderstanding the purpose of the meeting. Because one of the artifacts of sprint planning is a sprint backlog, many teams obsess over getting the sprint backlog perfect. These teams try to identify every last task and put a perfectly precise estimate on each task.

But that's not the goal of sprint planning. The goal of sprint planning is to select the right set of product backlog items to work on during the sprint and to feel that each has been discussed enough that the team is prepared to work on it.

Focusing too much on the tasks and their estimates leads teams to spend too much time in sprint planning. The tasks and the estimates are necessary, but they are tools a team should use to decide which are the right set of product backlog items to select for a sprint.

Kristin and Sondra: Estimating is really hard. How can we get the best estimates of story size?

Mike: Estimating is definitely hard, but there are a few things teams can do that help.

First, try to keep most estimates—or at least the most important estimates—within about one order of magnitude. There are studies that have shown humans are pretty good across an order of magnitude but that we are bad beyond that.

Second, estimate in relative rather than absolute terms. Rather than saying, "this will take five days," say "this (one story) will take about as long as that (story)." Then use velocity to determine how long each of those things will take. Not only is relative estimating more accurate, teams can do it more quickly. With relative estimating, the team does not need to think of all of the substeps, estimate each, and add them up. They only need to find something similar and use the same estimate.

Finally, rather than think of putting an estimate on a product backlog item, think of putting the product backlog item in the right bucket. I coach teams to do this by preidentifying a set of values they can assign as estimates. We'll commonly use values like 1, 2, 3, 5, 8, and 13, which is, of course, the Fibonacci sequence. Each number represents a bucket of that size. When estimating a product backlog item, the goal is to put the item in the right bucket. If the team thinks something is a 10, it goes in the 13 bucket because it's too big for the 8 bucket.

Kristin and Sondra: Should bugs, maintenance, or technical debt be part of the backlog?

Mike: They should definitely be part of the product backlog. The product backlog contains everything the product owner would like to do with the product. It the product owner wants those items addressed, they belong on the product backlog.

References and Further Reading

Anderson, David J. (2003). *Agile management for software engineering: Applying the theory of constraints for business results*. Upper Saddle River, NJ: Prentice Hall.

Beck, Kent. (2000). *Extreme Programming explained*. Boston: Addison-Wesley.

Beck, Kent, and Fowler, Martin. (2001). *Planning Extreme Programming*. Boston: Addison-Wesley.

Chandramouli, Subramanian, and Dutt, Saikat. (2012). *PMI Agile Certified Practitioner—Excel with ease*. Delhi: Pearson Education India.

Coad, Peter, De Luca, Jeff, and Lefebvre, Eric. (1999). *Java modeling in color with UML: Enterprise components and process*. Upper Saddle River, NJ: Prentice Hall.

Cockburn, Alistair. (2004). *Crystal clear: A human-powered methodology for small teams*. Boston: Addison-Wesley.

Cohn, Mike. (2005). *Agile estimating and planning*. Upper Saddle River, NJ: Prentice Hall.

Cohn, Mike. (2010). *Succeeding with Agile: Software development using Scrum*. Boston: Addison-Wesley.

Cunningham, Ward. (2012). Technical debt. http://c2.com/cgi/wiki?TechnicalDebt.

De Luca, Jeff. (2003). Getting flexible with planning. *De Luca on FDD Newsletter*, 1. http://www.featuredrivendevelopment.com/node/508.

DSDM. (2011). Dynamic Systems Development Method. http://dsdmofagilemethodology.wikidot.com.

Jones, Capers. (2007). *Estimating software costs*. New York: McGraw-Hill

McConnell, Steve. (2006). *Software estimation: Demystifying the black art*. Redmond, WA: Microsoft Press.

Mugridge, Rick, and Cunningham, Ward. (2005). *Fit for developing software: Framework for integrated tests (Robert C. Martin Series)*. Upper Saddle River, NJ: Prentice Hall.

Nash, Adam. (2009). Guide to product planning: Three feature buckets. Blog entry, July 22. http://blog.adamnash.com/2009/07/22/guide-to-product-planning-three-feature-buckets.

Palmer, Stephen R., and Felsing, John M. (2002). *A practical guide to feature-driven development*. Upper Saddle River, NJ: Prentice Hall.

Pichler, Roman. (2010). *Agile product management with Scrum: Creating products that customers love*. Boston: Addison-Wesley.

Poppendieck, Mary, and Poppendieck, Tom. (2006). *Implementing Lean software development: From concept to cash*. Boston: Addison-Wesley.

Pressman, Roger. (2005). *Software engineering—A practitioner's approach* (6th ed.). Boston, MA: McGraw-Hill.

Rubin, Kenneth. (2012). *Essential Scrum: A practical guide to the most popular Agile process*. Boston: Addison-Wesley.

Shore, James. (2010). The planning game. http://www.jamesshore.com/Agile-Book/the_planning_game.html.

Shore, James, and Warden, Shane. (2007). *The art of Agile development*. Sebastopol, CA: O'Reilly Media.

Stellman, Andrew, and Greene, Jennifer. (2005). *Applied software project management*. Sebastopol, CA: O'Reilly Media.

Sterling, Chris, and Barton, Brent. (2010). *Managing software debt: Building for inevitable change*. Boston: Addison-Wesley.

Sutherland, Jeff. (2011). Ten year Agile retrospective: How we can improve in the next ten years. http://msdn.microsoft.com/en-us/library/hh350860(v=vs.100).aspx.

Sutherland, Jeff, van Solingen, Rini, and Rustenberg, Eelco. (2012). *The power of Scrum*. Seattle, WA: CreateSpace Independent Publishing Platform.

Wells, Don. (1999). Release planning. http://www.extremeprogramming.org/rules/planninggame.html.

Wiegers, Karl. (2006). *More about software requirements: Thorny issues and practical advice*. Redmond, WA: Microsoft Press.

Wu, Liming. (1997). The comparison of the software cost estimating methods. http://www.compapp.dcu.ie/~renaat/ca421/LWu1.html.

Review Questions

Review 1

1. What is the name of the feature list of requirements?
2. What does DEEP stand for?
3. Should features provided by the competition influence prioritization?

4. Whose viewpoint is used in value stream mapping?
5. In the Kano model, do delighters sustain over time?

Review 2

6. What is *ideal time*?
7. Why is the Fibonacci sequence preferred over regular numbering for estimating?
8. What happens during product backlog grooming?
9. What does velocity tell a team?
10. What is *intentional technical debt*?

Review 3

11. What is an output from the Sprint planning meeting?
12. In the XP planning game, during which phase is customer prioritization completed?
13. Describe at least two ways that teams can incorporate maintenance work into sprint planning.

    a.

    b.
14. In Agile, what constraint is split into two distinct considerations?
15. If you want to remove resources from a project and the scope is fixed, what needs to change on the project?

Review 4

16. What is *relative sizing*?
17. How do you handle discrepancies in planning poker?
18. With wide-band Delphi, how are the estimates gathered?
19. Who owns the estimates in XP?
20. Is the product owner a chicken or a pig in the Sprint planning meeting?

Chapter 7

Testing, Quality, and Integration

Learning Objectives

- Understand how Agile methods can help improve product quality
- Learn how to use tools such as paired programming, test-driven development (TDD), and refactoring
- See an example of test-driven development and refactoring in action
- Understand manual, automated, and customer testing
- Read an interview with an Agile quality expert

In this chapter, we discuss how quality can be maintained and even enhanced using Agile tools. Sprints are short and do not offer extensive time for testing; therefore, incorporating testing and various testing tools is of critical importance. One of the key tenets of Agile is "frequent verification and validation" of working software, so this chapter focuses on different testing approaches, such as test-driven development, acceptance test-driven development, integrated testing, regression testing, and unit testing. We show how test-driven development and refactoring are done using an example of a blackjack game, and end the chapter by comparing manual, automated, and customer testing techniques.

Quality

The Agile Manifesto principle "Continuous attention to technical excellence and good design enhances agility" emphasizes that quality is a central theme for Agile development. Agile coach Tim Ottinger (personal communication, 2013) offers some important insight behind the philosophy of creating quality code:

> Testing does enhance quality, but it is really more of a discipline for helping developers work safely on code in "brain-sized" chunks. It's more about problem decomposition and managing cognitive load than about quality.
>
> On the other hand, the tests abide after the programming is done, and all of those unit tests (microtests) we write while doing TDD are there to help us know if the code we are currently working on breaks any existing code.
>
> Likewise, the acceptance test-driven development (ATDD) tests let us know if we've broken any behavior that the product's sponsors or customers are counting on.
>
> Since the difficulty and cost of fixing a mistake increase the longer the defect is undetected, this is primarily a cost-saving (and face-saving) measure.
>
> And yet, it does increase quality.

Ottinger reminds us that creating quality software is more than just using a set of tools: Quality starts with creating an environment where team members can do their best work.

Creating a Quality-Focused Culture

Creating a culture that is relentlessly focused on quality requires a lot more than just writing a quality plan and tracking to that plan, as has been the norm with organizations using a Waterfall approach. Quality needs to be at the basis of the organization's culture.

The most fundamental difference between Waterfall and Agile methodologies is that Waterfall takes a more reactionary approach, whereas Agile emphasizes that teams must be proactive about quality. For example, in many Waterfall projects, code from the various supporting areas such as the user interface and the back-end database may not be integrated until the development work is completed. Each individual area may have done unit testing on their specific code, but they have no sense of how well that code will work with the other code that is needed to make a working product. By the time it finally comes together in Waterfall, the code is no longer fresh in the minds of the developers and can often take longer to fix. The team of developers might also be suddenly overwhelmed with a huge backlog of defects that need to be fixed. Agile, on the other hand, advocates for daily builds that integrate all of the current code for the product. If the build breaks, the team is immediately alerted (often by a flashing light or other visual cue) and the developers can resolve the problem quickly, because the details of the code are fresh in their minds and there is a lot less new code to work through. This keeps defects backlogs at a much more manageable level for the team. Agile teams also use specific tools such as pair programming, test-driven development, and refactoring to continually manage product quality.

Pair Programming

Pair programming, an idea that was introduced by the XP methodology, consists of two programmers sitting side by side with a shared workstation. Each person in the pair is either the **driver**, the one writing the code, or the **observer,** who oversees the code as it is being written. Typically these roles are switched regularly during a pairing session. The driver is tasked with inputting quality working code while the observer thinks of ideas on how to optimize the code and points out any problems that arise. Developers are encouraged to pair with a variety of different people on the team for optimal learning and to familiarize themselves with all areas of the code. Testers and other functional areas can also benefit from participating in pair programming.

Pair programming offers several important benefits that contribute to the quality of the product. The first is that both programmers are learning from each other and becoming more familiar with different aspects of the product. This is important for continual improvement and cross-training, but also helps expedite code defects as they arise during the build. The second benefit is that pair programming allows each developer to focus on his or her specific role; there is a lot less cognitive overload when a developer can concentrate on getting the code working while letting the pairing partner focus on things such as performance optimization or possible bugs. Finally, pairing can also build trust and encourage more regular communication between team members.

Test-Driven Development (Unit Testing)

Test-driven development (TDD) originated with XP and has become a widely adopted approach for developers to test their code. Unlike traditional Waterfall approaches, where the developers first write the code and test it afterward, TDD requires that developers first write automated test cases and then write only the code necessary to make the test cases pass with no issues. This encourages the developers to think through the requirements before writing the code, encourages only the code that is needed is written, and ensures that each piece of the code has gone through an initial quality check before formal testing.

So how do you write a test for each individual piece of code that you intend to write?

1. Decide what language the code will be written in, and then ensure that you have the correct testing framework to use with that language. For example, if you are coding in Java, then you would use JUnit.
2. Start by writing a test for the simplest case that can be used for the method. If you run this test, it should fail because you have not written the code to make it pass.
3. Write the least amount of code possible to make the test pass.
4. If it passes, you can move on to the next test case for that method (or the next method if that one is complete). If it does not pass, you need to modify the code until the test passes.

This process is continued for all of the code that is written for the product. These test cases are used not only for unit testing code during development, but also to create an automated test suite used to regularly test the product.

Refactored Code

Fowler et al. (1999) authored the seminal book on refactoring, *Refactoring: Improving the Design of Existing Code*. The book defines **refactoring** as "the process of changing a software system in such a way that it does not alter the external behavior of the code yet improves its internal structure" (p. 16). Refactoring does not mean you are debugging your code, but rather cleaning it up so that extraneous code is removed and it complies with other patterns or structures that may exist in the product. Refactoring is a process to ensure that the least amount of code is written to pass a failing test.

The idea of refactoring originated from the mathematical term *equivalence,* where equations are continually reduced until no additional reductions can be made. The same is true with code: You are not ultimately changing the functions, but you are reducing them to the simplest form possible that keeps the code functioning as it was intended. Steve Wozniak, cofounder of Apple, used the idea of refactoring when they were creating the first Apple computer. He started with x number of parts, say 25, then he tried to build the same computer with 20 parts, then 15, and so on. He kept reducing the number until he was certain that he had the minimum parts, hence the fewest potential break points (see Figure 7.1).

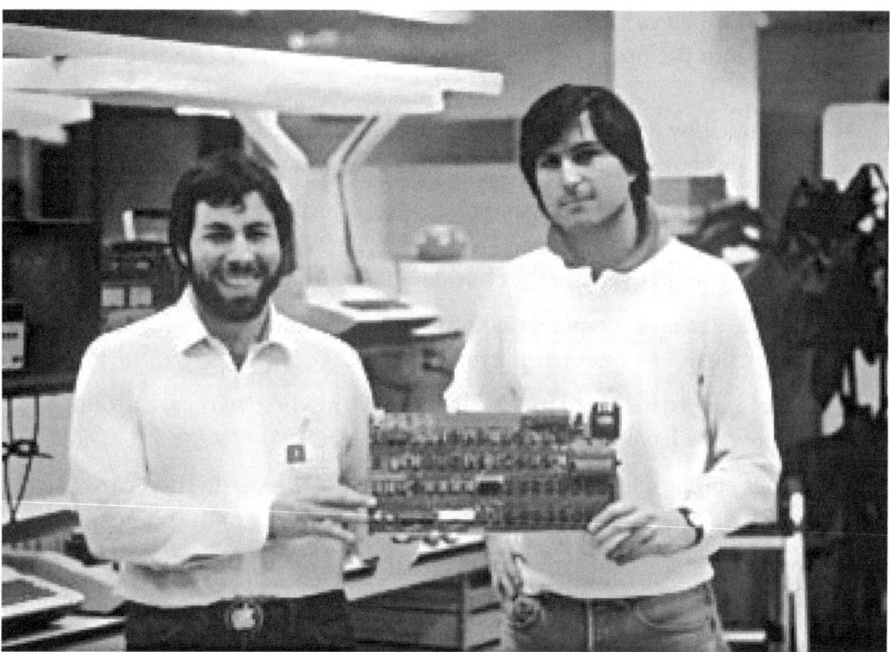

Figure 7.1 *Steve Wozniak and Steve Jobs showing their minimalist computer design*

The idea of coupling comes into play when you are refactoring code. Coupling is the extent to which a program module depends on other modules within the program. Martin (2008) encourages decoupling the code, or making each piece less dependent on other pieces and more individually testable. The primary benefit of decoupling is that it reduces the number of changes that are required if you want to use a different module. For example, if your product is dependent on an SQL database and your team decides they instead want to use a non-SQL database, then the rework required would be minimized and the likelihood of introducing new defects would be reduced.

A TDD and Refactoring Example

Let's look at an example from Cayman Design that includes test-driven development and refactored code.

Cayman Design secured a new assignment to create a blackjack game for an online casino. It is important that the game is as problem-free as possible to gain the trust of online players and also so the casino does not lose money from a code defect.

Their plan involved starting the first sprint by incorporating the basic rules of blackjack into the program. Here are the basic blackjack requirements:

- The game always starts by the dealer and player each receiving two cards. The dealer has one card facing up and one card facing down.
- The goal is to get as close as possible to a card total of 21 without going over 21. The player that gets closest to 21 without going over wins the hand. If you go over 21 it is considered a "bust" and you lose the game.
- If the dealer and the player end up with the same total, then it is considered a "push" and neither player wins.
- The player or the dealer gets blackjack if his first two cards total 21. If both players have blackjack, then it is a push.
- Numerical cards are worth the number on the card. Face cards (jack, queen, king) are worth 10. An ace is worth either 1 or 11 points.
- After the first two cards are dealt, the player can either "stand" (not request additional cards) or "hit" (request one or more additional cards). A player can continue to hit until he thinks he has a number closer than the dealer to 21, he gets blackjack, or he busts. The dealer must continue to hit until he has a total of 17 or more.

Cayman Design assigns two of their strongest software engineers to pair program and to develop some initial working code for the customer to review; they want to ensure that the code passes the test-driven development cases that the developers prepared before writing the code. They agreed to start by confirming that all of the rules of blackjack for a player and a dealer are followed. Each test case is written in JUnit (www.junit.org), a popular testing framework for Java, because the team will be writing the blackjack game in Java code. The team will start by writing test cases for the `playHand()` method. This method plays a single hand of blackjack and returns the winning player. If it is a tie, the method returns a Java "null" object that in this case means there will not be a winner. The team starts by setting up the JUnit test parameters as described in the following steps:

1. Set up the JUnit test class.

```
@RunWith(MockitoJUnitRunner.class)
public class GameTest extends TestCase {
```

2. Create an artificial card deck using a mocking framework. This allows the tester to predetermine what cards will be drawn from the deck to support

the test case. If this is not done, the card deck would contain random cards.

```
@Mock CardDeck mockDeck;
```

3. Create a mock user interface to allow the test to predetermine the user's moves. A mock is used so that a tester can override the real methods on an object, which allows the tester to predetermine the results a method will return.

```
@Mock
private PlayerInterface playerInterface;

private Player player;

private Dealer dealer;
```

4. Define the class that is being tested; in this example, it is the `Game` class.

```
private Game classUnderTest;
```

5. Define the cards that will be used in the test.

```
//test data
private Card ace = new Card(14, Card.Suite.Hearts);
private Card queen = new Card(12, Card.Suite.Spades);
private Card two = new Card(2, Card.Suite.Spades);
private Card five = new Card(5, Card.Suite.Diamonds);
private Card nine = new Card(9, Card.Suite.Diamonds);
private Card four = new Card(4, Card.Suite.Hearts);
```

6. Set up the objects that are being used by other methods in the test. The `@Before` annotation tells JUnit to run the `setUp` method before running any of the other tests.

```
@Before
public void setUp() throws Exception {
    player = new Player("testPlayer", 1000);
    dealer = new Dealer("testDealer", mockDeck );
    classUnderTest = new Game(player, dealer,
playerInterface);
```

Now that the setup is complete, the team is ready to write the first test. They work through the following scenarios to create tests to validate the method to play a single hand of blackjack. The simplest method that can be tested for the blackjack game is to deal two cards, so the first test written will test that the dealer successfully deals two cards to the player.

Create the first test by using the `@Test` annotation; this tells JUnit that the method is a test method. The method name should describe exactly what the test will be doing. Tests can be run individually or as a batch.

Test Scenario 1

Define the first test method after the `@Test` annotation. This annotation is required at the start of each test method you write; it tells JUnit to include the test in the current test suite. It is a best practice to make the method name as descriptive as possible so that any developer can read through the test case to easily understand what the code should be doing. In this case we name the method `testDealFirstTwoCardsToPlayerSecondTwoCardsToDealer` because the test validates the first two cards will go to the player and the second two cards will go to the dealer.

```
 @Test
  public void testDealFirstTwoCardsToPlayerSecondTwoCardsTo
Dealer(){
```

The next step is to set up two new variables; one will store the expected dealer's hand and the other will store the expected player's hand.

```
    List expectedDealerHand = newArrayList(queen, nine);
    List expectedPlayerHand = newArrayList(nine, four);
```

The `when` statement that follows defines the result of the `getMoveFromPlayer` method on the mock `playerInterface` (see previous Player Interface mock). Now when the `getMoveFromPlayer` method is called in the code under test, it will always return the move "stand." This ensures the player does not draw more than two cards for this test.

```
    when(playerInterface.getMoveFromPlayer()).thenReturn
(Game.PlayerMove.stand);
```

The next `when` statement sets the results of the `drawCard` method to return the sequence of cards to match the expected dealer and player hands just defined. So, the first two cards drawn are four and nine and the second two are nine and queen.

```
    when(mockDeck.drawCard()).thenReturn(four).
thenReturn(nine).thenReturn(nine).thenReturn(queen);
```

This line executes the `playHand()` method in the code under test with the mock objects previously defined. If the code is written correctly, it should result in the player drawing the first two cards (four and nine), and the dealer drawing the next two cards (queen and nine).

```
    classUnderTest.playHand();
```

The first `assertEquals` statement checks that the player's hand is equal to the `expectedPlayerHand` defined at the start of this test. In other words, it checks that the player gets the first two cards in the deck, which we set to be four and nine. If this is not true, the test will fail.

```
    assertEquals(player.getHand(),expectedPlayerHand);
```

The final `assertEquals` does the same check to make sure the dealer gets the next two cards in the deck. If either of these asserts fails, then the whole test fails.

```
    assertEquals(dealer.getHand(), expectedDealerHand);
  }
```

Here is the code that passes the first test:

```
public Player playHand(){
```

The first two lines call the dealer's `dealCard` method twice to deal the first two cards to the player face up. The `dealCard` method internally calls the `drawCard()` method on the `mockDeck` to get the cards. So, the dealer will deal the same cards we loaded the deck with in the test case. We pass the value `false` to the dealer's `dealCard` method to indicate that the card is not dealt face down.

```
    player.acceptNewCard(dealer.dealCard(false));
    player.acceptNewCard(dealer.dealCard(false));
```

The second two lines call the dealer's `dealCards` method to deal the second two cards to the dealer: one face up, and one face down.

```
    dealer.acceptNewCard(dealer.dealCard(false));
    dealer.acceptNewCard(dealer.dealCard(true));
```

For now, the `playHand` method just returns `null` because we are not concerned with the winner at this point.

```
        return null;
  }
```

In the next three test cases, we assume the dealer and the player both have two cards, and verify the `playHand` method behaves correctly in all possible blackjack scenarios: dealer and player have blackjack, dealer has blackjack, player has blackjack. You will also notice that we moved the code for dealing the first two cards into its own method called `dealFirstTwoCards`. This is a common type of code refactoring known as *method extraction*.

Test Scenario 2: Dealer and Player Both Have Blackjack

The expected action is that both players have blackjack, resulting in a push, and neither the player nor the dealer wins.

```
@Test
  public void testPushWhenDealerAndPlayerBothHaveBlackjack()
throws Exception{
```

Tell the mock user interface to always return the move "stand" when "get move from player" is called.

```
when(playerInterface.getMoveFromPlayer()).thenReturn(Game
.PlayerMove.stand);
```

Tell the mock deck to first return a queen and an ace to the player, then return a queen and an ace to the dealer, resulting in two blackjacks.

```
when(mockDeck.drawCard()).thenReturn(queen).thenReturn(ace)
.thenReturn(queen).thenReturn(ace);
```

If the player wins, then the test should return a "player winner," or if the dealer wins, it should return "dealer winner." If there is no winner, as expected in this test, the `playHand` method should return `null`.

```
    Player winner = classUnderTest.playHand();
```

`assertNull` checks that the winner equals null and if not, the test fails.

```
    assertNull(winner);
  }
```

This is the end of second test.

Here is the code that passes the second test:

```
public Player playHand(){
    dealFirstTwoCards();
```

An `if` clause was added here to return `null` (signifying a tie or push) if the dealer and the player both have blackjack.

```
    if (hasBlackjack(dealer) && hasBlackjack(player)) {
        return null;
    }
    return null;
}
```

Note that the only code that was added from scenario 1 is the code that returns `null` if both the dealer and the player have blackjack.

Test Scenario 3: Dealer Has Blackjack and Player Does Not

The expected action for test scenario 3 is for the dealer to have blackjack and win the game and the player does not win.

```
@Test
  public void testDealerWinsWhenDealerHasBlackjackAndPlayerDoes
Not() throws Exception{
```

Tell the mock user interface to always return the move "stand" when "get move from player" is called.

```
when(playerInterface.getMoveFromPlayer()).thenReturn(Game
.PlayerMove.stand);
```

Tell the mock deck to first return a queen and a nine to the player, then return a queen and an ace to the dealer, resulting in the dealer getting blackjack.

```
when(mockDeck.drawCard()).thenReturn(queen).thenReturn(nine)
.thenReturn(queen).thenReturn(ace);
```

Run the test on `playHand`.

```
    Player winner = classUnderTest.playHand();
```

Check that the dealer is the winner. If not, the test will fail.

```
    assertSame(winner, dealer);
  }
```

Here is the code that passes the third test:

```
public Player playHand(){
    dealFirstTwoCards();
    if (hasBlackjack(dealer) && hasBlackjack(player)) {
         return null;
    }
```

A new `if` block is added here to check if the dealer has blackjack and to return the dealer as the winner if this is the case.

```
    if (hasBlackjack(dealer)){
         return dealer;
    }
    return null;
  }
```

Note that the code from scenarios 1 and 2 has remained the same and the only thing added was the code to return that the dealer has won if the dealer has blackjack and the player does not.

Test Scenario 4: Player Has Blackjack and Dealer Does Not

The expected action for test scenario 4 is for the player to have blackjack and win the game and the dealer does not win.

```
@Test
public void testPlayerWinsWhenPlayerHasBlackjackAndDealerDoes
Not() throws Exception{
```

> **Exercise**
>
> Write the test case to verify that the `playHand` method returns the player object when the player gets blackjack. Hint: it will be very similar to test scenario 3.

Here is the code that passes the fourth test:

```
public Player playHand(){
    dealFirstTwoCards();
    if (hasBlackjack(dealer) && hasBlackjack(player)) {
      return null;
    }
```

```
    if (hasBlackjack(dealer)){
      return dealer;
    }
    if (hasBlackjack(player)) {
      return player;

    }
    return null;
  }
```

More Complex Test Cases

The next set of test cases start to test what happens when the game moves past the initial hand and the player gets to decide whether to hit or stand. We can predetermine how many cards the player draws by mocking the `getMoveFromPlayer` method. As always, we start with the simplest cases, where either the player or the dealer busts and then the game is over. In the remaining test cases, we assume the existence of two methods: one for dealing the cards to the player (`dealCardsToPlayer`), and one for dealing the cards to the dealer (`drawDealerCards`). The `dealCardsToPlayer` method prompts for the player's move and keeps dealing cards until the player stands or busts. The `drawDealerCards` method is similar, but forces the dealer to draw on 16 and stand on 17 or above. Of course, the code for these methods should be test driven as well.

Test Scenario 5: Dealer Wins Because the Player Busts

In test scenario 5, the expected action is that the player busts and the dealer wins the game.

```
@Test
 public void testDealerWinsWhenPlayerBusts() throws Exception{
```

The first move is to hit and the player busts because the cards total over 21.

```
when(playerInterface.getMoveFromPlayer()).thenReturn(Game
.PlayerMove.hit).thenReturn(Game.PlayerMove.stand);
```

As always, the first two cards go to the player, who gets a queen and a two. The second two cards go to the dealer, who also gets a queen and a two. The player takes the option to hit and draws a queen; at this point, the player is over 21 and busts. The dealer does not need to draw because the player busted.

```
when(mockDeck.drawCard()).thenReturn(queen).thenReturn(two)
.thenReturn(queen).thenReturn(two).thenReturn(queen);
    Player winner = classUnderTest.playHand();
```

The test checks that the dealer wins. If not, the test fails.

```
    assertSame(winner, dealer);
```

Here is the code that passes scenario 5:

```
public Player playHand(){
   dealFirstTwoCards();
    if (hasBlackjack(dealer) && hasBlackjack(player)) {
            return null;
    }
    if (hasBlackjack(dealer)){
      return dealer;
    }
    if (hasBlackjack(player)) {
      return player;
    }
```

We added the following code to call a method that deals new cards to the player. The method keeps prompting the player for a new move until the player chooses to stand or busts.

```
    dealCardsToPlayer();
```

The following `if` block returns the dealer as the winner if the value of the player's hand is over 21 (player busts).

```
    if (isPlayerBusted(player)){
      return dealer;
    }
return null;
}
```

Test Scenario 6: Player Wins Because the Dealer Busts

In test scenario 6, the expected action is that the dealer busts and the player wins the game.

```
@Test
public void testPlayerWinsWhenDealerBusts() throws Exception{

when(playerInterface.getMoveFromPlayer()).thenReturn(Game
.PlayerMove.hit).thenReturn(Game.PlayerMove.stand);

when(mockDeck.drawCard()).thenReturn(queen).thenReturn(two)
.thenReturn(queen).thenReturn(two)
       .thenReturn(five).thenReturn(queen);
    Player winner = classUnderTest.playHand();
    assertSame(winner, player);

  }
```

Here is the code that passes scenario 6:

```
Public Player playHand() {

  dealFirstTwoCards();

  if (hasBlackjack(dealer) && hasBlackjack(player)) {
    return null;
  }
  if (hasBlackjack(dealer)){
    return dealer;
  }
  if (hasBlackjack(player)) {
    return player;
  }
  dealCardsToPlayer();
  if (isPlayerBusted(player)){
     return dealer;
  }
```

The following `drawDealerCards` method will continue drawing cards until the value of the dealer's hand is greater than 16. The dealer must hit 16.

```
drawDealerCards();
```

The following `if` block returns the player as the winner if the dealer's hand is over 21.

```
  if (isPlayerBusted(dealer))
    return player;
  }
  return null;
}
```

Test Cases to Compare

The remaining test cases cover what happens when we actually need to compare the value of the dealer's hand to the value of the player's hand to determine the winner. This needs to be done only if there are no blackjacks or busts. The code that is written to pass these test cases will be put into a private method named `findWinnerBasedOnCardValue`. This new method gets called at the end of the `playHand` method we have been working with all along. From this point on, we will focus on the changes to the new `findWinnerBasedOnCardValue` method because the `playHand` method does not change.

Test Scenario 7: Player Wins Because of a Higher Hand Value

The expected action is that the player wins because the player's hand had a higher value than the dealer's hand.

```
@Test
public void
testPlayerWinsWhenPlayerHasHigherHandValueAnd
NoBustsOrBlackjack() throws Exception {

when(playerInterface.getMoveFromPlayer()).thenReturn
(Game.PlayerMove.stand);

when(mockDeck.drawCard()).thenReturn(queen).thenReturn
(nine).thenReturn(queen).thenReturn(five)
    .thenReturn(two);
    Player winner = classUnderTest.playHand();
    assertSame(winner, player);
  }
```

The code that passes scenario 7 is the final version of the `playHand` method.

```
public Player playHand(){
    dealFirstTwoCards();
    if (hasBlackjack(dealer) && hasBlackjack(player)) {
      return null;
    }
```

```
    if (hasBlackjack(dealer)){
      return dealer;
    }
    if (hasBlackjack(player)) {
      return player;
    }
    dealCardsToPlayer();
    if (isPlayerBusted(player)){
      return dealer;
    }
    drawDealerCards();
    if (isPlayerBusted(dealer)) {
      return player;
    }
    return findWinnerBasedOnCardValue();
  }
private Player findWinnerBasedOnCardValue(){
```

The following lines of code compare the player's hand to the dealer's hand, and the method returns the player as the winner if the player has a higher hand.

```
  if (player.getValueOfHand() > dealer.getValueOfHand() ) {
    return player;
  }
  return null;
}
```

Test Scenario 8: Dealer Wins Because of a Higher Hand Value

The expected action is that the dealer wins because the dealer's hand had a higher value than the player's hand. The player starts off with a queen and a five. The dealer starts off with a queen and a nine. The player hits once and then stands on 17. The dealer wins with 19.

```
@Test
public void
testDealerWinsWhenDealerHasHigherHandValueAnd
NoBustsOrBlackjack() throws Exception {

when(playerInterface.getMoveFromPlayer()).thenReturn(Game
.PlayerMove.hit).thenReturn(Game.PlayerMove.stand);

when(mockDeck.drawCard()).thenReturn(queen).thenReturn(five)
.thenReturn(queen).thenReturn(nine)
        .thenReturn(two);
```

```
    Player winner = classUnderTest.playHand();
    assertSame(winner, dealer);
  }
```

The following code allows scenario 8 to pass.

```
private Player findWinnerBasedOnCardValue(Player player1,
Player player2){

  if (player.getValueOfHand() > dealer.getValueOfHand() ) {
    return player;
  }
```

This line of code compares the player and dealer hand values again and returns the dealer if the player hand value is less than the dealer hand value.

```
  else if (player.getValueOfHand() < dealer.getValueOfHand()) {
    return dealer;
  }
  else {
    return null;
  }

}
```

Test Scenario 9: Dealer and Player Tie with the Same Hand Value

The expected action is that there is a tie between the dealer and the player, resulting in a push.

```
@Test
public void testPushWhenDealerAndPlayerHaveSameHandValue()
throws Exception {

when(playerInterface.getMoveFromPlayer()).thenReturn(Game
.PlayerMove.stand);

when(mockDeck.drawCard()).thenReturn(queen).thenReturn(nine)
.thenReturn(queen).thenReturn(nine);
    Player winner = classUnderTest.playHand();
    assertNull(winner);
  }

  }
```

The following example shows the code that passes scenario 9.

> **Note**
>
> There are no changes from the code for scenario 8 because we have already tested for two of the three possible outcomes. The tie case is the fall-through case that must be there for the code to compile.

```
private Player findWinnerBasedOnCardValue(Player player1,
Player player2){

  if (player.getValueOfHand() > dealer.getValueOfHand() ) {
    return player;
  }

  else if (player.getValueOfHand() < dealer.getValueOfHand()) {
    return dealer;
  }
```

This is the fall-through case that returns `null` (indicating a tie) when the player hand value is equal to the dealer hand value.

```
  else {
    return null;
```

> **Review 1** At this point, the reader should be able to answer Review Questions 1–5.

Minimizing Defect Backlog

The best-case scenario when creating a product is to carefully write the code so that defects are never introduced. Although most developers would prefer to spend all of their time writing new and innovative code, to err is human, and defects happen in even the most thoughtfully developed products.

To create a quality product, there has to be a continuous focus on defect detection during all phases of development, from finding a bug while pairing to running regular integration tests. Joel Spolsky (2000), blogger and former employee at Microsoft, writes about one of the early releases of Microsoft Word. The project was behind, and recovering the schedule became the highest priority. The developers threw together whatever code was necessary to make the features work, and often had to work late into the night. It comes as no surprise that this mode of operation introduced a lot of product defects that had to be fixed at the end of the cycle, which created an even greater delay in product delivery. The team held a lessons learned session (this was before the days of retrospectives) and as a result implemented a new rule that fixing defects always took priority over writing new code. Spolsky argues that the longer you wait to fix a bug, the more the organization will ultimately pay in time and money. Developers can usually find and fix bugs much faster if the code is fresh in their minds. If it has been months since a developer looked at a section of the code, then it is highly likely that another team member has modified that code, making it more difficult to fix. If a bug is found in the field, you risk a hit to product reputation and the loss of valuable customers.

Defects are typically found in the early phases of development during unit testing, where developers test their own code, through paired programming, or by using TDD. These are important points to find defects, but these bugs are found in isolated pieces of the code. Often many of the defects arise when the code from various parts of the product come together as an integrated product; this is known as *integration build*. Integration builds can happen whenever code is completed; however, many Waterfall projects have traditionally used weekly (or monthly) scheduled builds. The thought behind weekly builds was that they would collect all of the code that was changed or added for that week and come in Monday to review any bugs that may have been introduced. Some of the Waterfall teams used even less regular build schedules and waited until all of the code was completed before they did an integration build. You can imagine the defect backlog they were faced with when a month's worth of development work finally came together.

Consistent with the Agile Manifesto, which states, "Working software is the primary measure of progress," Agile promotes continual integration builds. This means that as soon as the code is checked in, it is integrated with the overall product build. This does not mean the updates are part of the live product; it simply means that a new integrated build is always available to the product development team for testing. Some Agile teams are so focused on finding defects quickly that they have implemented a system where a siren or alarm goes off when new code breaks a build; the siren alerts the entire team that there is a problem and allows them to respond immediately. Developers do not want their code to be the one that causes the embarrassing noise, so they are motivated to carefully test before they check anything in for a build.

Manual, Automated, and Customer Testing

A product development team has two options when testing whether the code is working as it was designed.

Manual Testing

The first is **manual testing,** where a human tester must progress through each step or look over the product to make sure nothing about the code or design is defective. Manual testing can be very time-consuming and is subject to human error, but is often necessary in cases where the feature cannot be automated or if it is a visual update such as a background color that must match the rest of the product. Manual testing is often used when validation of the user interface is required.

Automated Testing

The other option is **automated testing,** which uses software that is independent of the software being tested to execute tests without human intervention and compare the results against the desired outcome. A single test or a string of tests can be automated, but running a series of tests tends to provide the most benefit. An automated test can be anything such as a series of clicks in a user interface, executing commands in a command-line interface, or checking that data is appropriately stored in a database. Table 7.1 summarizes the different types of testing that benefit from automation.

Gherkin Example

The testers at Cayman Design have agreed to use behavior-driven acceptance tests to confirm the blackjack game design with their business team. This allows their business counterparts to participate in the code design process without needing to have a deep knowledge of the code. They are starting with the scenarios used in the test-driven development cases that are based on the user stories their product owner created for their first sprint. To write the test in Gherkin language, they first need to describe the feature in the "Feature" line and the scenario they are testing in the "Scenario" line. From there they use the

Table 7.1 *Types of Testing That Benefit from Automation*

Test	Definition	Agile Considerations for Automation	Example
Microtests	Individual unit tests that run while the code is being developed. They test an individual behavior in a single object.	Pro: Fast and automated check for quality while the code is being developed. Con: Will not detect system-level defects.	Tests a small portion of the code (less than 12 lines) and only a few classes in an object.
Acceptance	Acceptance tests are performed to ensure that the product functions meet the agreed-upon requirements. Acceptance tests can be performed by the test team when acting as a mock customer or by a customer before formally accepting a contracted product.	Pro: Can be read by nonprogrammers. Con: Slow to execute.	Behavior-Driven Testing (e.g., Gherkin, JBehave)—a tool that tests the behavior of a product. The test code is written in "business readable language," meaning the test language can be read and understood by team members who are not familiar with programming languages. See "Gherkin Example."

Regression	Testing to see if new code has broken code that already exists in the product.	Pro: Quickly determines if new code has broken existing code. Typically the code is run against a select set of tests (sometimes referred to as a "regression bucket") that provide good coverage of the product functions. Con: Usually does not cover all test cases and cannot detect system-level problems.	JUnits tests can be run against every new build to verify that previously working code still functions properly.
System	Testing all components of the product together on all supported platforms emulating the customer experience.	Pro: Tests the full system. Con: Tests can take significant time and money and may require external dependencies such as special hardware.	Testing an app to make sure it works on both Android and iOS operating systems.
User Interface	Automating the clicks through a graphical or command-line interface.	Pro: Allows user interface testing to be part of the regression and speeds up user interface testing. Con: Some features are difficult to automate and may miss some critical bugs.	Selenium (docs.seleniumhq.org) will automatically test web pages to make sure all features (e.g., buttons, links, mouse overs) are functioning.

"Given" line to describe the current condition and the "And," "When," and "Then" lines to explain how the scenario proceeds from there.

Feature: The game returns a null winner when both the dealer and the player have blackjack.

Scenario: Both the dealer and the player have blackjack
Given the initial round of cards have been dealt
And neither player has busted
When the dealer and player review their cards
And the dealer has blackjack
And the player has blackjack
Then the game returns a null winner
And neither the dealer nor the player wins the game

Scenario: * Continue with the next scenario

The product owner and the business analyst agree that the code accurately represents their goals from the user story, and the developers proceed to include these tests in their automated system tests to ensure the product continues to operate as designed.

Customer Feedback

Customer feedback can take many forms. Alpha tests are used to allow customers to try early versions of the code. Beta tests are similar in that they allow customers to try out the product before it is released generally to the public, but the product has been through much more extensive testing by the development team. Usability testing involves observing the customer interacting with the product to understand where there may be opportunities to improve the ease of use.

Alpha, beta, and usability testing are not unique to Agile and have been used for years during software development projects. Agile does advocate for new techniques that involve regular engagement with the customer. In some of the more extreme cases, the customers are actually part of the development team. The teams that use this approach tend to be the development teams that are creating product for internal use, such as an insurance company including an insurance agent when they are developing a new tool for their sales team. It is more common to find customers involved on a weekly or monthly cadence depending on the length of the sprint or development cycle. Some companies use what is often called a *customer council,* where the development team meets with the customers to review ideas or working code. Other companies invite the customers to participate in the stakeholder feedback sessions; companies such as IBM started using a customer feedback method called **transparent development**. In projects using transparent development, the code is made available to customers on a server at all stages of development so they can provide feedback anytime they wish. No matter what approach you use to get customer feedback, it is important to remember the Agile Manifesto value that emphasizes, "It is more important that the customer become intimately involved with the product development team than to focus on the terms and conditions of the project."

Review 2 At this point, the reader should be able to answer Review Questions 6–11.

Conclusion

One of the most important benefits of moving to a more Agile approach to developing software is the emphasis on quality. Tools such as pair programming, test-driven development, and refactoring offer techniques that build in quality from the beginning. Introducing automated testing and regular customer feedback are also best practices that help ensure issues are found early in the process and can be addressed quickly.

Summary

- Creating a quality culture is more than using new tools or techniques; it is also creating an environment where team members are not overwhelmed and can focus on creating the best product possible.
- As teams start to develop with more agility, it is important that they integrate new practices that allow them to find issues early and address them as quickly as possible.
- Pair programming is a technique where two team members sit together using a shared keyboard and screen to develop code. The driver is the person writing the code and the observer is providing real-time feedback.
- Test-driven development requires developers to first write automated test cases and then write only the code necessary to make the test cases pass with no issues.
- Refactoring does not mean you are debugging your code, but rather that you are cleaning it up so that extraneous code is removed and complies with other patterns or structures that may exist in the product.

- Agile approaches emphasize the importance of keeping the defect backlog to an absolute minimum.
- Manual testing requires step-by-step human intervention to execute each test case, and automated testing uses software that is independent of the software being tested to execute tests without human intervention and compare the results against the desired outcome.
- Customer testing can be performed in many ways, such as alpha, beta, or usability testing. Agile methodologies encourage early and regular feedback from customers during the development process.

Interview with Tim Ottinger

Tim Ottinger is a recognized Agile coach and author with more than 30 years of software development experience. He has shared his software development knowledge with both small and large corporations around the world and is a regular speaker at conferences.

Tim contributed his software development insight in *Clean Code*, *Pragmatic Bookshelf* magazine, the *C++ Report*, *Software Quality Connection*, and other publications. He coauthored *Agile in a Flash*, with Jeff Langr in 2011.

Kristin and Sondra: Which of the Agile tools that you've helped companies adopt have had the most positive influence on product quality?

Tim: The switch to TDD and the switch to pair programming are the most positive, transformative changes programmers can make. Code becomes clearer, easier to write, harder to get lost in, more certain to run . . . it's amazing.

Unit testing frameworks, then, are of key importance. All of the xUnit frameworks are pretty good, and usually they are extendable enough that any project in any language can learn to make good use of them.

Microtests are the workhorse tests of the Agile project. Usually, 80% of the tests will be small, fast-running microtests, and they will be run many times every hour. Some tools like "Autotest" for Ruby, "sniffer" for Python, or "Infinitest" for Java will run microtests continually as you write your code. You don't even have to push a button to get immediate feedback!

Integration/Acceptance/Behavior Testing

Acceptance tests are usually specified by a customer or business analyst (in Scrum it's the product owner, in XP it is the customer, but often the tests are coauthored by test automation engineers or programmers). These tests are usually written before the code is written, to guide the programmers who are writing the code.

The tests are considered "executable specifications" and will typically be written in either an English-like language called "Gherkin" or else in something derived from Ward Cunningham's Framework for Integrated Test (FIT) syntax for behavior-driven testing [http://fit.c2.com/wiki.cgi?IntroductionToFit].

Part of the value proposition of these tests is that they are writeable and readable by nonprogrammers. This is an important benefit if you have nonprogrammers involved with your teams, and can be good documentation even if you do not.

Some teams have only technical members, and will sometimes write system tests in their chosen programming language. If they do, they usually separate them in some way from the fast unit tests (microtests) because tests in this middle layer run much more slowly and require much more setup than microtests.

Often these tests are only run once or twice a day, sometimes only when code is otherwise considered "done," or in some cases only by a build server running Jenkins or Hudson or Anthill (or another code integration tool). They tend to be slow, and that makes running the tests frequently an unattractive option.

System Testing

System testing tools are always useful, because they test a full, running system instead of testing just parts. However, they are troublesome for the same reason.

While I might run 10,000 unit tests in a minute, having to stand up a full system with its network components and databases and user interfaces will ensure that it takes many seconds (even minutes) to prepare a test bed (sandbox). A test bed is a development environment that allows for the isolated testing of a particular module outside a production environment.

This is worse if the test bed requires other external partners (or simulators) to be running.

Once the test bed is running our system, communicating through a user interface requires something like Selenium, Watir, LDTP, Squish, or Mechanize. These tools take time and resources to run also. Web testers have to spin up browsers or connect to the windowing system.

System tests tend to be fragile. If they are using the positioning or names of UI elements, then a change to naming or position will cause these expensive tests to break and need maintenance. This is particularly true of the "record and playback" tests.

The fragile test problem is worse when it comes to validating output. It is hard to avoid overspecifying (such as setting an entire report to be the expected result, instead of checking that it contains the right information). In a fragile test, even a change in the date or time might cause a test to fail.

Due to the systems requirements and the slowness of system tests, they often cannot be run on the developers' desktops, and are only run on special equipment after all the microtests and integration tests have successfully completed.

System testing is important and has value, but it is expensive even if automated, and building robust enough tests is a whole skill set.

On-Target Testing

If the development team is building code to run on a mobile device or an embedded component of some larger system, it is necessary that the project have tests that run on actual target hardware. These tests are a bit harder to set up and a bit more expensive to run than system tests and may require special hardware rigs to make them run.

In Agile teams, we want all our code to pass automated tests on actual hardware as soon as possible, so that we can discover and address risks as soon as possible. After all, testing is a risk-management discipline even in Agile teams. The sooner we know we are in trouble, the sooner we can learn from it and adjust our techniques and designs.

Manual Testing

It's worth mentioning that a lot of manual testing is still done in Agile projects, but not the dull, repetitive work. Anything that can be better done by a machine is automated. What's left is creative, destructive, clever human testing. Automated tests never approach the system with a misunderstanding of how to use it. Automated tests don't care if the experience is not pleasant. Automated tests don't notice that the screen has funky colors.

Automated tests never surprise us by entering the wrong kind of data into an input field or by executing a gesture the programmers didn't expect.

The idea is to leave as much room for manual, creative, human testing as possible by automating everything else.

Kristin and Sondra: If an organization is moving to Agile development methodologies, where should they start to improve the quality of their code?

Tim: It's good to start with testing disciplines. Pair programming and TDD are good starting points, but there are a bunch of other disciplines that tie into doing those well. A team should educate itself about quality code and how to refactor.

One of Industrial Logic's e-learning courses begins by teaching code smells (indications something may be wrong with the code), then how to refactor, then how to write microtests, and then how to test-drive code, and finally how to transform legacy code into testable code. I think it's a very wise progression. A team doesn't have to buy our products, but they will benefit from learning these disciplines, however possible.

There is a book written by the various Object Mentor employees and gathered, edited, and managed by Robert C. Martin; the book is called *Clean Code*. Developers could get a lot of help from reading and studying this book.

The other thing that I find helpful is to study code katas, which are programming exercises that help you practice your art through exercises and repetition. The word "kata" comes from the Japanese term for practicing detailed patterns of movement. The Internet is full of code katas, in video and written prose form, and each of them shows techniques of test-driving code from concept through to finished algorithm.

Kristin and Sondra: Automated testing is not unique to Agile. Teams using the Waterfall methodology have been using automated testing for many years. In your view, what is the major difference in how automated testing is used between the two methodologies?

Tim: The difference is that Agile processes encourage automation when it comes to testing, meaning that Agile teams prefer the test processes to be continual and without manual intervention. We probably don't spend any more or less time than non-Agile teams who automate tests; we just run them all the time. We do spend a lot less time than teams who test all their code manually. Automated tests make testing and debugging much quicker.

References and Further Reading

Beck, Kent. (2002). *Test-driven development: By example*. Boston: Addison-Wesley.

Crispin, Lisa, and Gregory, Janet. (2009). *Agile testing: A practical guide for testers and Agile teams*. Boston: Addison-Wesley.

Fowler, Martin, Beck, Kent, Brant, John, Opdyke, William, and Roberts, Don. (1999). *Refactoring: Improving the design of existing code*. Boston: Addison-Wesley.

Gherkin. https://github.com/cucumber/cucumber/wiki/gherkin.

Langr, Jeff, and Ottinger, Tim. (2011). *Agile in a flash: Speed learning Agile software development*. Frisco, TX: Pragmatic Bookshelf.

Loveland, S., Miller, G., Prewitt, R., and Shannon, M. (2005). *Software testing techniques: Finding the defects that matter*. Hingham, MA: Charles River Media.

Martin, Robert. (2008). *Clean code: A handbook of Agile software craftsmanship*. Upper Saddle River, NJ: Prentice Hall.

Ottinger, Tim. (2013). Personal communication.

Spolsky, Joel. (2000). The Joel test: 12 steps to better code. http://www.joelonsoftware.com/articles/fog0000000043.html.

Review Questions

Review 1

1. Why is it better to find defects earlier rather than later in the product development cycle?
2. What are the benefits of pair programming?
3. How does test-driven development improve code quality?
4. What are the benefits of refactoring code?
5. What is the benefit of decoupling code?

Review 2

6. What risk may you encounter when doing regression testing?
7. What is the difference between alpha and beta testing?
8. What is the difference between manual and automated testing?
9. What is the difference between acceptance and system testing?
10. What is a "business readable language"?
11. How is customer testing different in Agile development environments?

Chapter 8

Tracking and Reporting

Learning Objectives

- Understand Kanban, its effectiveness, and when it is used
- Learn the definition of work in progress (WIP) limits and how they can identify bottlenecks in processes
- Explore different tracking mechanisms used in XP, Scrum, Lean, DSDM, and Crystal
- Understand burn charts, both burn-up for release management and burn-down for sprint tracking
- Examine feature-driven development (FDD) parking lots and how they assist in tracking large and complex projects
- Learn the different strategies for tracking quality through an iteration
- Understand the importance of meetings in tracking progress and course correcting
- Learn the purpose and desired outcome for each meeting—the daily stand-up, the Sprint review, and the retrospective
- Consider the metrics for measuring the success of Agile projects

The previous chapters have led us to this point—where we need to track and report on our progress and results. All of our efforts to prepare the requirements (Chapter 5), plan and groom the activities (Chapter 6), and test our code (Chapter 7) are critical steps toward producing quality software that will meet the customer's needs and deliver business value. This chapter is focused on tracking and measuring our success and quickly identifying the areas that need attention and improvement. We review the tools that are used in tracking, such as Kanban task boards, burn charts, information radiators, and progress charts. We show how quality is built into the process and then discuss the meetings or ceremonies where progress is measured and adjustments are made, if necessary. We explain how to define success within Agile, including the ever-important metric of customer satisfaction.

Kanban

Kanban is a methodology that we have not focused on because it is fundamentally different from the others that we have discussed. Most of the Agile methodologies deliver working software in a time-boxed fashion, meaning that the work proceeds in iterations, or sprints. Conversely, Kanban operates in a "continuous flow" model, meaning that there is no time box for development; tasks are continuously added to the backlog and removed as they are completed. Kanban has three primary characteristics:

- **Visualize the workflow**
    - A Kanban board maps the steps of the workflow in columns across a board.
    - Items, or tasks, are represented on cards or sticky notes and are tracked as they move through the workflow steps.
- **Limit work in progress (WIP)**
    - Assign limits to each column, or workflow step, so that no one group or person can be overloaded with work.
    - The WIP limits naturally identify bottlenecks in the process so they can be addressed, in keeping with the Lean principles.

- **Measure the lead time**
  - By understanding the workflow and removing the bottlenecks, the teams will discover the time it takes for a task to move from creation to resolution, thus providing the organization with metrics for lead time (Kniberg and Skarin 2010, p. 20).

How does Kanban compare with Scrum? Scrum is a great fit for products/projects with a time-boxed workflow, such as product development efforts, that can progress in a series of sprints or iterations. On the other hand, Kanban is a better fit for an unpredictable workflow, unplanned work, and development tasks that require deployment in less time than a typical iteration. For example, Kanban is a great fit for help desk tickets and custom software support where small tickets are continually created and require speedy resolution.

Let's look at Cayman Design for examples. The new calendar option, where customers can buy print calendars with weather-related historical information, is new product development. It makes sense for that work to progress on a sprint cycle, with new features added in each sprint until the entire product is ready for release.

Our product that is in production, however, may have issues that our current customers need addressed, and we have a support team that works those tickets. One customer may report an issue with the browser Chrome; the support team needs to log that ticket, investigate it, write code to correct the issue, and then push that code to production. The customer would not want to wait for that story to be groomed, prioritized, estimated, and put into a sprint and then worked on—they need it fixed right away. This is where Kanban is a great option because it shares all of the Agile elements that make this work so well—collaboration, clear prioritization, small increments of work, fast delivery of working software—and moves it to a continuous workflow.

Kanban Board

Teams often use white boards and sticky notes to create the Kanban board, but any visual tool can be used, from a chalkboard to a large sheet of paper and markers. There are also software programs that create online Kanban boards, which is helpful for distributed teams.

Looking at a specific example, we have five columns on our Kanban board: "backlog," "not started," "in progress," "testing," and "completed." Because workflow stages can vary based on the nature of the work, the columns will change to match the needs of the particular team.

- **Backlog**—The product owner puts all of the requirements (stories) on sticky notes in priority order. The estimated effort of the requirement is also noted. This list could be quite lengthy, depending on the size of the backlog.

- **Not started**—These stories have been selected by a developer and are therefore assigned, but the development work has yet to begin. This is equivalent to a "pending" queue, or the next items to be worked.
- **In progress**—These are the requirements that are currently being coded by a developer.
- **Testing**—This is when the testing is done to ensure that the code is working as intended.
- **Completed**—The requirements in this column are considered ready to be delivered to a customer.

Work in Progress (WIP) Limit

Kanban allows for limiting the amount of work (stories) in a given stage at any point in time; this limit is commonly referred to as the **work in progress (WIP) limit**. WIP limits help organizations to identify where there are bottlenecks in their processes. One of the key tenets of Agile is increased transparency, and the Kanban WIP limits bring attention and focus to the areas of the business where things are slowing down so we can quickly address and correct the situation.

For example, on our Kanban board, we have the following WIP limits:

Backlog: No limit

Not started: WIP limit of 5

In progress: WIP limit of 4

Testing: WIP limit of 3

Completed: No limit

By having these limits, we can identify where our bottlenecks are. Let's walk through an example to see how this works. Take a look at Table 8.1.

In this rudimentary example, all of the WIP limits have been reached, and each person is working diligently on his or her tasks. If the developer finishes task D, he cannot move it into testing because their queue is already full. He must wait until task A, B, or C is completed in testing and moved to completion before task D can be pulled into the testing queue. To move task D into testing now would violate the testing WIP limit of 3.

Therefore, our developer who has completed task D cannot pull task H in from the "not started" queue, because adding that task to the "in progress" queue would violate the WIP limit of 4.

Table 8.1 *Example Kanban Board with WIP Limits*

Backlog	Not Started (5)	In Progress (4)	Testing (3)	Completed
Task M	Task H	Task D	Task A	
Task N	Task I	Task E	Task B	
Task O	Task J	Task F	Task C	
Task P	Task K	Task G		
Task Q	Task L			
Task R				
Task S				

There are many reasons why this is valuable and reinforces the values of Agile. Perhaps the developers are moving very fast and, as an unfortunate result, they are writing buggy code. Thus, the testing queue is backed up because they cannot get tasks A, B and C to pass testing. The developers are finishing more tasks but they cannot move them to testing yet—and they cannot pick up any new tasks. Therefore, the developers can help the testers with their tasks; the testing queue will get cleared, and the developers will understand that the better code they write, the more smoothly the process will go.

The WIP limits also prevent the product owner (or executives) from forcing too much work on the team. The "not started" queue has a WIP limit of 5, so those represent the stories or tasks that are well defined and prioritized. Just as Scrum limits the amount of work by allowing the team to commit only to what they can reasonably finish in the duration of a sprint, the WIP limits accomplish the same goal by limiting how much work can be in each queue.

In this example, WIP limits are set by the number of tasks, but as you can imagine, not all tasks are equal; some tasks are much larger or more complex than others, so some teams set their WIP limits by the number of story points, which were described in detail in Chapter 6, "Grooming and Planning." WIP limits could also be based on hours required to complete the task. Setting and enforcing WIP limits can be challenging for teams, so some teams that are new to Kanban start with the workflow and the Kanban board and add WIP limits later, when they are more comfortable with the process.

The WIP limits also help with the third characteristic of Kanban—the ability to measure lead time. Just as a Scrum team will establish their velocity, Kanban teams need to understand the time it takes for a task to flow from beginning to end. The team could then predict that if a task is accepted into the development queue on Tuesday, it will typically be released on Friday, barring any unforeseen circumstances.

The Kanban principles are built into Lean software development, because Lean is very focused on cumulative flow diagrams and visual controls (Anderson 2003, p. 93). Lean principles focus on eliminating waste, specifically "muda," "mura," and "muri"; an effective Kanban board will address all three. "Muda" is waste created by an activity in the process that adds no value; value stream mapping, which we discussed in Chapter 6, is designed to identify and eliminate muda. When diagramming the workflow to define the columns in Kanban, muda would be evident as a step that is not valuable. "Mura" is the waste generated by unevenness in operations. With the visibility of the Kanban board, we can easily see the work flowing through the system—or across the board—to isolate inefficiencies where work is uneven. Finally, there is "muri," which is the overburdening of people or equipment with more work than they can reasonably manage. The WIP limits in Kanban detect muri by clearly identifying bottlenecks in the process where more work is being added than can effectively be delivered (Tera TPS 2012).

Kanban is a wonderful alternative for teams who want to embrace all of the values and principles of Agile but whose work is unpredictable and difficult to plan. In many organizations, both Scrum and Kanban are utilized, depending on the makeup of the work.

Review 1 At this point, the reader should be able to answer Review Questions 1–5.

Tracking

Regardless of the particular methodology being used, tracking progress is critical to Agile. Increased transparency and the desire to eliminate surprises make tracking essential to effectively managing an Agile project. We explore several tracking mechanisms and philosophies in detail.

Extreme Programming (XP)

XP takes tracking so seriously that one of their roles is that of a tracker, as we first described in Chapter 4, "Describing the Different Roles." The tracker talks to the developers daily and asks two questions—how many ideal days have they worked on a task, and how many ideal days do they have remaining (Beck and Fowler 2000, p. 79). You may recall from Chapter 6 that ideal days or ideal time is the amount of time a task would take under ideal circumstances, with no interruptions, phone calls, meetings, etc.

The authors of *Planning Extreme Programming*, Kent Beck and Martin Fowler, emphasize that the tracker should talk to each developer about the task status (2000, p. 79); this reinforces the importance of face-to-face communication so the tracker can ensure that he or she obtaining accurate and realistic responses from the developer. Scrum addresses this in a similar fashion, through the use of the daily stand-up meeting, described later in the chapter.

Burn Charts

Burn charts are a mechanism to be transparent about the progress of a release or iteration so the team can decide if they need to alter their approach to the work in order to honor their commitments. By being able to easily see their actual progress charted against the planned progress, they have actionable data to inform their decisions.

Burn-Up Charts

Burn-up charts are a way to depict progress toward a product's release goal. Typically, time is on the X axis, either in sprints, months, or quarters, and the Y axis represents the release at completion. The Y axis can be either story points or feature descriptions.

In Figure 8.1, the black line is the cadence that we expect to see relative to the number of story points delivered in each sprint; the gray line represents actual story points delivered.

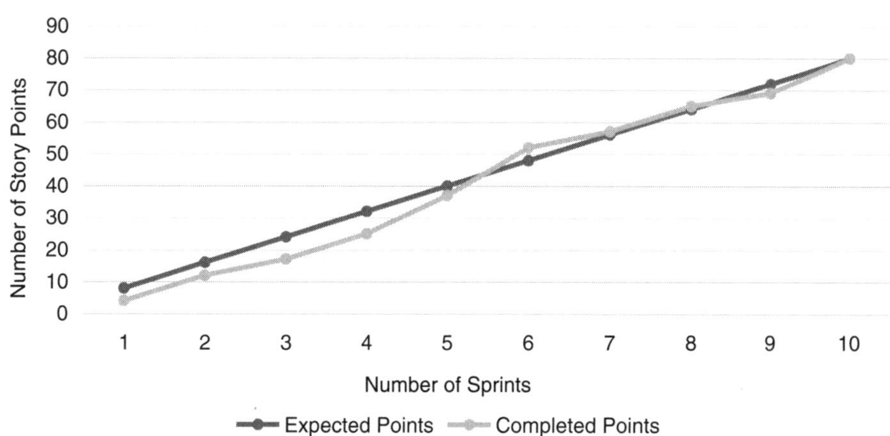

Figure 8.1 *Example burn-up chart by expected points*

In Figure 8.2, we have a slightly different view. Here we see the black line as the number of story points that we need to achieve to meet our release goals. Our gray "actual" line tracks upward, and we meet the goal after sprint 10.

Figure 8.3 shows the feature milestones that we need to complete each quarter to realize the vision for this product. The actual progress is then tracked against these features, as completed.

Although Figures 8.1 and 8.2 do reveal the progress that the team is making, the charts may not convey the necessary information to stakeholders. It is interesting to note the team's velocity and how quickly they are delivering story points, but that does not necessarily mean that the product is producing the right deliverables. Figure 8.3 shows the actual features that are delivered to the

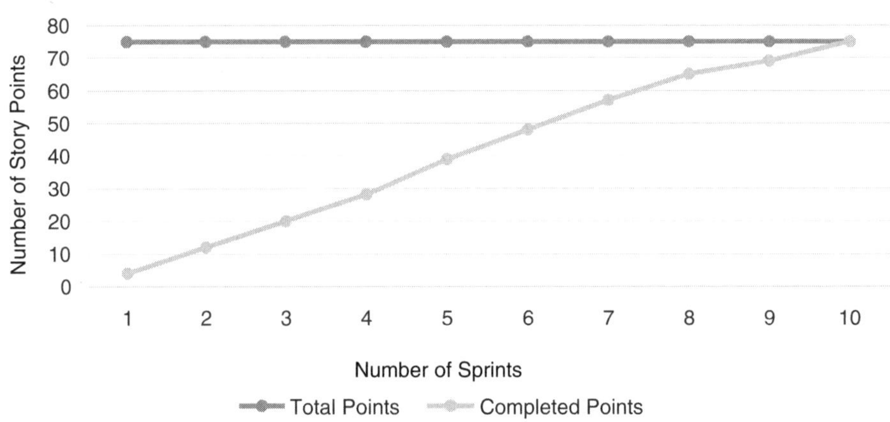

Figure 8.2 *Example burn-up chart by total points*

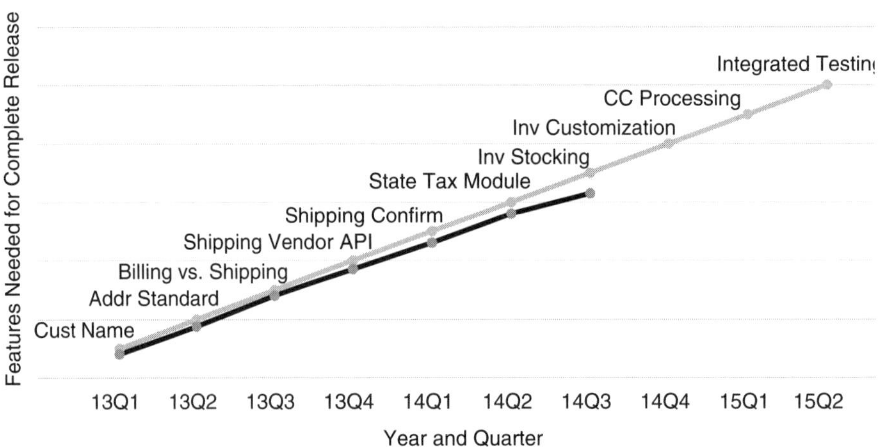

Figure 8.3 *Burn-up chart by feature*

marketplace. Executives often prefer this view because they can easily see the feature delivery progress (Cockburn 2004b).

Burn-Down Charts

Burn-down charts serve a different purpose: These are the daily status checks for the team relative to where they expected to be at a particular point in time. This is a critical tracking element within a sprint or iteration to ensure that any necessary course correction is identified and addressed as early as possible.

As described in Chapter 6, a few critical activities take place during the Sprint planning meeting. First, the developers choose the tasks that they want to own. After they select the tasks, they estimate the hours that they believe each task will take them to complete. Before Sprint planning, most activities are at the user story level, and they are estimated in story points. Once Sprint planning is completed, stories are broken down into tasks, and tasks are estimated in hours. Now that the developer is known, and he or she has small increments of work, it is easier to estimate the actual amount of time a task will take. Therefore, the team can see the total number of hours allocated to the sprint and track their actual progress against the target.

The black "expected" line represents the ideal sprint progress if the same level of work was completed every day. You can tell from the chart in Figure 8.4 that our sprint got off of a rocky start because our gray "actual" line was above the "expected" line for several days. Whenever this happens, the team must determine if they are able to finish the expected amount of work within the sprint. In this case, the team recovered nicely, and with three days

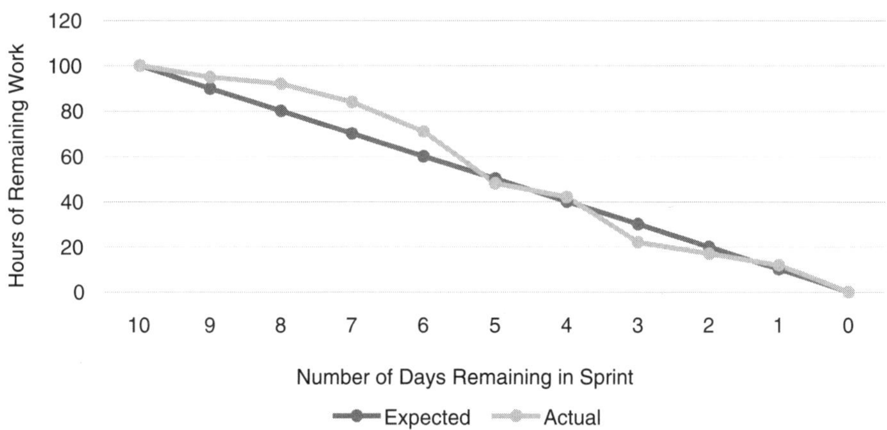

Figure 8.4 *Burn-down chart 1*

remaining in the sprint, they were actually ahead of schedule. They finished the last day with all of the work completed.

The next example in Figure 8.5 does not paint as pretty a picture.

As you can see from this chart, something went horribly wrong on day 5. Perhaps several team members were out sick with the flu; or the team uncovered a significant problem with the database; or a production issue occurred and the entire development team was pulled off the sprint to work on the live issue; or a story ended up being significantly more difficult than originally thought. In any case, the burn-down clearly shows that the sprint is in jeopardy, and we can see this almost immediately. The team has several options to try to remedy the situation. For example, they can reassign tasks to the most competent developers to speed things up, or they can work long hours (with lots of caffeine) to make up the difference (noting that this is not a sustainable way to manage work). They can also negotiate with the product owner about the situation and the best resolution. The product owner should be involved in all discussions because he or she will need to determine which stories are removed from the sprint, if necessary. No one ever wants this to happen, but when it does, having the product owner determine the appropriate work to complete—based on priority and business value—is still far better than not knowing and just having the IT teams fail to deliver.

Although the example represented in Figure 8.5 is not ideal, it is still positive. Without Agile and this level of transparency, we would have situations of unknown risk, dates missed, and customers disappointed.

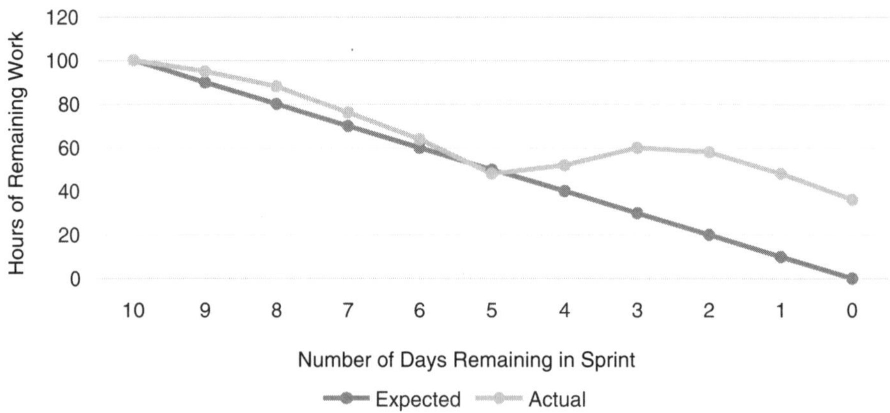

Figure 8.5 *Burn-down chart 2*

Exercise

Create a burn-down chart for the Cayman Design team in this scenario: They have committed to a two-week sprint (ten working days) and plan to accomplish 120 hours of work in that time. What would their ideal line look like?

Insert "actuals" if they were above the line, or behind on their work, for days 6, 7, 8.

Insert "actuals" if they were below the line, or ahead on their work, for days 9, 10, 11.

Information Radiators

Information radiators (see Figure 8.6) are anything posted in the team members' physical space that they will walk by or see on a regular basis. The idea is that the information radiates into the team's subconscious because they encounter the information regularly. Radiators work in much the same way as advertisements on billboards along the freeway: They encourage you to think about ideas because they are presented to you regularly. For some Agile teams, the

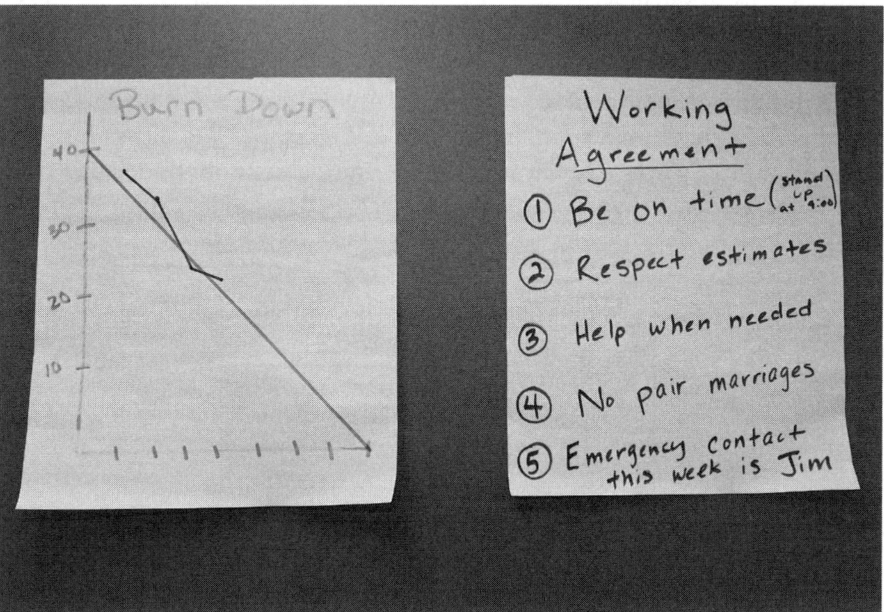

Figure 8.6 *Information radiators*

information radiator might be some best practices posted on a white board, such as "We will not write new code until all defects are closed." Other teams may post the daily status in a common area so the team members know what is going on with the project and maintain a sense of urgency. Some teams may even use information radiators to promote a positive culture and post birthdays or promotions for everyone to see. Regardless of how a team decides to use information radiators, they are a helpful tool to promote team communication.

Feature-Driven Development (FDD) Parking Lots

FDD incorporates an excellent way to track progress on larger projects where many activities are contributing to a cohesive whole. For our Cayman Design project, we want to create and sell weather-related calendars to customers; this is a large departure from the other features in our weather app because we have to consider inventory, shipping, and payment details. An example of an FDD parking lot might look like what is shown in Figure 8.7.

This tells us that the feature "Collect Customer Information" consists of seven stories totaling 32 points. At this moment, we are 75% complete, and the feature is needed by August 2014. The color on the story can indicate its health, this particular story being yellow, meaning it is in jeopardy. Although this is an interesting depiction of information, it is not necessarily more valuable than any of the other Agile tools we have discussed—that is, until you add many other components, and then the picture painted by the FDD parking lot is incredibly useful (see Figure 8.8).

From this parking lot view, you can get an immediate sense for the project health, even though we are looking at a total of 66 stories and 325 points. You can add teams/owners to each parking lot and define a more detailed color scheme as needed for your particular project. FDD's model-driven approach

Collect Customer Information
7 Stories
32 Points
75% Complete
Color: Yellow
Aug-14

Figure 8.7 *FDD parking lot partial view*

Customer Data		
Collect Customer Information	Capture Order Details	Gather Payment Information
7 Stories	9 Stories	6 Stories
32 Points	46 Points	31 Points
75% Complete	25% Complete	50% Complete
Color: Yellow	Color: Red	Color: Green
Aug-14	Aug-14	Sep-14

Inventory Management	
Inventory Stocking	Calendar Customization
14 Stories	8 Stories
55 Points	42 Points
50% Complete	0% Complete
Color: Green	Color: Yellow
Oct-14	Oct-14

Shipping Information		
Standardize Addresses for Shipping	API to Shipping Vendor	Confirmation Details Sent to Customer
4 Stories	10 Stories	8 Stories
20 Points	65 Points	34 Points
50% Complete	25% Complete	0% Complete
Color: Yellow	Color: Red	Color: Green
Aug-14	Aug-14	Sep-14

Figure 8.8 *FDD parking lot full view*

allows it to scale to support large, complex projects (De Luca 2012; Griffiths 2007; Highsmith 2012).

Other Progress Charts

Gantt (percent complete) and stoplight (red, yellow, or green status) charts have been the most common status-tracking tools in software development projects for many years. Although there is nothing about the Agile methodology that would prevent Gantt or stoplight charts from providing useful information, Agile teams have embraced tracking tools that help the teams focus on their daily status.

Tracking Quality

Agile endorses the idea of writing quality code throughout the development process through pair programming and test-driven development, which we discussed in depth in Chapter 7, "Testing, Quality, and Integration." Despite these preventive measures, poor quality can still be introduced into the product. There are several approaches to tracking the quality of a product during an iteration.

Build Status

Once a developer has completed testing of his or her code, the first check for quality is to look for errors when the code becomes integrated in the product build on the server. If a previously error-free build is indicating that there are errors, then the development and test team have a very clear indication that there may be a problem with the new code. These defects are found quickly because Agile teams are doing regular builds. It is also easier to narrow down the defect location in the code because typically only small amounts of code are added with each build.

The team can track how many builds introduce errors over time, but this is not commonly measured. The Agile teams that utilize a siren or alarm with a build error often create an environment where defects are avoided at all costs and build errors become a rarer occurrence.

Defects

Defects are a normal part of the product development process. In Waterfall development, quality is sometimes measured as a ratio such as the number of defects introduced per 1,000 lines of new code or the number of defects detected compared to the number that the developers were able to close in a given week. These metrics can also be used while doing Agile development, and in fact some teams create a defect burn-down chart similar to the sprint burn-down chart as a visual representation of the defect closures. If the defect burn-down chart is not trending down, then the team knows that either defect closure is not being prioritized by the developers or the new code is continuing to have more and more problems. In either case, the team should focus immediately on defect closure.

Test Cases

An important part of the testers' role is to write test cases that will uncover the defects in the code to ensure the highest-quality product is released to customers. These tests should cover both the functionality and the usability of the product.

In Waterfall projects, testers would review the design documents and requirements, write an overall test plan, write individual test cases for the requirements, and then execute the test cases when the developers had finished coding and document the results. If a defect was found during a test case in Waterfall, it would be documented and prioritized, and the tester would track it through resolution.

Agile development works differently because testing is considered more of a whole-team activity that happens throughout the iteration. Lisa Crispin and Janet Gregory's book, *Agile Testing: A Practical Guide for Testers and Agile Teams* (2009), uses the Agile testing quadrants (see Figure 8.9) to describe how an Agile tester can think through the different types of tests that need to be performed during the iteration. We covered testing in detail in Chapter 7, but for the purposes of using test cases to assess the quality of the product, it is important to make sure that all aspects of the product (e.g., technical, usability, performance) are sufficiently covered. Savvy Scrum masters know that if very few defects are found during testing, that may mean that the code is of high quality, or it could mean that the product was not sufficiently tested. It is important to question the team if too many or too few defects are found during an iteration.

Review 2 At this point, the reader should be able to answer Review Questions 6–10.

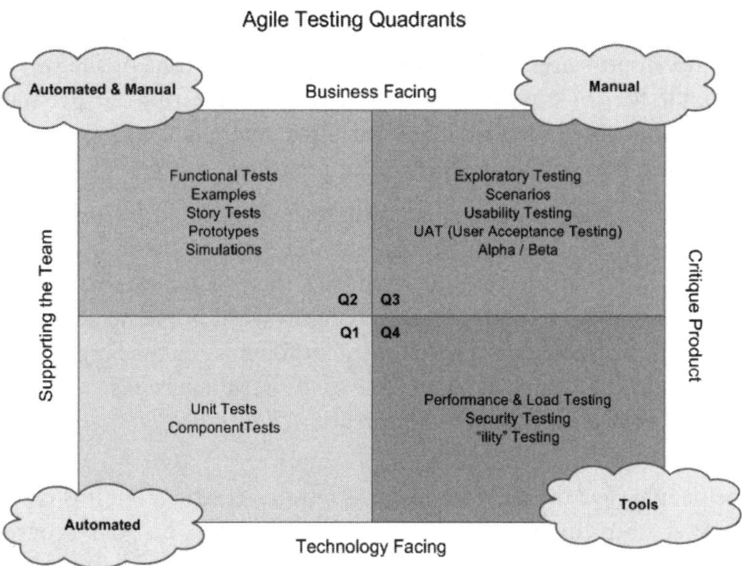

Figure 8.9 *Crispin and Gregory's (2009) Agile testing quadrants*

Source: Crispin, Lisa, and Gregory, Janet. 2009. *Agile Testing: A Practical Guide for Testers and Agile Teams*. Boston: Addison-Wesley, p. 98.

Meetings or Ceremonies

Because the teams are working hard during the sprint or iteration to design, code, and test the requirements, we need a mechanism to keep track of their progress and make sure everything is working well on the teams. Similar to how the XP tracker asks each developer how things are going, Scrum, Lean, and DSDM all recommend a daily stand-up meeting, sometimes called the daily Scrum.

Daily Stand-Up Meeting

Development teams use the **daily stand-up meeting** (see Figure 8.10) to do a quick status check and prepare the team for the day. These meetings usually take less than 15 minutes and provide an opportunity to understand the team's progress in the iteration. Each team member answers three key questions during the daily stand-up meeting:

- *What did I do yesterday?* This is an opportunity for a developer to share what tasks were closed yesterday or if something was more difficult than expected or will require more time.
- *What am I planning to do today?* This information helps the team know the developer's area of focus for the day and also if he or she will be unavailable for some portion of time because of meetings or personal considerations. By understanding what a teammate is working on, the other team members can align their work, if necessary.
- *Is there anything blocking my progress?* This could be anything that is preventing advancement, from a technical issue to the lack of a test environment to a clarification question with the product owner. The key is to share challenges to keep things moving forward in the iteration. The output of this discussion serves as the action items for the Scrum master. As you will recall from Chapter 4, one of the Scrum master's primary roles is to clear roadblocks or impediments.

Some people view the daily stand-up as a status meeting, but it is much more than that: A status meeting is simply informing others on your progress in a static and single-threaded way, but the daily stand-up meeting is an opportunity for team calibration. If one team member reports struggles with a task, then other team members can jump in and help. This help might be sitting together to solve the problem or offering to take ownership of other tasks to allow the teammate to continue working on the troublesome task. Within Agile, the team succeeds or fails together. To ensure that commitments are kept, the team needs

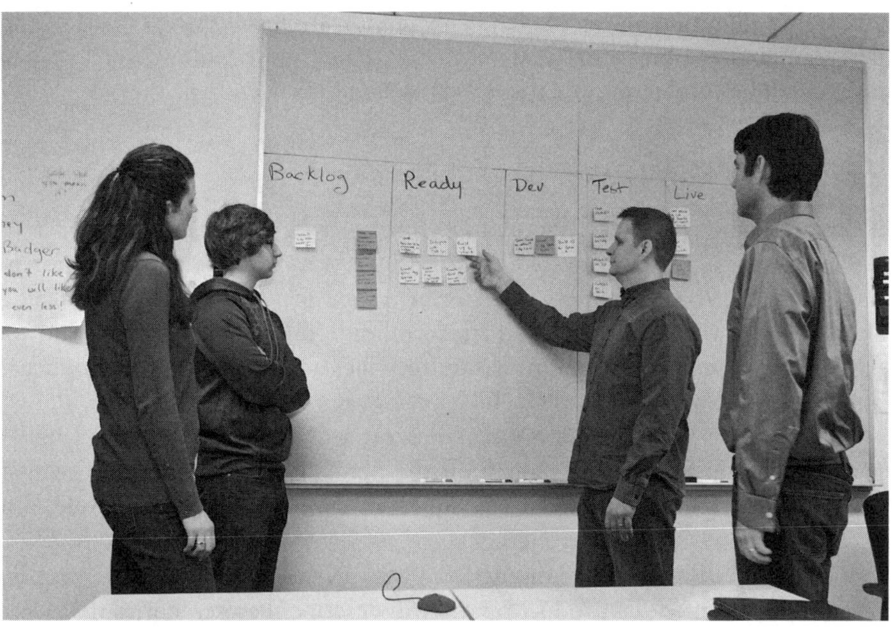

Figure 8.10 *Daily stand-up*

to band together to deliver on all tasks. The daily stand-up meeting provides a forum for teammates to calibrate on the work remaining and support each other to success.

There are a few other important parameters for the daily stand-up meeting. First, the meeting is open to everyone, meaning that stakeholders and extended team members are welcome to attend, but only the "pigs," as described in Chapter 4, may talk. The reason for this distinction relates to the goal of the meeting—*it is about team calibration.* Although a stakeholder may have an opinion to share, the daily stand-up meeting is probably not the right forum. Also, because the daily stand-up is designed as a short meeting, where the participants actually stand up to prevent the meeting from lasting longer than necessary, it is not the right place for problem solving. When a developer or tester is answering the three questions, it is often easy to start brainstorming and problem solving as part of the discussion. The Scrum master needs to control the meeting and push certain discussions "offline," meaning that they should be discussed after the meeting.

When introducing the daily stand-up to new Agile teams, there can be hesitation about a daily meeting. People often believe they do not have time to meet every single day, and they initially view it as unnecessary overhead. However, if the daily stand-up meeting is run well, with a focus on information sharing and team calibration, it can accelerate a team toward meeting their goals. High-performing teams often find that other longer and more tedious meetings can be avoided by conducting an effective daily stand-up.

Sprint Review or Demo

A Sprint review, or Sprint demo, is a meeting hosted by the team that is open to a wide audience including extended team members, stakeholders, and potentially even external customers. The sprint review provides the opportunity to showcase the working software to inform and educate the organization on what has been completed and to gather feedback to ensure that the product is delivering on expectations.

The session is not intended to be a large, professional meeting with a lengthy presentation. In fact, most teams limit the "prep" time for the demo to two hours or less; we want the teams to spend their time writing great code, not producing pretty PowerPoint slides.

The person who leads the discussion varies by team and may even vary by Sprint review. Often the product owner will describe the user stories that were tackled during the sprint, and the Scrum master will demonstrate the working software. On other teams, the product owner runs the entire meeting, because having a nontechnical person work through the software demonstrates its usability. On still other teams, the developers do the demonstration because they feel a great sense of ownership for the value that they have created with the software. Within Extreme Programming (XP), many teams have the customer (product owner) lead the demonstration because the entire team wants to showcase their work, and the customer should demonstrate the progress that has been made on the features (Beck and Fowler 2000, p. 83).

If the feedback is particularly negative, the team will need to evaluate whether they should make the new feature publicly available. Positive feedback validates that the new feature is ready for deployment. In Chapter 4, we mentioned that one of the product owner's responsibilities was to "accept or reject" the completed user stories; this should be done either before or at the Sprint review meeting. If the stakeholders offer opportunities for improvement, those can be documented as potential new requirements. The product owner is responsible for collecting all of the feedback and determining what items will be addressed in future sprints and their relative priority. Stakeholders should not assume that all feedback will be incorporated. The product owner should evaluate the business value of each suggestion and compare it against the items in the product backlog.

Retrospectives

Retrospectives are an important part of Agile software development as a forum for open communication among team members and as a tool for continual improvement. The Agile Manifesto emphasizes team retrospectives in this principle: "At regular intervals, the team reflects on how to become more effective, then tunes and adjusts its behavior accordingly." A retrospective is a team meeting at the end of an iteration where the team has the opportunity to inspect and adapt their teamwork (Derby and Larsen 2006, loc. 144). One method for facilitating the discussion is to pass out note cards and ask participants to jot down their observations into categories; the categories could be "stop doing," "start doing," and "continue," as in Table 8.2 (Cohn, http://www.mountaingoatsoftware.com/agile/scrum/sprint-retrospective).

Retrospectives allow the teams to discuss the workflow and how that can be enhanced, but the bigger value comes in the sense of teamwork and trust that is emphasized during this meeting.

Gathering the team together to talk about how they are getting along can be awkward and uncomfortable, but it is the surest way to improve things. There are a number of ways to manage retrospectives to make the conversation more natural, while ensuring that the key concerns are addressed effectively. In their 2006 book *Agile Retrospectives: Making Good Teams Great*, Esther Derby and Diana Larsen present a number of ideas for teams to use to frame the conversation in a way that is nonconfrontational but allows the key issues to be addressed. Agile's concept of team self-organization, collaboration, and continuous improvement makes the retrospective a critical meeting to have for the growth and development of the team.

One idea from the book is brilliant in its simplicity. The authors call it "Prioritizing with Dots," and it helps to prioritize the items that the team wants to work on; here is a synopsis (Derby and Larsen, 2006, loc. 1319).

Table 8.2 *Example Retrospective Comments*

Start Doing	Stop Doing	Continue Doing
Recalculate velocity after each iteration Enroll the team in a clean coding course Encourage testers to pair program with developers	Allow the daily stand-up meeting to last more than 15 minutes Write new code when unresolved defects exist	Team lunch on Fridays Retrospectives Customer feedback sessions

Have team members write down specific action items that they would like the team to address on a sticky note, note card, white board, etc. Post each suggestion with no judgment or priority. After every idea is on the board, give each participant three small stickers; these could be small sticky notes, colored dots, or even labels from the printer. Each person places the three stickers on any action item(s) he or she considers most important; all three stickers could be put on a single item, for example, or they could put one each on three different items. When the exercise is completed, the team knows that the action item with the most stickers is the top priority. Based on the sticker allocation, you can decide how many action items you want to address. There is nothing magical about the number three—each person could vote five times or eight; teams should use whatever number works best to achieve their goals.

Retrospectives are an important vehicle for the team to continuously grow together as an entity, which will make their work environment more productive and more enjoyable.

Measuring Success in Agile

How do you know if an Agile project is successful? This topic has sparked a great deal of debate, because some Waterfall metrics drive the wrong behavior and thus are inappropriate. Rally Software has developed a nice framework for measuring performance, in which they suggest four categories of measurement (Maccherone 2013):

- Do it fast
- Do it right
- Do it on time
- Keep doing it

These parameters align well with the core values and principles of Agile. In the "do it fast" category, we can measure the teams' productivity and their responsiveness. In the "do it right" category, we are measuring quality and customer satisfaction. When we "do it on time," we demonstrate a predictable cadence for when working software is delivered. Under "keep doing it," we want to measure employee satisfaction, which is a critical component of sustainability as referenced in the Agile principles.

Truly, the absolute best measure of success for Agile teams is customer satisfaction. If your organization is delivering high-quality software that meets the needs of the users and is delivered quickly and predictably, then your customer satisfaction scores should be steadily (or dramatically) improving.

Review 3 At this point, the reader should be able to answer Review Questions 11–15.

Conclusion

Tracking and reporting are critical to Agile projects because of the focus on transparency and continuous improvement. Kanban is an Agile methodology that tracks items through the workflow and uses the Lean principles to remove bottlenecks or waste. Tracking mechanisms within all of the Agile methodologies will help the teams determine when and how to adjust to ensure delivery on their commitments. Burn charts, information radiators, FDD parking lots, and quality tracking measures all provide valuable information to the teams. The meeting structure also reinforces the tracking and reporting measures, with the daily stand-up providing real-time feedback on progress and allowing the team to calibrate on the remaining work. The Sprint demo or review is a forum for stakeholders to see the working software and provide feedback. Finally, the Sprint retrospective helps the team to inspect and adapt their relationships and team effectiveness. It is important to measure the overall performance of an Agile project, and customer satisfaction is a meaningful way to ensure that the organization is delivering business value to the marketplace.

Summary

- Kanban is an Agile methodology that is better suited for work that is unpredictable or difficult to plan, such as help desk tickets and custom software requests.
- Kanban focuses on three goals—visualize the workflow, limit the work in progress (WIP), and measure the lead time.
- Limiting the work in progress, referred to as setting WIP limits, helps teams to identify and correct bottlenecks in the workflow.

- There are three types of waste, according to Lean principles. Muda is waste created by steps that add no value. Mura is waste created in the unevenness of the process. Muri is the waste created by overburdening the people or systems in the process.
- Burn charts provide the team with real-time status on progress and deliverables.
- Burn-up charts are designed to map incremental delivery against the release targets. Burn-down charts are used within a sprint to ensure that tasks are being completed in a timely fashion that will lead to a successful iteration.
- Information radiators are any data, metrics, or values that are helpful to the team, displayed visibly in the work area so the information "radiates" throughout the space.
- Feature-driven development (FDD) uses parking lots to provide visibility to large, complex projects so stakeholders and team members can easily see how the project is progressing.
- Tracking quality is important in Agile, and teams need to track the build status to ensure that no new defects were introduced. Bug or defect resolution is important to track to ensure quality is purposefully measured and reported.
- The daily stand-up meeting allows the team members to discuss what they completed yesterday, what they are working on today, and what, if anything, is standing in their way.
- The daily stand-up meeting is designed to be only 15 minutes each day, and only the team members (the pigs) are allowed to talk.
- The daily stand-up meeting is an opportunity for the team to calibrate on their work to ensure that all deliverables are met by the end of the sprint.
- The Sprint review or demo is the opportunity to showcase working software to stakeholders to solicit their feedback. Data gathered in the demo is considered by the product owner for possible adjustments to priorities and user stories in the backlog.
- Sprint retrospectives are an opportunity for the team to get together to discuss the team dynamics and effectiveness.
- Measuring success in Agile projects can be challenging, because many of the old Waterfall metrics no longer apply or would actually drive the wrong behavior.

- Although there are many ways to measure success through productivity, speed to market, responsiveness, and predictability, the number one measure of success is customer satisfaction. If we are producing working, high-quality software quickly in response to market needs, customer satisfaction should reflect our success.

Review 4 At this point, the reader should be able to answer Review Questions 16–20.

Interview with Kent McDonald

Kent J. McDonald is an Agile coach who has helped many organizations understand and solve the problems they face. He is actively involved in the both the Agile software development and Business Analysis communities, as he has seen where companies succeed and fail in their Agile implementations. By sharing those stories at BeyondRequirements.com, TechWell.com, and ProjectConnections.com and through his speaking and coaching engagements, he is actively helping businesses move forward. Kent's influence is global, as he recently served as the conference chair for the highly acclaimed Agile 2013 conference for the Agile Alliance.

Kristin and Sondra: In your experience, which status-tracking method is best for teams who are new to Agile?

Kent: They go by a variety of names—information radiators, big visible charts, story board. My friend Chris Matts calls them visualization boards. Basically, make the work visible by taking large white boards—it's helpful to have them on wheels—that are split into columns; the location of a card representing a story indicates that story's status. Teams that I have worked with will often have two boards—a discovery board that indicates the progress of getting stories ready for an iteration, and a delivery board which reflects the progress of stories in an iteration.

Kristin and Sondra: How should teams calculate their initial velocity estimate?

Kent: There are a couple of methods that I know of. One is based on commitment-based planning. The product owner (PO) and team get together along with a stack of sized stories. The product owner picks the first story, reads it, team discusses it, and then decides whether they can commit to delivering it in that iteration. Product owner then picks the next story, reads it, team discusses, then PO asks team, "Can you commit to this story along with the one(s) you already committed to?" This process continues until the team says they are full and cannot bring on any additional stories. The team can then add up the story points for those stories and use that as their initial velocity, until they have some iterations of actual experience.

Kristin and Sondra: Is there a point where a team works at a consistent velocity?

Kent: That is desirable, and can usually happen if the composition of the team stays consistent. If you are constantly changing the members of the team, the velocity will never stabilize and velocity, which is intended to be a guide for planning purposes, is basically useless. That is one argument for keeping the same team together and bringing work to the team.

Kristin and Sondra: How should a team determine their work in progress (WIP) limit?

Kent: Most teams I've worked with recently work in an iterative fashion, so the WIP limit ends up being the number of stories they bring into an iteration. If I were looking to create a WIP limit for given stages in the team's process (say Dev in Progress), I would base the WIP limit on the number of people who would be working on stories in that column. Say you have four people on your team and you have decided to pair on everything; you may set your WIP limit for Dev in Progress at 2.

Kristin and Sondra: How do most of the Agile teams you work with allocate time for defect resolution?

Kent: This partly depends on what your definition of "defect" is. First off, I don't consider problems that are identified with stories under development in the current iteration as defects; fixing these things is just part of getting to "done." Assuming that you are doing all your testing in the same iteration in which the story is developed (which is what you want to have happen), then the only defects are those that escape into production. I usually treat defects as another story and add them to the backlog for consideration with other stories. If the defect is dramatically impacting the operation of the system, those defects may get pushed up to the top of the backlog. If the team is also dealing with production support and has items come up that have to be addressed quickly (for example, cannot be included in the backlog), then the time the team spends addressing those production issues usually gets factored into the velocity. The team's actual velocity may be a few points lower than optimal because the team had to spend some time fixing production issues. If the team sees this happening quite a bit, the important question is not how to allocate time to resolve defects, it's looking at the team's process to figure out where defects are typically introduced and correct that issue.

References and Further Reading

Anderson, David J. (2003). *Agile management for software engineering: Applying the theory of constraints for business results*. Upper Saddle River, NJ: Prentice Hall.

Anderson, David J. (2010). *Kanban: Successful evolutionary change for your technology business*. Sequim, WA: Blue Hole Press.

Beck, Kent, and Fowler, Martin. (2000). *Planning Extreme Programming*. Boston: Addison-Wesley.

Cockburn, Alistair. (2004a). *Crystal clear: A human-powered methodology for small teams*. Boston: Addison-Wesley.

Cockburn, Alistair. (2004b). Earned value and burn charts. Blog entry, June 22. http://alistair.cockburn.us/Earned-value+and+burn+charts.

Cohn, Mike. Sprint retrospectives. http://www.mountaingoatsoftware.com/agile/scrum/sprint-retrospective.

Cohn, M. (2010). *Succeeding with Agile: Software development using Scrum*. Boston: Addison-Wesley.

Crispin, Lisa, and Gregory, Janet. (2009). *Agile testing: A practical guide for testers and Agile teams*. Boston: Addison-Wesley.

De Luca, Jeff. (2012). FDD implementation. http://www.nebulon.com/articles/fdd/fddimplementations.html.

Derby, Esther, and Larsen, Diana. (2006). *Agile retrospectives: Making good teams great*. Frisco, TX: Pragmatic Bookshelf. Kindle edition.

Griffiths, Mike. (2007). Summarizing progress with parking lot diagrams. http://leadinganswers.typepad.com/leading_answers/files/summarizing_progress_with_parking_lot_diagrams.pdf.

Griffiths, Mike. (2012). *PMI-ACP exam prep, premier edition: A course in a book for passing the PMI Agile Certified Practitioner (PMI-ACP) exam*. Minnetonka, MN: RMC Publications.

Highsmith, Jim. (2002). *Agile software development ecosystems*. Boston: Addison-Wesley.

Highsmith, Jim. (2012). Managing larger projects with feature-driven development. http://www.nebulon.com/pr/cutterlargefdd.html.

Kniberg, Henrik. (2012). *Lean from the trenches: Managing large-scale projects with Kanban.* Dallas, TX: Pragmatic Bookshelf.

Kniberg, Henrik, and Skarin, Mattias. (2010). *Kanban and Scrum—Making the most of both.* Raleigh, NC: Lulu.com.

Maccherone, Larry. (2013). The seven deadly sins of Agile measurement: Sins #2 and #3. Blog entry, July 31. http://www.rallydev.com/community/agile/seven-deadly-sins-agile-measurement-sins-2-and-3.

Palmer, Stephen, and Felsing, Mac. (2002). *A practical guide to feature-driven development.* Upper Saddle River, NJ: Prentice Hall.

Poppendieck, Mary, and Poppendieck, Tom. (2003). *Lean software development: An Agile toolkit.* Boston: Addison-Wesley.

Sutherland, Jeff, and Schwaber, Ken. (2013). *The Scrum guide.* https://www.scrum.org/Portals/0/Documents/Scrum%20Guides/2013/Scrum-Guide.pdf#zoom=100.

Tera Prudent Solutions Pty Ltd. (2012). Waste reduction by MUDA, MURA and MURI. http://www.tera-tps.com.au/Pdf/MUDA.pdf.

Review Questions

Review 1

1. How is Kanban different from the other Agile methodologies, specifically Scrum?
2. What do the columns on a typical Kanban board represent?
3. Why would a team implement a work in progress (WIP) limit?
4. What are the three forms of waste from the Lean principles?
5. What types of work is Kanban well suited for?

Review 2

6. What are “information radiators,” and how do they help Agile teams?
7. What is the difference between a burn-up chart and a burn-down chart?

8. How do you know from a burn-down chart if you are behind schedule?
9. What is an "FDD parking lot"?
10. How can a team track their defect resolution?

Review 3

11. What three key questions are answered by team members during a daily stand-up meeting?
12. Who typically gets assigned action items during a daily stand-up meeting?
13. What does the daily stand-up meeting provide to the team beyond simply giving status?
14. What is the purpose of a Sprint demo or review?
15. Why is it important for a team to hold a retrospective session?

Review 4

16. What is the best indicator of success in Agile?
17. Who should lead the Sprint demo or review?
18. If the daily stand-up meeting allows you to assess the effectiveness of the sprint and the Sprint demo allows you to assess the effectiveness of the product, what are you assessing in the Sprint retrospective?
19. Who writes and executes the test cases?
20. How is stakeholder feedback collected in the Sprint review, and what is done with that feedback?

Chapter 9

Agile beyond IT

Learning Objectives

- Learn how the Agile values apply to bringing products to market, beyond the development efforts
- Understand ways to systematically collaborate with the marketplace through discovery and validation
- Explore the changing dynamics for marketing of products with the proliferation of new channels and the complexities of brand management with social media
- Review how wireframes and prototypes can be used in the marketplace to inform priorities for Agile software development teams
- Learn how to be Agile when launching products by managing features, limiting the initial audience, and pursuing continuous enhancements
- Take the Agile concepts beyond IT and product development and see how other corporate organizations can benefit from Agile values and principles
- Discover how Marketing has taken Agile to a whole new level of discipline by creating their own manifesto

It is important to appreciate that delivering a successful product to the marketplace does not end when the code is deployed in a production environment; numerous other activities must take place before, during, and after the software development efforts to ensure a product's success. The very first Agile principle is "Our highest priority is to satisfy the customer through early and continuous delivery of valuable software" (http://www.agilemanifesto.org). Satisfying the customer means that we must have a clear understanding of who the customer is, what his or her needs are, how to introduce the product, and how to gather customer feedback. The first part of the chapter focuses on the delivery elements of software development.

We then explore how the Agile principles and values can easily apply to other organizations, such as HR, finance, legal, and more. Finally, we deep dive into how some marketing professionals have adopted Agile in a vigorous and disciplined way.

Products beyond Software Development

Taking a product to market is a delicate and sometimes risky effort that requires thoughtful initiatives and robust feedback loops—much like the software development process. To explore the "go to market" aspects of product development, we refer to the four Agile values and see how they are applied.

Customer Collaboration

Throughout the entire process of taking a product to market and introducing it to end users, we need to be collaborating. We need to be focused on what customers, prospects, and the marketplace in general are looking for so we can ensure that we are building the right thing, that the right stories are being captured in the product backlog, and that they are given the appropriate priority. So how do we collaborate with customers to gain that feedback?

Pragmatic Marketing (http://www.pragmaticmarketing.com) breaks down the data-gathering process into two categories—discovery and validation. The discovery phase is about listening to customers and others in the marketplace; it is very qualitative in nature. The validation phase is about confirming that what you learned in discovery is an accurate assessment of many, rather than the pain points or wishes of just a few. The validation phase adds quantitative data to the qualitative information that was collected in discovery.

Discovery

There are several ways to collaborate with customers during this phase, and the most common is interviews; this is where product owners spend time with actual customers asking them very open-ended questions, such as "What is the biggest challenge for your company today?" "What keeps you awake at night?" The hope is that these open-ended questions will get the customers talking, and a skilled product owner can then start to piece together product or feature solutions that will solve the customer's pain points. Determining whom to interview in the discovery process is important to make sure that you receive input from different sources and with very different perspectives. You definitely want to gather feedback from your existing customers, because they know your product and its strengths and weaknesses and can provide valuable insights for additional features, usability enhancements, and workflow improvements. However, they should not be the only ones you reach out to because they have already purchased your product. You also need to collaborate with the audience who will help your product to grow. For this information, the product owner needs to spend time with prospects, people who showed an interest in the product but either have not made a purchase decision yet or have chosen a competitor. This audience is critical because they are making an assessment of how your product stacks up against the other available options, and since they are in the mind-set of evaluation, they can provide the product owner with candid feedback on the product's strengths and weaknesses.

One-on-one interviews are the best way to gather data from customers and prospects. They can be time-consuming and possibly expensive, but the data gathered can be extremely helpful.

Another method of collecting qualitative data is through focus groups, which are gatherings of users who are walked through a series of questions about a product or business problem by a facilitator to ascertain their opinions and impressions. The company sponsors focus groups, and the participants usually receive some type of compensation—anything from a free meal to a gift card. This group approach allows a company to collect data from multiple participants, but there is a risk that the group members will influence one another, so you might not receive the same quality of information, or degree of candor, that you would get in one-on-one interviews.

Validation

Validation involves applying the information learned in discovery to a wider audience to test its relevancy. The most common way of performing validation is through a survey because it is an inexpensive way to collect data from many people.

Regarding our weather application from Cayman Design, we have conducted interviews with several end users and have found that our customers are seeking three new features: (1) sale of weather-related apparel such as umbrellas and snow boots, (2) digital alerts about significant world weather events such as hurricanes and tornadoes, and (3) the ability to receive inbound texts/e-mail about the daily weather in their location. To find out which feature has the greatest interest, we can then put together a quick user survey for our customers who visit our web site. Survey response rates can vary, with most being between 10% and 30% (Kaplowitz et al. 2004), so you have to allow the right amount of time and incentives to collect statistically valid information. Gathering the quantitative data to marry with our qualitative research ensures that we are making sound business decisions based on fact, rather than opinions.

In our example, the survey results reveal that item #3 is the most popular response, so we can factor this data into our product backlog prioritization. The danger with this example, however, and a trap that many companies fall into when conducting surveys, is that we are considering only our existing customer base: They are the most likely to respond because they already have a relationship with the company. Getting survey responses from prospects or the general public is much more difficult, but you will gain tremendous insights if you can find a way to tap into other audiences.

Other quantitative data can be gathered by conducting experiments such as A/B or multivariant testing. In a Web environment, this type of testing presents some users with a one-page layout or design and others with the same information in a different layout or design to see which delivers greater results (Laja 2013a).

For the Cayman Design weather application, we can have two home pages: One contains the top weather story from a global perspective, and the other displays local weather based on the location information we receive from users' browsers. In both instances, the users are instructed to send a link to friends and family asking them to visit the web site; this is an example of A/B testing, where the global home page is A and the local home page is B. We can then study the results to see which home page resulted in more link forwarding. From that data, we know more about which home page will help us to achieve our goals and drive more business value.

Multivariant testing follows the same principle but increases the number of variables. For example, the global home page could be blue, pink, and purple and have font sizes of 10, 12, and 14. Again, each different combination would appear to a random audience, usually in rotation, and the data will indicate which combination produces the most desirable results. This is an example of validation because we are adding a quantitative measure to a qualitative suggestion. This testing can produce compelling results, but our product owner must again be cognizant of the limited audience—only existing customers—that would participate in this type of diagnostic.

Beyond discussions with actual users or prospects, another way to collect market insights is through market studies and analyst feedback. This would be only loosely related to the Agile concept of customer collaboration because the product owner is not hearing feedback directly from customers or prospects. The information can still be quite valuable; companies such as Gartner (www.gartner.com) and Forrester (www.forrester.com) invest significant time and money collecting statistically valid market insights. Examples of both Gartner and Forrester reports are included here (see Figures 9.1 and 9.2). Many other analyst firms produce similar market insights.

Using this type of research from analyst organizations can be very helpful when it comes to understanding the marketplace and validating assumptions. Good product owners will rely on a wide set of resources to ensure that the Agile teams are always working on the deliverables that will generate the highest business value.

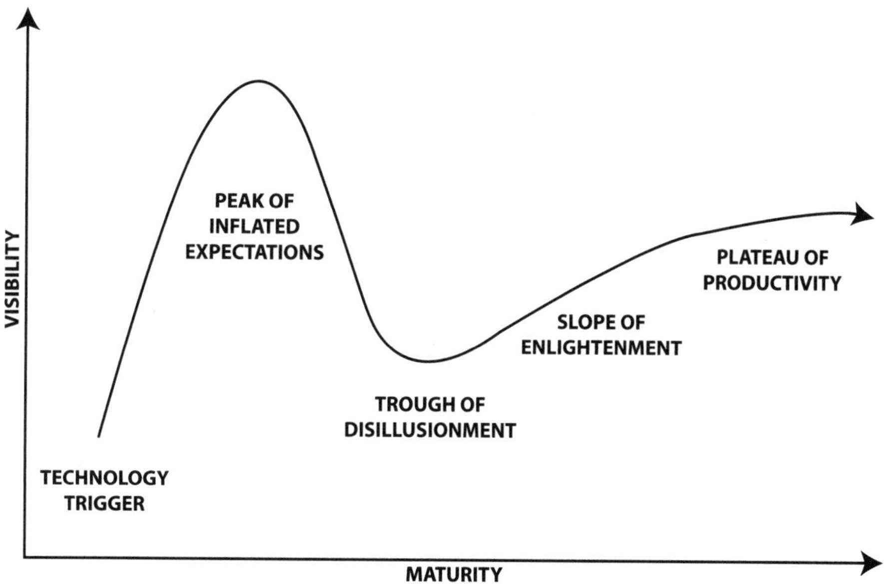

Figure 9.1 *Example graphic from Gartner Research—The Gartner Hype Cycle*

Source: Gartner, Research Methodology, http://www.gartner.com/technology/home.jsp.

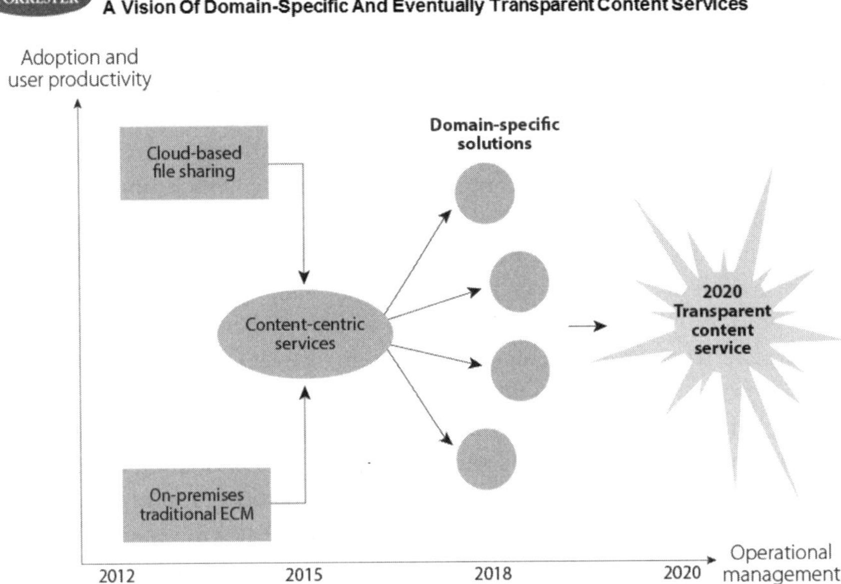

Figure 9.2 *Example of a graphic from Forrester Research*

Source: Graphic from "*Trends in Mobility, Cloud Computing, and Analytics Shake Up ECM,*" Forrester Research, Inc., January 11, 2013.

Responsiveness to Change

Delivering working software to the marketplace is what Agile is focused on, and we have discussed the need to respond to change when it comes to evolving requirements for how the product should work in the earlier chapters. Responsiveness to change also affects how that product is introduced to the marketplace and what tools and methods are used to generate interest and sales.

In recent years, the ways consumers are marketed to and the options that are available have changed dramatically. We explore these changes and why being Agile is essential to ensure that the product resonates in the marketplace.

Introduction of New Channels

The generations before us had only a handful of ways that marketing touched their lives: dynamic advertisements on TV and radio; print advertisements on billboards and in magazine and newspapers; and direct mail pieces. Now we have banner advertisements on web sites and targeted "posts" on social media tools such as Twitter, Instagram, and Facebook. We even have television shows and movies featuring product placement, where you can see your favorite character drinking a Coca-Cola or eating a McDonald's hamburger. This explosion of advertising and customer connection mediums creates tremendous challenges for marketers, who have to understand where their buyers reside and how best to reach them. Because a new social media channel could appear literally overnight, marketers must be responsive to change. Their marketing plans must be Agile, and they must be able to adapt to a continuously evolving marketplace.

Brand Management

Another driver for marketing to be more responsive to change is new considerations for what is known as "brand management." Seth Godin (2009a) defines a brand as "the set of expectations, memories, stories and relationships that, taken together, account for a consumer's decision to choose one product or service over another."

Just a generation ago, the brand was defined and managed by the company. Through press releases, web sites, and advertising, experts in marketing told consumers how to feel about the brand. The best marketers established emotional connections with the consumers, and they spent their time and money controlling the customer information flow relative to the brand.

Technology has changed that. Consumers are now much more in control of the brand through their comments, "likes," tweets, and social interactions; to survive, marketers must be Agile and respond to this changing environment. Social media has literally changed how organizations deal with customer service issues because previously, a single bad interaction was known only to the customer and the company; now, an angry consumer can share his or her experience with the world via YouTube, Twitter, and all the other social media channels. If marketers fail to embrace the Agile value of responsiveness to change, then the product that the development teams have worked so hard to create may not make an impact in the market.

Feedback Cycle

Another example of the need to respond to change is the length of the feedback cycle. Historically, it might have taken several months for sales results to be reported so marketers could know the impacts of their efforts. Now, the feedback cycles can be nearly instantaneous, with Google Analytics and Omniture reporting real-time information about web site and app traffic and visitors' behaviors.

On the positive side, the proliferation of channels and the short feedback cycles allow marketers to apply the Lean principles to their work. We have small campaigns with quick feedback for the opportunity to continuously learn and to adapt our efforts—just like the development teams do.

One of the challenges with this short feedback cycle is the sheer amount of data that is available. Marketers must be able to sift through mountains of data to discern the elements that are most impactful. A number of tools can help with this, and "big data" is getting more attention and product offerings to assist in this very task.

Clearly, marketers are living in a dynamic and evolving world, and their ability to respond to change is critical to their survival.

Review 1 At this point, the reader should be able to answer Review Questions 1–5.

Working Software

The next Agile value that we investigate is working software over comprehensive documentation. Working software is the output that is taken to the marketplace; and although the IT and product teams spend time making sure that we build the right product and build it right, we need the marketing teams to craft messaging about what differentiates our product from others in a crowded marketplace.

Delighting the End User

In Chapter 6, "Grooming and Planning," we introduced the Kano method of prioritization, and software that "delights" the end user. This is a marketers' dream: The delight factor can be used for competitive advantage as a differentiator, which is the process of distinguishing a product or service in the marketplace, showing how it is different and better than other available options.

If a product offers the same features as the competition, it can be referred to as a "me too" product; that is harder to position and sell. When you think of purchasing a laptop, you are often guided by the differentiating features in options such as battery life, screen size, or processing speed. The product whose differentiators best match your needs and expectations will be the one that you choose, so marketers need to clearly understand and articulate what makes their product special—and delightful.

Wireframes and Prototypes

As introduced in Chapter 5, "The New Way to Collect and Document Requirements," wireframes and prototypes can help with the Agile processes by creating something that users can react to without a heavy investment of IT resources.

These tools are helpful to our marketing teams because they provide a tangible representation of the product to take to focus groups or potential users to elicit early feedback. Roman Pichler reminds us that "the key to effective experimentation is to generate the necessary knowledge rapidly by implementing and testing prototypes and mock-ups" (Pichler 2010, loc. 886).

A wireframe is a visual mock-up of how a web site or workflow could perform. It is typically low-fidelity and is sometimes referred to as a "skeleton," "outline," or "blueprint" (Shorr 2011).

Marketing can work with the usability experts (user experience designers) to produce wireframes that the marketers can put in front of customers and prospects. Not only does this help the product owner to gain valuable product feedback, but it also helps the marketing team to know what resonates with the buying public and what features they should emphasize.

Prototypes do include development resources, but to a much lesser extent than a full product. Prototypes are typically simplistic working models of a product used to demonstrate features and functionality (Rouse 2005).

As you have an existing customer walking through the prototype for a new feature offering, the marketing team can be learning right along with the product owner. For example, our persona Sam, the executive business traveler, is going through the prototype and stumbles on the airport name to gather weather at his travel destination. Sam may not know the proper name of the airport—George Bush Intercontinental Airport in Houston, Texas, or Eppley Airfield in Omaha, Nebraska—but he does know the three-digit airport code because it is written on his ticket. If our application can translate IAH to the Houston airport for Sam, it is a tremendous value. Marketing now has a key differentiator that they can highlight in the marketing materials—airport codes accepted and converted—and the prototype analysis helped to identify this unique value-added feature.

Metric and Data Driven

We already mentioned that the influx of marketing data can help marketers be smarter about their messaging and placement, but working software can also help with marketing efforts. Data collectors can be written into the software code, which can help marketing to improve their efforts. For example, our weather application sometimes delivers "No Results Found" when a user enters search criteria. The application collects whatever was input for every failure. Then marketing, along with the product owner, can analyze the results and determine how the product could be adapted. Here might be another opportunity to learn the importance of airport codes because MCI is entered multiple times without delivering results. We know that MCI is Kansas City International Airport, so we can add the airport look-up differentiator.

Usage statistics are wonderful and can help hone a conversation, but when marketing and development work together to insert other data collectors into the working software, additional insights can be gained that can propel the product forward in user adoption.

Individuals and Interactions

Embracing the Agile Manifesto value of individuals and interactions over processes and tools means getting everyone closer to the customer, and in a truly Agile organization, this does mean everyone. Of course the people in marketing and the product owner are talking directly to the customers, understanding their needs and gathering feedback. Great Agile organizations extend that level of collaboration to the development teams: When developers can hear customer feedback firsthand, they gain a much deeper appreciation for the complexities of the business problem that the company is trying to solve. If the marketing organization, for example, is hosting focus groups as previously described, inviting some members of the development team to listen in can be a great opportunity to make the customer or end user more tangible and "real" to the developers.

Another option is to invite developers to listen to customer service calls alongside the customer service representatives (CSRs). Hearing the end user questions and watching the CSRs navigate to find the answers can bring a heightened awareness to the impact of software decisions. Developers that participate in interactions like this expand their knowledge and understanding.

Speaking to the Market with Agility

There are a number of ways to effectively market products built with Agile development teams. Some Agile purists are uncomfortable committing dates and features to the marketplace, but in most industries, it is not optional: Existing customers and late-stage prospects demand to know when and how the product will evolve. We outline several ways to balance these two sides.

Managing Features

As initially discussed in Chapter 5, when operating with Agile software development, the iterative nature of the work and the continual adjustments in priority can make it difficult for the marketing and sales teams to know what expectations to set with the marketplace. One method of managing this issue is to define the high-level features that will be included in a release and commit to the release date; the flexibility is maintained in the definition of the features. If the teams run into minimal roadblocks and everything comes together well, then the delivered features will be very rich and full of options, but if they find things more difficult and time-consuming than estimated, then the delivered features will be more basic and simple. Let's look at an example to explore this idea.

We have committed in our Cayman Design weather application to selling weather-related calendars via our web site. The features include the ability to order a calendar using the nearest Farmer's Almanac information for weather patterns through history. We know with certainty that several base features will be included in the initial release: The calendars will be 12 months, can be shipped anywhere in the United States, and can be paid for online via a credit card. Marketing and sales can immediately begin discussing the product and these base features with confidence.

As a development team, we envision a much richer feature set, encompassing all of the items in Table 9.1; and we can adjust scope, if necessary, as the project progresses. With the careful prioritization in Agile, we know that the top bullet (in italics) for each element is the most important, and anything listed below it is a lower priority. Therefore, if resource constraints or unexpected complexities arise, we can easily de-scope the lower items and still deliver our commitment to the marketplace.

This method of component management allows the flexibility of Agile to be combined with making market commitments and enforcing dates.

Table 9.1 *Managing Scope to Committed Features*

Committed Features	Possible Components
12-month calendar	• *All calendars are January through December* • Calendars can be ordered for the current year or next year only • Calendars can be customized to whatever start month is desired • Calendars can be ordered for up to 5 years in advance • 3-month, 6-month, and 9-month calendars are available at a discounted price

(Continues)

Table 9.1 *Managing Scope to Committed Features (Continued)*

Committed Features	Possible Components
Information from the nearest Farmer's Almanac	• *We have loaded data from 10 Farmer's Almanacs based on the most populated states/regions* • Load data for 50 Farmer's Almanacs, one for every US state • Load data from every available Farmer's Almanac for the highest level of precision
Shipped anywhere in the US	• *Ship using one vendor with state taxation based on an open source tax module* • Ship using one vendor with state taxation based on a robust and more exact integrated tax module • Expand shipping to three shipping vendors for customers to choose from
Paid for online via a credit card	• *Accept MasterCard and Visa with settlement processed through a 3rd party* • Add American Express and Discover with settlement processed through a 3rd party • Add ACH payments for transactions directly through banking institutions

Limited Audience

Another way to deliver things to the market while maintaining flexibility is to perform a soft launch, which is release to a limited audience with little or no marketing announcing the new feature (McMahon 2013). This can be an ideal option when you are unsure exactly how the product or feature is going to be received in the marketplace and it is crucial to gather feedback from your customers. Care needs to be taken in executing a soft launch because you want to include customers who are candid and constructive in their feedback and are also interested in seeing the company succeed. Inviting angry, dissatisfied customers to participate in a soft launch is typically a bad idea, because they are looking for errors or deficiencies and are more judgmental than constructive in their feedback.

The customers that participate in a soft launch are called "beta users." A soft launch might also be referred to as a "beta launch" or "pilot."

Continuous Enhancements

The final example of speaking to the marketplace with agility is the concept of *continuous enhancements*. As more companies are practicing Lean software and product development, consumers are getting more accustomed to the initial release being simplistic and seeing new features deployed very quickly. Eric Ries, the founder of the Lean Startup movement, refers to this as *continuous deployment*—and, at the extreme, has seen companies release software updates multiple times per day (Ries 2011, p. 191).

When you operate in this type of environment, there is no need to worry about customer expectations and due dates because you are adapting and releasing so frequently that they are never an issue.

Review 2 At this point, the reader should be able to answer Review Questions 6–10.

Agile in Other Organizations

As Agile has transformed development organizations around the world, other departments have taken notice and begun adopting Agile principles for themselves. The simplicity and practicality of the Agile values and principles are appealing in many circumstances. In this section, we examine the pieces of Agile that are being used and, specifically, deep dive in a marketing initiative to embed the principles even deeper.

Tools for Broad Use

When thinking about the Agile tools and framework, there are many applications of the concepts of trust, transparency, teamwork, self-organization, frequent delivery, close collaboration, continuous improvement, and rapid feedback loops. We examine a few concepts that can easily be introduced.

Working Agreement

As included in Chapter 4, "Describing the Different Roles," working agreements help the team to establish the values and norms that will govern their interactions. Working agreements are great because they are established when things are relatively calm and stress levels are low. Then, if things go wrong and behavior starts to get off track, the team can refer to the working agreement to reestablish proper conduct. For example, the team's working agreement says the following: *We are a learning organization, therefore the knowledge owner needs to be respectful to those learning and take time educating others so we can become less single-threaded.*

When a crisis occurs and we are busy and overwhelmed, you can imagine a scenario like the following unfolding: "Dave, I am sorry to interrupt but I am trying to kick off the XYZ process and I am getting an error that I have never seen before."

Without a working agreement, Dave might say, "Sarah, can't you see that I am busy? I don't have time to train you on every little thing!" If this were to occur in an Agile environment, Sarah could respond, "Sorry. I was just trying to honor our working agreement principle that we are a learning organization, and I really want to understand this so you don't have to always do these types of tasks." By being able to refer to the working agreement, Sarah can defuse a potential personality conflict by just calling out what was agreed upon.

Any organization that is striving to improve its teamwork can implement a working agreement; it could be assembly line workers on a manufacturing floor or finance teams who are trying to close the books every month. The keys to a successful working agreement are that everyone has an opportunity to participate in its creation, that it is visible and referenced often, and that it is updated as the team evolves and team dynamics change.

Fist of Five

Also introduced in Chapter 4, "fist of five" is a voting mechanism that allows every voice in the room to be heard and counted. This certainly has applications beyond development, because every team is faced with some sort of dilemma that requires making difficult decisions. For example, the facilities team could have a cost-saving initiative and they have two options that will achieve the financial goal—reducing the heat in the building by one degree or altering the trash pick-up cycle to every other day instead of every day. Neither option is ideal, and both have consequences that should be discussed. When the team decides to go with the temperature change, they can vote using fist of five to ensure that everyone is supportive of the direction.

Definition of "Done"

This concept, described in detail in Chapter 6, can be helpful in a number of situations, particularly when a deliverable is being handed off from one individual or group to another. A good example is the annual review process, when a manager completes paperwork regarding a team member's performance. When is someone "done" with a review? Has it been added to a corporate system, or is it okay to be handwritten? Has it been reviewed by a superior before it is delivered to the employee? Does the employee need to sign it? All of these elements could influence the definition of done. One manager might be celebrating completion because all of the handwritten reviews were delivered to the employees, but human resources might think nothing has started because the system has not been properly updated.

These Agile tools can be used in corporate departments and university settings, and even within families.

Agile Marketing

One organization has taken their Agile adoption to the next level by writing their own manifesto. In this section, we detail the tenets of the Agile Marketing Manifesto to develop a better understanding of how the core Agile values and principles are being applied.

A group of cutting-edge marketers met in San Francisco in June 2012 and started brainstorming the ideas and needs around the evolution of marketing. One of the key participants, Jim Ewel (2012), said, "Agile Marketing is *NOT* just another tool in the toolbox. It's *NOT* about the application of Scrum or Kanban to manage the marketing process. Agile Marketing is a movement, a quest, a revolution, with all that implies—emotion, radicalism, religious fervor." As you can see, for the people that care deeply about this topic, there is a good deal of energy and enthusiasm.

Since that meeting, other Agilists have expressed some skepticism that a new manifesto was actually required since we already have other organizations such as finance and legal that are adopting Agile principles without creating their own manifesto (Muldoon 2012; Skeels 2012). Whether or not a manifesto specifically for marketing is truly necessary, we cannot deny the enthusiasm and effort that have gone into this concept. Let's review the seven values of the Agile Marketing Manifesto to get a better understanding.

Validated Learning over Opinions and Conventions

Since marketing is designed to elicit emotional reactions to create a connection with a product or brand, many aspects are somewhat subjective: "How does this make you feel?" "Do you think this is funny?" "Does this image make you want to buy xyz?" This tenet of the Agile Marketing Manifesto expresses that opinions are interesting, but marketing decisions should be driven by data that is validated. Using quantitative tools, such as surveys and A/B testing described earlier in the chapter, is important to bring objectivity to a discussion.

Customer-Focused Collaboration over Silos and Hierarchy

Just as the Agile Manifesto places high importance on customer engagement and collaboration, the marketing teams have found that they also suffer from organizational structures that sometimes distance them from customer feedback. If you have a marketing organization that separates market research from public relations from product marketing, you run the risk of losing the customer's viewpoint between the organizational silos. Some marketing organizations separate functions to cultivate expertise, but this could result in a fragmentation of the customer's experience (Allan 2013).

Adaptive and Iterative Campaigns over Big-Bang Campaigns

Breaking development down into small deliverables and incorporating the learnings from each iteration are central to the success of Agile. This allows us to learn as we go and continuously enhance the product. Marketing campaigns are no different: To presume that you know all of the requirements up front and that nothing is going to change during the execution of the campaign is as detrimental for marketers as it is for developers. Marketing is also an iterative process where we learn from our mistakes and focus on continuous improvement (Smith 2009).

The Process of Customer Discovery over Static Prediction

Again, the similarities between marketing activities and development are interesting. Large marketing campaigns make assumptions about how consumers are likely to respond. This element of the manifesto targets the feedback loop—customers will not always respond as predicted, and sometimes their behaviors can lead to better-than-expected results, if that feedback can be effectively incorporated.

Flexible versus Rigid Planning

This principle seems obvious to those who embrace Agile: Rigidity has no place in our world, because we are continuously inspecting and adapting. This was likely included in the Agile Marketing Manifesto because the structure of most marketing relationships is very "statement of work" (SOW) driven, with an agency clearly defining deliverables up front, in the contract, so that clients can predict what they will be paying for. It continues to be a challenge for marketing agencies to operate in a truly Agile fashion when their client base has yet to embrace the iterative, inspect-and-adapt concept. Jack Skeels, of AgencyAgile, recalls, "I once spent a month in 'discussion' with the Client's lawyer on a single definition of what constitutes 'change' in an Agile frame" (Skeels 2013).

Responding to Change over Following a Plan

This value comes straight from the Agile Manifesto, so it should sound very familiar. It is equally important to the people in marketing since, as we already described, the change in the marketing landscape is accelerating and unpredictable.

Many Small Experiments over a Few Large Bets

This value again speaks against the instinct to overplan and allows marketers to learn and adjust. It suggests that a small Twitter campaign plus a targeted direct-mail piece plus a single billboard in a densely populated urban area can be executed simultaneously with relatively small investments. Then, based on the results, we can expand the experiment that worked best into a more national campaign.

As you can see, there are not completely new ideas in the Agile Marketing Manifesto but more of an adaptation for a discipline that finds itself directly affected by Agile development and in the midst of a revolution within its own sector.

Exercise

Document three examples where developing software is similar to developing a marketing campaign. How do the values of the Agile Manifesto affect both activities? Of the 12 principles of Agile, are there any that simply do not apply to marketing? Please explain your response.

Review 3 At this point, the reader should be able to answer Review Questions 11–15.

Conclusion

Agile has truly transformed people's lives. Those working in software development that have adopted the Agile values and principles addressed in this book are certainly performing their work differently, and hopefully they are happier and more productive than ever before. Agile makes so much sense in the simplicity and efficacy of its design that other organizations and institutions are adopting it. Think about how Agile could affect your life outside of the obvious software development career. Could you be more effective with face-to-face conversations? Could you empower people so the greatest ideas can rise to the top? Can you focus on sustainability so that you do not wear yourself down to the point of burning out? We could go on and on with examples, and we hope that you are now inspired and excited about all of the Agile possibilities.

We hope that this textbook has enhanced your understanding of this way of thinking and developing software. Most importantly, we hope it has made you thirst for continuous learning. There are numerous practitioner books, blogs, conferences, and forums where you can expand your learning and share your own experiences.

We close this book with a great quote from Jim Highsmith, one of the signers of the Agile Manifesto: "Stop doing Agile. Start being Agile" (2013).

Good luck!

Summary

- To effectively deliver Agile software to the customers that desire it, we must think through the impacts of data gathering and marketing.
- When collaborating with customers and prospects, we need to consider two distinct methods of collecting information—discovery and validation.
- Discovery is about gathering feedback from customers, prospects, or the general public in the form of interviews or focus groups. In discovery, we are gathering qualitative feedback.
- Validation is about adding statistical validity to the information gathered in discovery. By conducting surveys or doing A/B or multivariant testing, we are adding quantitative information to our findings.
- Analyst organizations such as Gartner and Forrester can help with market analysis by providing research reports on market trends, buying behaviors, industry pain points, and much more.
- Marketing has many challenges in bringing products to market because new channels are appearing at a rapid pace; Twitter, Instagram, and Facebook may be replaced as the mainstream channels as new options arise.
- Social media has also affected the concept of brand management because companies are no longer exclusively in control of their brand in the marketplace; a terrible customer service experience that goes viral in social media can create impressions and fears that the company will have a hard time managing.

- Gathering input and feedback is critical in product development as we try to "delight" end users with elements that differentiate our product from the competition.
- Wireframes and prototypes are a good vehicle to collect feedback from existing or potential users without utilizing expensive development resources.
- Incorporating "counters" and data gathering mechanisms into code can provide additional insights on customer behavior and opportunities for improving usability.
- Developers should welcome the chance to hear feedback straight from end users by listening to customer service calls or participating in focus groups.
- Bringing Agile products to market can be tricky when balancing marketing and sales needs for a delivery date and feature expectations. By managing the scope within a committed feature, the necessary flexibility (and agility) can be maintained.
- A soft launch to beta or pilot users is a great option for getting something new to the marketplace but only to a limited audience.
- Lean product and software development allows for continuous enhancements where new features are launched frequently, so customers become accustomed to an ever-evolving platform.
- Organizations outside of IT are also benefiting from the principles of Agile by introducing working agreements, fist of five, definition of done, and more to their workflows.
- Agile marketing enthusiasts have taken things a step further by creating their own Agile Marketing Manifesto.
- The seven tenets of the Agile Marketing Manifesto parallel the original but are specific to the challenges in marketing today.
- Agile can transform organizations, companies, and people's lives when deployed correctly and enthusiastically. We hope that you are inspired.

Review 4 At this point, the reader should be able to answer Review Questions 16–20.

Interview with Travis Arnold

Travis Arnold was a key figure at the SprintZero meeting where the Agile Marketing Manifesto first came to light. His role was pivotal, as he was responsible for bringing together various opinions and ideas into a cohesive whole. As founder of Harbinger Labs, Travis is a passionate digital strategist specializing in creating strategic marketing plans and developing and integrating marketing platforms. Through his work, he helps brands with search marketing (SEO and PPC), analytics, content strategy and development, e-mail marketing, CRM, and marketing automation technology. Travis regularly blogs at www.harbingerlabs.com about content marketing, design, personas, marketing strategies, and more. He also has a deep appreciation for a great taco.

Kristin and Sondra: How did the Agile Marketing Manifesto come to be?

Travis: It started with a few Agile marketing practitioners pulling together what they believed were the key principles and values of Agile marketing. At that point (late 2010), there were six or seven separate interpretations of an Agile marketing manifesto. It was John Cass and Jim Ewel who wanted to organize everything that had been written into an organized set of values. They brought me in during the planning phase for SprintZero, the first Agile marketing conference. My role was to analyze the previous "manifestos" and pull out the commonalities between them and provide that list for an un-conference session at SprintZero. What resulted is what you can find at Agilemarketingmanifesto.org: seven values that are independent of the Agile development manifesto that inspired us. It's been really cool to see more and more people adopt some or all of the values in their orgs. It's very gratifying.

Kristin and Sondra: How do you reconcile the Agile desire to be iterative and responsive with the marketing need to inform the marketplace of what is coming?

Travis: It's not as challenging as you'd think, and in some cases makes for better campaigns. Just because an organization is using Agile for marketing, doesn't mean longer-lifespan projects don't exist. What is different is how the work is organized and rolled out. Like all Agile methods, it starts with a plan. From that plan, work, timelines, and milestones are created and rolled out. Once something is complete it's reviewed, edited, if necessary, and scheduled for deployment. If any market or product changes were to occur prelaunch, the work would be reintroduced into the sprint and the changes would be made. In Agile marketing, big projects are broken up into digestible chunks, making them easier to work through. This also helps reduce production bottlenecks that occur when attacking a big project all at once.

Kristin and Sondra: Can marketing actually help the Agile process?

Travis: I think so. Marketing and development are very similar in how they work. You have a buyer/user and you ship something. Development ships products, marketing ships materials in one form or another. Both departments are working with the same user, just at very different points in the life cycle. Marketing can and should pass along persona information to development to help them get a clearer picture of the user. In an ideal world, marketing and development would work closer to improve the user experience from the "just shopping" phase to the "logged-in user" phase.

Kristin and Sondra: Does Lean product development deliver enough to the marketplace?

Travis: It's not delivering more that is important, it's delivering what is right. Delivering a minimally viable product that solves my exact problem as a buyer is better than a more refined product that doesn't. We've been seeing more products that solve one core problem first, then iterate from there to include what is right for their buyers. I'd rather have a product that does three things better than anyone else than one that does ten things subpar.

Kristin and Sondra: What are the tricks that the best teams do to deliver amazing products?

Travis: I said it earlier, but the planning phase is so important to the mechanics of an Agile marketing process. When you're working fast and focused, having that two- or three-week plan for reference helps reduce bottlenecks. Another big part of the equation is involving your people each and every day. Daily stand-ups help identify problems and provide an outlet to celebrate success each and every day. DON'T SKIP THE STAND-UPS! They are important for team building and keeping the momentum going. Also, take a page from Google and give your team "free time." Free time helps flex the creativity muscles and oftentimes stirs up great ideas for product/marketing improvements.

References and Further Reading

Allan, Scott. (2013). Removing marketing silos to better understand the customer journey. http://marketingland.com/removing-marketing-silos-to-better-understand-the-customer-journey-47789.

Ewel, Jim. (2012). Agile Marketing Manifesto. Blog entry. http://www.agilemarketing.net/making-manifesto.

Foxworthy, Jim. (2008). Maybe your opinion IS relevant! http://www.pragmaticmarketing.com/resources/maybe-your-opinion-is-relevant.

Freeling, Anthony. (2011). *Agile marketing: How to innovate faster, cheaper and with lower risk*. Seattle, WA: Goldingtons Press.

Gartner Research. (2014). Research methodologies. http://www.gartner.com/it/products/research/methodologies/research_hype.jsp.

Godin, Seth. (2009a). Blog entry. http://sethgodin.typepad.com/seths_blog/2009/12/define-brand.html.

Godin, Seth. (2009b). *Purple cow, new edition: Transform your business by being remarkable*. New York: Penguin.

Goward, Chris. (2012). *You should test that: Conversion optimization for more leads, sales and profit or the art and science of optimized marketing*. Hoboken, NJ: Sybex.

Highsmith, Jim. (2002). *Agile software development ecosystems*. Boston: Addison-Wesley.

Highsmith, Jim. (2013). Stop "doing Agile" start "being Agile." http://www.thoughtworks.com/events/stop-doing-agile-start-being-agile.

Kaplowitz, Michael, Hadlock, Timothy, and Levine, Ralph. (2004). *A comparison of web and mail survey response rates*. American Association for Public Opinion Research. http://www.uwyo.edu/studentaff/_files/docs/survey_calendar/kaplovitz_hadlock_levine_a_comparison_of_web_and_mail_survey_reponse_rates.pdf.

Laja, Peep. (2013a). "How to build a strong A/B testing plan that gets results." Blog entry. May 24. http://conversionxl.com/how-to-build-a-strong-ab-testing-plan-that-gets-results/#.

Laja, Peep. (2013b). *How to build websites that sell: The scientific approach to websites*. Seattle, WA: Amazon Digital Services.

Le Clair, Craig, and Owens, Leslie. (2013). Trends in mobility, cloud computing, and analytics shake up ECM. Cambridge, MA: Forrester Research.

McMahon, Mary. (2013). What is a soft launch? http://www.wisegeek.com/what-is-a-soft-launch.htm.

Muldoon, Nick. (2012). SprintZero—The physics of Agile marketing wrap up. Blog entry. http://www.nicholasmuldoon.com/2012/06/sprintzero-the-physics-of-agile-marketing-wrap-up.

Pichler, Roman. (2010). *Agile product management with Scrum: Creating products that customers love*. Boston: Addison-Wesley. Kindle edition.

Poppendieck, Mary, and Poppendieck, Tom. (2006). *Implementing Lean software development: From concept to cash*. Boston: Addison-Wesley.

Ries, Eric. (2011). *The Lean startup: How today's entrepreneurs use continuous innovation to create radically successful businesses*. New York: Crown.

Rouse, Margaret. (2005). Prototype. http://searchcio-midmarket.techtarget.com/definition/prototype.

Shorr, Brad. (2011). The benefits of wireframing a design. http://sixrevisions.com/user-interface/wireframing-benefits.

Skeels, Jack. (2012). Defining Agile marketing: You say you want a manifesto? Blog entry, September 17. http://agencyagile.com/defining-agile-marketing-you-say-you-want-a-manifesto.

Skeels, Jack. (2013). Considerations for Agile-based delivery contracts between agencies and clients. Blog entry, April 1. http://agencyagile.com/considerations-for-agile-based-delivery-contracts-between-agencies-and-clients/.

Smith, Will. (2009). Marketing is an iterative process. http://www.notwillsmith.com/work/marketing-is-an-iterative-process.

Stull, Craig, Myers, Phil, and Scott, David Meerman. (2010). *Tuned in: Uncover the extraordinary opportunities that lead to business breakthroughs*. Hoboken, NJ: Wiley.

Taber, David. (2013). *Salesforce.com secrets of success: Best practices for growth and profitability* (2nd ed.). Upper Saddle River, NJ: Prentice Hall.

Review Questions

Review 1

1. According to Pragmatic Marketing, what are the two categories of customer data gathering?
2. Does a focus group provide qualitative or quantitative feedback?
3. What audience might be missing from focus groups and surveys?

4. What is "A/B testing"?
5. Name at least three social media channels that are influencing buying behavior today.

Review 2

6. What is an example of a product differentiator for frozen pizza?
7. How involved are development resources in the creation of wireframes and prototypes?
8. Should developers participate in focus groups? Why or why not?
9. When Agile development efforts are committed to the marketplace through marketing and sales, how can the development team maintain flexibility?
10. What is a "soft launch"?

Review 3

11. How does a college professor apply a definition of done in the classroom?
12. How does a working agreement influence teamwork?
13. Where and when was the Agile Marketing Manifesto created?
14. What are some examples of silos in the marketing organization?
15. What are some of the traits of large marketing campaigns that mirror Waterfall software development?

Review 4

16. Why is it important for developers to understand how products are delivered in the marketplace?
17. Are there any departments or institutions that would not benefit from Agile? Please explain your answer.
18. What does it mean to stop "doing" Agile and start "being" Agile?
19. Since the Agile principles are easy to understand, does that mean they are easy to implement? Please explain your answer.
20. What are the four values of Agile?

Appendix

John Deere Case Study

John Deere, a global leader in agricultural and construction heavy equipment headquartered in Moline, Illinois, may not be the first company that comes to mind when you think about Agile software development. Many are surprised to learn that John Deere has a large software development organization, called Intelligent Solutions Group (ISG), whose mission is to deliver innovative solutions that radically improve their customers' productivity, efficiency, yield, and, ultimately, profitability as they build and feed the world. This includes global positioning system (GPS) software displays for the tractors and the Web tools that allow their customers to manage the data that is collected from the tractor for precision agriculture (see Figure A.1).

Figure A.1 *Farmer using the ISG GPS*

Like any company that has withstood the test of time, John Deere values innovation, one of their core values, and supports creative solutions to business and technological problems. In 2010, John Deere was facing a challenge that many technology companies were facing—they needed a way to deliver increased value to their customers more quickly. The Waterfall methodology they were using limited their ability to develop and deliver solutions that customers demanded; their response was to become an Agile software development organization. We caught up with three of their leaders to garner some insight about their transformation.

- **Tony Thelen**—Director, Solutions Infrastructure, Intelligent Solutions Group
- **Rob Roling**—Development Team Lead
- **Joyce Harris**—Product Owner

Interviewer: What led to the decision to go Agile?

Thelen: The realization that we needed to improve performance of our operations, particularly in regard to customer focus and responsiveness, quality, innovation, and employee engagement. We researched opportunities to improve and spoke with many in the industry to land on our final recommendation to move to an Agile software development structure.

Roling: Our need to deliver smaller features more often.

Interviewer: Was your movement to Agile a bottom-up movement or more of a top-down dictate?

Thelen: The business requirements to improve were driven from the top down; however, the solution of Agile being the manner to do this was bottom-up.

Roling: A few teams were given the option to try it and had success. Then other teams requested the opportunity to try it and it grew from there. It was a bottom-up movement with top-level support.

Interviewer: What was your biggest challenge as a leader rolling out Agile in a large organization?

Thelen: Managing expectations and ensuring we had the right skills and expertise to guide us through this journey. Thankfully, we had a few key individuals in the right positions to help us make these decisions and see the implementation all the way through.

Interviewer: Were all teams included, or was it a rolling implementation?

Thelen: We decided to ensure we had 100% of our operations converted inside a six-month window in order to achieve optimum impact and to help people engage the new process.

Roling: It was a rolling implementation.

Interviewer: Are all divisions of ISG doing Agile development? If so, has it worked better for some departments than others?

Thelen: All divisions of ISG are working in an Agile methodology, some more strict than others, but the protocols to what is Agile are applied everywhere. Depending on the nature of the projects being undertaken, we have seen some areas do better than others. Those projects that are very wide and far-reaching in scope have struggled to maintain expectations, but those that had a more narrow or short-term scope have generally fared much better.

Roling: I believe all ISG groups are doing Agile. It works better for web site development than vehicle display development. The vehicle displays are a component of John Deere equipment like tractors and combines. The software approval process for components on our equipment does take more time.

Interviewer: What form of Agile was chosen? How was that decision made? Do you have a variety, for example, Scrum, Kanban, XP?

Thelen: We do XP and TDD as a practice, but have used the Agile methodology to organize our people and our work streams. This was based on discussion with an industry Agile coach.

Roling: We started with basic Scrum and XP. Kanban has been adopted by a few teams lately and has been very successful.

Interviewer: What was the degree of executive sponsorship?

Thelen: We had full support of a senior vice president, president, and eventually the CEO to continue down this path.

Roling: ISG leadership bought into Agile early and promoted it.

Interviewer: How much did you rely on outside coaching to make the transition to Agile? Did you hire full-time Agile consultants? For how long?

Thelen: We relied on an external coach for a year to help us manage this transition, and have used this same coach to come in one year later to fine-tune our operations.

Roling: External coaching was a key to our success. It is important to have a mix of Agile coaches and XP coaches. We have had full-time Agile consultants for over two years.

Interviewer: What training programs do you have in place? How have those changed through the course of the implementation?

Thelen: We currently have two areas active in training—first are classes that introduce Agile concepts to employees, and secondly we sponsor attendance at industry conferences and in some cases hold summit meetings with key companies who are dealing with Agile at scale.

Interviewer: What roles were considered important initially? Has that changed as your implementation progressed?

Thelen: Many roles changed, as all had to adjust to a team-driven environment—all played key roles in supporting this change and supporting each other as the organization adapted.

Roling: Scrum masters were important initially. Most of our product owners also do the Scrum master role now. Initially we treated them separately.

Interviewer: How did you decide on the makeup of the original Scrum teams? Did you assign people to teams, or did you let individuals decide which team they would work on?

Roling: We assigned people to teams based on who they were currently working with already. We assigned many systems engineers as product owners.

Interviewer: Did you assign Scrum teams to a specific function, or can a Scrum team handle multiple functional areas?

Thelen: We assigned various product groups to Scrum teams supported by functional areas of expertise—marketing, engineering, program management, etc.

Roling: Scrum teams are typically skilled in a specific code base, and they can handle multiple features within that code base.

Interviewer: What were the cultural impacts of your adoption? Was there anything that was easier or harder than anticipated?

Thelen: Moving to a team-based structure was a difficult transition for many of our middle management layers—in some cases areas that were significantly reduced or eliminated altogether. The culture of ownership at the team level produced significant increases in employee engagement, innovation, and quality improvements. Having the appropriate level of metrics to measure our progress was and continues to be a difficult area.

Roling: Daily stand-up meetings [see Figure A.2] promoted more communication and transparency among Scrum team members. Team members started using paired programming to work out designs and debug defects. As team members worked together, they started tearing down cube walls and moving toward the collaborative workspace we have now.

Harris: Within my project group, adoption was a mixture of relief and victory. We had several folks who had experience with Agile elsewhere and a few teams who were being Agile before it was sanctioned by the enterprise. The feelings could be likened to underground freedom fighters that, once the tide has turned, can now fight openly for their cause. And, as in

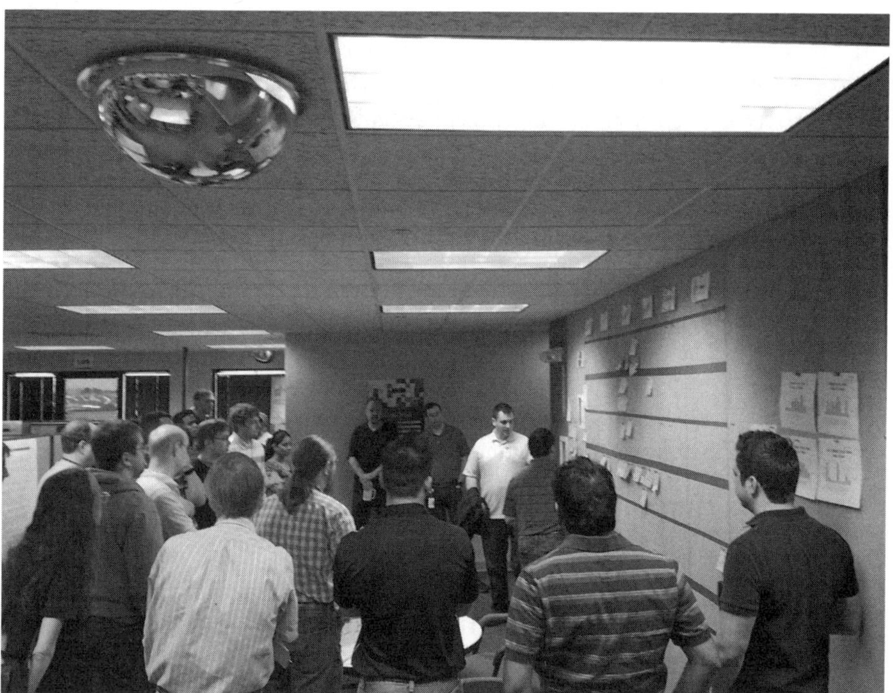

Figure A.2 *John Deere team during a daily stand-up meeting*

any revolution, there were some that resisted change and hung onto the old ways.

Easier: Management support for the adoption of XP practices such as pair programming.

Harder: Priority alignment across trains; what is #1 for solutions is #4 for displays, and the feature needs work done in both areas to provide value to the user. We knew it was going to be hard, but it has been harder even than we had imagined.

Interviewer: How have you had to adapt your management style for Agile?

Roling: Agile allowed me to empower my team, which has improved employee engagement.

Interviewer: Are you deploying code faster? more accurately? How do you measure the success of your implementation?

Thelen: We have been able to demonstrate step function improvements in quality, innovation, speed to market, and employee engagement. In some of these areas, we have demonstrated far beyond our expectations. With these successes, we have also been provided more opportunities that we are able to address in a timely manner, which has led to a need to better manage expectations of the enterprise as well as closely monitor our own internal commitments in portfolio management.

Roling: We are deploying code much faster and with higher quality. I measure success by how quickly we can release features to customers. We have a ways to go on releasing faster. Our next challenge is to get the rest of our organization to deliver at the same speed. For example, our marketing department continues bundling our features together and releasing them in large groups to minimize training overhead. We need to find a way to get our features out as they are developed instead of putting them on the shelf until we have a large bundle ready to go.

Interviewer: How do you collect user stories? What tools do you use?

Harris: There are a variety of methods to gather stories, depending on the size and scope. We have a formal process for gathering customer needs that marketing owns; Out of that, broad strategies are generated. Out of that come epics, features, and stories. These are created in a series of workshops with many stakeholders to refine the broad strategies. I participate in some workshops but once it gets to the feature level, I truly own it and work with the development team, user experience, and architecture to further break down and refine it into user stories (see Figure A.3).

Interviewer: What was the hardest part of the transition as a product owner?

Harris: Balancing between the voice of the customer and the realistic development challenges; having all the responsibility for how the features should be but none of the authority to make decisions to get things done (for example, getting people's time from other trains).

Interviewer: How are you measured as a product owner?

Harris: That's a very good question. I don't have a good answer. Different POs have different skill sets, so expectations are different for each. I am a senior software developer and have broad experience with our products and system, as well as relevant domain knowledge, so I operate on a level above a typical product owner with a single Scrum team, more of a systems engineer. We referred to it as "uber product owner." I still have

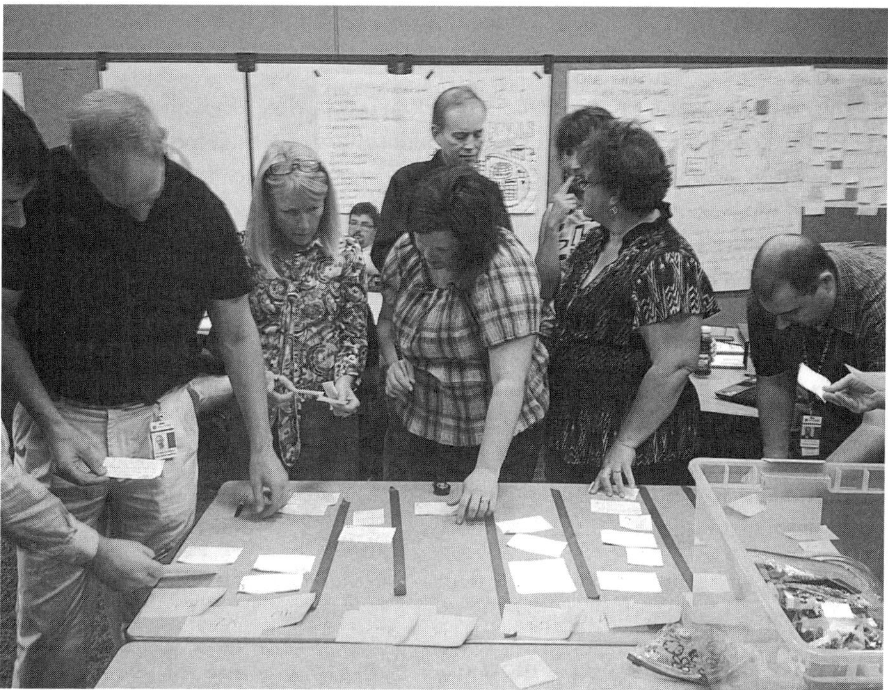

Figure A.3 *John Deere team participates in a card-sorting activity*

my primary Scrum team to provide detailed story direction, but I had a cluster of sister teams to coordinate interactions between components of the system.

Interviewer: Has your "go to market" strategy changed at all due to Agile? Are you communicating with the marketplace differently?

Thelen: We are adapting over time to new and more innovative ways to move value to the market—including in some cases daily and weekly delivery of value. As our capabilities evolve, there will be continued need to adapt and adjust the "go to market" strategy accordingly.

Interviewer: Has the move to Agile increased customer satisfaction with your products?

Thelen: Customer satisfaction has been primarily impacted through higher quality, faster speed to response on field issues, and in some cases more finely tuned features that meet customer needs by engaging customers earlier in the design process.

Roling: Our customers have noticed that we respond to defects faster, but we haven't released new features at a high frequency yet.

Harris: The product that my team developed was well received in the marketplace, and the actual rollout to production was a huge nonevent because we did incremental development and were able to act upon customer feedback prior to release. In the past, that feedback would've had to be scheduled and approved by higher levels of management, so it essentially never happened.

Interviewer: How much interaction do you have with customers?

Harris: I function more as a proxy product owner. The marketing product manager has frequent interaction with real customers. I make customer visits once or twice a year. However, since our domain is agriculture and I live in Iowa and come from a farming family, my informal interactions with customers are quite frequent.

Interviewer: What is the biggest benefit you have seen from using the Agile development methodology?

Harris: The ability to react more quickly to change. It is a lot easier to kill off bad ideas and mistaken assumptions.

Discussion Points

- Was there anything that surprised you about John Deere's transition to Agile software development?
- What role did executive sponsorship play in their transition?
- What impact did Agile methods have on their culture?
- How did Agile change their product outcomes?
- Is their definition of a product owner the same or different from what you have seen or experienced in other Agile organizations? How so?

Glossary

A/B testing A common practice to compare two ideas for effectiveness. Web sites, for example, might have two home pages that are presented to visitors on a random or targeted basis, and the actions taken from the two pages are measured to determine which one drives the desired behavior.

Acceptance criteria An indication of what is needed for a user story to be considered complete.

Acceptance tests Acceptance tests are performed to ensure that the product functions meet the agreed-upon requirements. They can be performed by the test team when acting as a mock customer, or by a customer before formally accepting a contracted product.

Accountability Accepting the consequences of your actions, whether good or bad.

Adaptive software development (ASD) An Agile methodology that focuses on speculation, collaboration, learning, and adapting the process to the work at hand.

Agile An umbrella term for a group of methodologies that follow the values and principles captured in the Agile Manifesto. Scrum is an example of an Agile methodology.

Agile Manifesto A philosophical foundation for effective software development, the Agile Manifesto was created by representatives from several Agile methodologies. It reads as follows:

We are uncovering better ways of developing software by doing it and helping others do it. Through this work we have come to value:

Individuals and interactions over processes and tools

Working software over comprehensive documentation

Customer collaboration over contract negotiation

Responding to change over following a plan

Alpha tests Tests that allow customers to try early versions of the code to provide feedback to the product team.

Automated testing Testing that uses software that is independent of the software being testing to execute tests without human intervention and compare the results against the desired outcome.

Backlog See Product backlog or Sprint backlog

Behavior-driven testing A tool that tests the behavior of a product. The test code is written in "business readable language," meaning the test language can be read and understood by team members who are not familiar with programming languages.

Beta tests The soft launch of a new product or features to a select group of people to gather feedback.

Beta users The customers who participate in a beta test or soft launch. In return for their candid feedback, they usually receive the product at a discount, or even for free.

Big bang This refers to a large program, project, or campaign that is unveiled when it is completed. Agile does not advocate a big-bang approach because we want to deliver frequently and collect feedback at regular intervals.

Big boss A role in XP assigned to the person who holds the team accountable and ensures that they do what they say they are going to do.

Bottleneck A point in the workflow where tasks queue up because there are not adequate resources to handle the workload. This is a form of waste that Lean principles address.

Brand management The conscious caring for the desired feelings and expectations that customers and prospects associate with a product.

Bugs See Defects

Build status When developers add new code to an existing code base, they complete a "build," and the build status shows if the added code broke any of the existing functionality.

Burn-down chart A chart showing how much work is remaining in the sprint.

Burn-up chart A graphical representation that shows work completed, such as the number of story points, for the project or release.

Business analyst (BA) A role, often in IT, of someone who clarifies requirements and assists with testing. A BA is usually not a developer but can be very useful on a team.

Business value This is a qualitative measure of the value that a particular effort will bring to the business; it could be increased revenue, decreased costs, improved customer experience, efficiency improvement, and much more. Business value is used to determine priority.

Cadence Represents the flow or rhythm of events and the pattern in which something is experienced.

Campaigns Typically refers to marketing efforts designed to attract a target market and drive them toward a purchase.

Change control A term often associated with Waterfall, this is the activity taken to modify the scope, date, or resources of a project; this process is put in place to ensure that changes are known, considered, and documented. Agile incorporates responses to change in the methodologies without a rigid process.

Chickens and pigs Refers to a cartoon about commitment: Chickens are involved in Agile efforts, but pigs are committed. For example, a stakeholder is a chicken; a developer is a pig.

Child story A smaller, more detailed user story that is created by breaking down an epic (parent story).

Classes A breakdown of architecture, systems, or sections of code within FDD, so specific developers work on specific classes of software, as opposed to the collective ownership of code used by XP and Scrum.

Coach An Agile coach guides an organization or team through an Agile transformation. In XP, a coach is someone who mentors and guides the team.

Code kata Programming exercises that help you practice your art through exercises and repetition. The word "kata" comes from the Japanese term for practicing detailed patterns of movement.

Collaboration The action of soliciting input and incorporating the ideas and opinions of others into the planned activity.

Continuous flow This is the way that Kanban projects progress, because an unpredictable stream of work comes into the team. With Scrum, in contrast, where the work progresses in a time-boxed fashion, there is a distinct start and end to a sprint.

Continuous improvement The activities in Agile that lead to getting smarter, more disciplined, and constantly learning, even through mistakes.

Continuous integration A software engineering practice in which isolated changes are immediately tested and reported on when they are added to a larger code base. The goal is to provide rapid feedback, so that if a defect is introduced into the code base, it can be identified and corrected as soon as possible. The usual rule is for each team member to submit work on a daily (or more frequent) basis and for a build to be conducted with each significant change.

Coupling The extent to which a program module depends on other modules within the program.

Course-correct Making modifications in your work, practices, or behavior based on new information.

Crowd sourcing The activity of gathering feedback from a broad group of people, typically through the use of social media, to gain more diverse input than typically comes from traditional customers or users.

Crystal A family of Agile methodologies (Crystal Clear, Crystal Yellow, Crystal Orange, etc.) whose unique characteristics are driven by several factors such as team size, system criticality, and project priorities. It addresses the realization that each project may require a slightly tailored set of policies, practices, and processes in order to meet its unique characteristics.

Culture The behaviors and practices that exist within an organization as the way to get things done; often these are unspoken norms that drive actions. Changing a culture is one of the challenges of an Agile implementation.

Customer council A reoccurring collaboration meeting where the development team meets with the customers to review ideas or working code.

Cycle time The time required to complete a cycle of an operation. It represents the point at which a request was initiated to the time in which it has been completed (delivered into production).

Daily scrum A short meeting (approximately 15 minutes) to share progress, report impediments, and make commitments.

DEEP An acronym coined by Mike Cohn describing a good product backlog: It is Detailed appropriately, Estimated, Emergent, and Prioritized.

Defect An item not functioning as stated in acceptance criteria or a test plan. "Defect" and "bug" are often used interchangeably.

Defect backlog The total number of defects that have yet to be fixed for a product.

Definition of "done" This is an Agile concept where the team agrees on what is considered "complete" before starting the work. Each team might have a slightly different definition of "done," which might include, for example, peer review or documentation. Every Agile team should include designing, coding, and testing in their definition of done.

Delight A desired state, from the Kano model, where customers are delighted with unique, value-added, and unexpected features in a product.

Demo See Sprint demo

Discovery An activity to solicit input from people about desired functionality or process improvements. Discovery could take the form of interviews or focus groups, for example.

Driver The team member who is writing the code during a paired programming session.

Dynamic System Development Method (DSDM) An Agile methodology based on the nine key principles that primarily revolve around business needs/value, active user involvement, empowered teams, frequent delivery, integrated testing, and stakeholder collaboration. Fitness for business purpose is the primary criterion for delivery and acceptance of a system, focusing on the useful 80% of the system that can be deployed in 20% of the time.

Epic A large user story that will take weeks or months to implement. An epic may also be referred to as a "parent story."

Estimation The process of agreeing on a size for the stories in a product backlog. This is done by the team, often by using planning poker. Also referred to as "sizing."

Extreme Programming (XP) An Agile methodology that promotes high customer involvement, rapid feedback loops, continuous testing, and close teamwork to deliver working software at very frequent intervals. Based on four simple values—simplicity, communication, feedback, courage—and 12 supporting practices.

Face-to-face communication One of the core tenets of Agile, advocating that people speak directly to one another so nonverbal cues can be received—such as body language and tone of voice—which might be lost or misinterpreted in an e-mail, for example.

Feature Describes capabilities identified by the stakeholder that provide some value for that person, typically accomplished in one or more stories.

Feature-Driven Development (FDD) An Agile methodology that is a model-driven, short-iteration process. It begins with establishing an overall model shape. Then it continues with a series of two-week "design by feature, build by feature" iterations. These features are small but useful in the eyes of the client. The rest of the development process is designed around feature delivery using eight practices.

Feedback Input from stakeholders and users about a system, workflow, idea, etc. Feedback is often opinions, not necessarily supported by data, but important nonetheless.

Fibonacci sequence A nonlinear number series (1, 2, 3, 5, 8, 13, 21, 34, 55, etc.) where the next number is derived by adding the previous two. This is used by development teams when sizing user stories, though most teams use a modified sequence.

Fist of five A process for determining agreement. When decisions need to be made, all team members hold up one to five fingers to show level of agreement. If anyone is below a three, the decision is discussed further until the entire team agrees with a three or above.

Focus group A targeted group of users or prospects that are asked questions and given information about future product features as a means of gathering qualitative feedback.

Framework for Integrated Test (FIT) Syntax for behavior-driven testing created by Ward Cunningham.

Frequent delivery One of the primary objectives of Agile is the frequent delivery of working software so that the team can collect feedback and adjust if necessary.

Gantt charts A method of measuring project progress as a percentage of completion. Agile adapts to changing requirements, so Gantt charts are seldom used because they are more relevant when the scope is fixed.

Gherkin A language used to write behavior-driven acceptance tests.

Grooming See Product backlog grooming

Human–computer interaction (HCI) The science of how people and systems can most optimally interact.

Ideal time (hours, days) The amount of time a task would take under ideal circumstances with no interruptions, phone calls, meetings, etc.

Impediment Anything that prevents the team from meeting their potential. The Scrum master is responsible for removing impediments, or escalating an impediment if necessary.

Implementation size story A user story that can be completed within the duration of a sprint or iteration. This is sometimes referred to a "child story" and is often created by breaking down an epic into smaller pieces.

Information radiators Data or graphs posted in the team members' physical space that are seen on a regular basis.

Integration build A build that pulls together code from various parts of the product to create the integrated product.

INVEST A model for writing good user stories based on the idea that they are Independent, Negotiable, Valuable, Estimatable, Small, and Testable.

Iteration A period of time, usually one to four weeks, in which the development team codes and tests one or more small features, resulting in potentially releasable software. "Iteration" and "sprint" are often used interchangeably.

Kanban A tool derived from Lean manufacturing and associated with the branch of Agile practices loosely referred to as Lean software development. Like a task board, Kanban visually represents the state of the work in progress; but unlike a task board, it constrains how much work in progress is permitted to occur at the same time (see Work in progress limits). The purpose of limiting the work in progress is to reduce bottlenecks and increase throughput by optimizing the segment of the value stream that is the subject of the Kanban. A principal difference between Kanban and Scrum is that Scrum limits the work in progress through time boxing (e.g., the sprint) and Kanban limits work in progress by limiting how much work may occur at one time (e.g., X number of tasks or stories).

Kano model A categorization method for customer needs starting with basic needs, moving to performance needs, and finally delighting the customer with unique, value-added, and unexpected functionality.

Kata See Code kata

Lean A term coined in manufacturing processes and applied to software development and IT operations. The main principle of Lean is eliminating waste. See Waste for more.

Lean software development An Agile methodology that owes many of its principles and practices to the Lean enterprise movement. Lean software development focuses the team on delivering value to the customer and on the efficiency of the "value stream," the mechanisms that deliver that value.

Level of effort (LOE) Specifies the expected amount of activity required to accomplish the task; sometimes used in early stages of estimation.

Manual testing Testing that requires a human tester, who must progress through each step or look over the product to make sure nothing about the code or design is defective.

Metrics Quantitative measures to determine success.

Microtests Individual unit tests that run while the code is being developed. They test an individual behavior in a single object.

MoSCoW An acronym used in DSDM to represent how features or actions should be prioritized: Must have, Should have, Could have, and Want to have.

Multivariant testing The same concept as A/B testing, but with more than two variables.

Mura, muri, muda See Waste

MVP (minimum viable product) A term used in Lean software development: the minimum features needed to address a problem in the marketplace.

Nonverbal Unspoken communication, such as body language, eye contact, fidgeting, and other cues to how a person is feeling, which might contradict what he or she is saying.

Observer The team member who is watching and offering suggestions to the driver during a paired programming session.

On-target testing When the development team is building code to run on a specific device, hardware, or an embedded component of some larger system, it is necessary that the project have tests that run on the actual target hardware.

Pair programming An Extreme Programming approach where two programmers sit side by side, using a shared workstation, to develop code. The pair consists of a driver and an observer.

Parent story The original "epic" size user story that has been broken down into one or more child stories.

Parking lots A tracking mechanism used in FDD for large projects. It is a visual representation of a broad scope so stakeholders can easily assess progress and areas of concern.

Persona A fictional user or customer of the system, used to help guide the prioritization, user experience, and features.

Pigs and chickens See Chickens and pigs

Pilot Another term for "soft launch" or "beta test."

Planning poker A game used during the estimation phase, where the team has playing cards with story points on them. After learning of a new user story and asking all necessary questions, the team members "throw" the cards that represent their viewpoints of the story size. Any discrepancies are discussed to ensure that everyone has a common understanding.

Portfolio management A portfolio is usually a collection of related projects whose management is complex because of multiple teams and interdependencies.

Pragmatic Marketing An organization (http://www.pragmaticmarketing.com) that provides best practices and certifications to product managers.

Priorities Priorities dictate the relative order of importance of actions. In Agile, priorities are set according to the business value anticipated by the organization.

Product backlog A prioritized list of user stories that the product owner would like completed.

Product backlog grooming A collaborative process to prepare the product backlog for sprint planning; this may include breaking down stories into smaller stories, writing new stories, improving poorly written stories, estimating stories, adding acceptance criteria, or doing longer range technical planning.

Product owner The person who holds the vision for the product and is responsible for maintaining, prioritizing, and updating the product backlog.

Project champion Term often used in DSDM for the project sponsor.

Project management office (PMO) This is the organization where project managers typically report. Many organizations have disbanded their PMO as the teams gain authority and responsibility.

Project sponsor The position in the organization with the authority and budget to allocate financial and human resources to a project. The project sponsor is typically the key executive stakeholder for an Agile effort.

Protoype A rudimentary working model of software or a product that can be demonstrated and used for gathering input.

Public commitment A planned goal or promise made to other individuals, which typically leads to a higher degree of success.

Quality assurance (QA) Testing activity that takes place within a sprint or iteration. The tester typically develops test plans, which are influenced by the acceptance criteria. These test plans are executed against the code, and defects are reported to the developer.

Rational unified process (RUP) An Agile methodology that provides an adaptive framework for individual projects.

Refactoring Constantly improving a product's internal design (i.e., rewriting code) without changing its behavior to make the product more reliable and adaptable.

Regression tests Testing to see if new code has broken code that already exists in the product.

Relative sizing An estimation technique where a previous effort is used as the baseline and new efforts are compared to it.

Release The transition of an increment of a potentially shippable product from the development team into routine use by customers. Releases typically happen when one or more sprints have resulted in enough product value to outweigh the cost to deploy it.

Release management or release planning The activity of organized release scope and dates to meet the needs of the business and the marketplace.

Retrospective meeting A session where the team and the Scrum master reflect on the process and make commitments to improve.

Rework The action of redoing something after it has been completed due to new information or lessons learned. In the Waterfall methodology, rework had a negative connotation because it indicated error; in Agile, rework is a natural consequence of continuous improvement.

Roadmaps A tool product owners and product management use to share the release plan to customers and stakeholders.

Scalable Agile Framework (SAFe) An Agile software development methodology created by Dean Leffingwell that helps teams scale Agile and Lean techniques to enterprise scale.

Scope The breadth of requirements to be considered in a project. As the project scope grows, the time it will take to deliver may be extended, or additional resources may need to be added.

Scrum An Agile methodology that provides a framework for the iterative development of complex products, particularly software. Scrum is composed of a series of short iterations, called "sprints," each of which ends with the delivery of an increment of working software.

Scrum master A servant leader to the team, who is responsible for removing impediments and making sure the process runs smoothly so the team can be as productive as possible.

Scrum team A cross-functional group that is responsible for delivering the software or product. The Scrum team is encouraged to be self-organizing and to take collective responsibility for all work commitments and outcomes. Scrum teams respond to requirements (often presented as user stories) by collectively defining the tasks, task assignments, and the level of effort estimates.

Self-managing team See Self-organizing team

Self-organizing team A team that is provided a goal and allowed to work together to determine the best way to reach that goal instead of being told how to reach it.

ShuHaRi An Aikido term meaning "to learn a skill or technique." First you are in the "Shu" phase, when you must mimic your teacher precisely to master the basics. Next is "Ha," where you start to learn from other teachers that help you build on your skills, and you begin to gain knowledge about the history and theoretical basis for the technique. Finally, you reach the "Ri" phase, where you become the teacher and make new contributions to the technique.

Silos Organizational boundaries that inhibit collaboration.

Simplicity Striving to find the least complex or the minimalistic solution to the problem or opportunity.

Sizing An estimating technique that defines the relative measure of the effort involved with delivering a particular story. Also referred to as "estimating."

SME See Subject matter expert

Soft launch Presentation of a product or feature to a small group of customers to gather initial feedback and impressions.

Software development (engineering) Systematic, disciplined, and quantifiable approaches to the development, operation, and maintenance of software, and the study of these approaches; that is, the application of engineering to software.

Spike A story or task aimed at answering a question or gathering information, rather than at producing shippable product.

Sprint An iteration of work during which an increment of product functionality is implemented.

Sprint backlog A list of the tasks necessary to complete the sprint. Tasks are defined by the team.

Sprint demo or sprint review At the end of an iteration, the team will demonstrate the working software that they just developed. This is an informal meeting, open to everyone, including external stakeholders. The team receives feedback, which is used to influence future sprints.

Sprint goal Also known as "sprint theme"; the focus of the work for a single sprint.

Sprint planning meeting A meeting between the team and the product owner to plan the sprint and agree on the commitment.

Sprint retro See Retrospective meeting

Stakeholders These are people who are either directly or indirectly affected by the project. Internal stakeholders are inside the company and could range from users of the system to the CEO, depending on the size and scope of the project. External stakeholders are outside the company, and could range from users of the system to shareholders of stock in the company.

Stakeholder feedback sessions See Sprint demo

Stoplight charts A visual representation of project health; green indicates smooth progress, yellow indicates that risk factors need to be tracked, and red means the project is in trouble and needs intervention.

Story See User story

Story points The Scrum unit of measurement for estimating complexity of user stories; an arbitrary measure Scrum teams use to measure the effort required to implement a story. The number tells the team how hard the story is; "hard" could be related to complexity, unknowns, and/or effort. The Fibonacci sequence is often used to "point" stories.

Subject matter expert (SME) A person with deep knowledge of a system or process; SMEs are often key contributors to projects.

Survey A tool used to validate an assumption or hypothesis by querying many people to solicit opinions and impressions. The data is accumulated in the hopes of finding statistically valid trends.

Sustainable development One of the Agile principles, sustainable development means that you are not overworking the team, so they can maintain their pace over an extended period of time.

System tests Testing all components of the product together on all supported platforms, emulating the customer experience.

Task User stories are broken down into tasks during the Sprint planning session, and the team selects the ones that they are going to "own."

Task board A visual display of how work is progressing. Typically shown in grid form, where the columns represent the work stages (i.e., Design, Development, Testing), and items are moved across the board as the effort progresses. Task boards are commonly used with Scrum and are essential in Kanban.

Teamwork The ability of a group of people to act as a cohesive unit.

Technical debt Includes those internal things that the team chooses not to do now, but which will impede future development if left undone. There are two kinds of technical debt: Unintended technical debt is simply the consequences of the team's learning curve; intentional technical debt is incurred as trade-offs are made in the development process, such as choosing to write something quickly but suboptimally so the team can learn as they go. Technical debt also includes deferred refactoring.

Technical excellence One of the principles of Agile is to strive for technical excellence, which includes well thought-out architecture and design decisions as well as quality and discipline in your practices and preparation.

Test cases Repeatable scenarios to test existing and new functionality to ensure that the code works as designed and does not cause problems with any existing functionality.

Test-driven development (TDD) An Extreme Programming approach that requires developers to first write automated test cases, then write only the code necessary to make the test cases pass with no issues.

Time-boxed A term commonly used with Scrum or other methodologies where the work progresses over a predetermined time period, such as a two-week sprint. This contrasts with Kanban, which is referred to as "continuous flow," since there is no start or end date to a Kanban project.

Tracker Within XP, the tracker is the role that ensures that the project stays on track, often checking in with the development team daily.

Transparency Openly sharing the details of an effort, including progress, roadblocks, concerns, risks, and successes.

Transparent development Product code is made available to customers on a server at all stages of development so they can provide feedback anytime they wish.

Triple constraint A term commonly used in project management to refer to the interdependencies between scope, time, and resources. If you lose resources on a project, for example, you need to either reduce the scope or extend the time.

Trust This is the belief that your teammates will take the best course of action when faced with a decision, even if you are not there to participate.

UED User experience designer—See UX/UI designers.

Usability The ease with which an application can be used.

Use cases A process flow or action that will be taken by a user of the system. Use cases are part of the requirements in RUP.

User acceptance testing (UAT) The process of verifying that a solution works for the user; it is not system testing and is not performed by the development or Scrum team. Some teams include UAT in their definition of done. This is also referred to as "business testing."

User story A requirement, feature, and/or unit of business value that can be estimated and tested. Stories are the basic unit of communication, planning, and negotiation between the Scrum team, business owners, and the product owner. Stories consist of the following elements:

A description, usually in business terms

A size, for rough estimation purposes, generally expressed in story points, such as 1, 2, 3, 5, 8, and 13

An acceptance test, giving a short description of how the story will be validated

UX/UI designers User experience designers (or user interface designers), the people with background and education in the area of usability or the user experience.

Validation An activity where qualitative feedback, typically gathered in discovery, is quantified with activities such as surveys.

Value stream mapping An exercise where the process flow is mapped entirely from the customer's perspective to identify where value is added and removed.

Velocity The rate at which a team completes work, often measured in story points.

Vision A conceptual idea of how things should be at some point in the future.

Waste Eliminating waste is the top priority of Lean. The manufacturing (and Japanese) origins refer to three kinds of waste:

Muda—an activity in the process that adds no value

Mura—waste generated by unevenness in operations

Muri—overburdening the people or equipment in this system with more work than they can reasonably manage

Waterfall In Waterfall methodology, software development is done in a linear or sequential fashion: A task cannot begin until the one before it is completed.

Wide-band Delphi A form of estimation where participants anonymously write their size estimates on cards, and the moderator shares the estimates with the group; differences are discussed and the process is then repeated. It is a more formal and structured way to perform estimation.

Wireframes A visual depiction of a process flow that helps users can get a feel for workflow and usability before code is written. Sometimes referred to as "blueprints" or "skeletons."

Work in progress (WIP) limits A characteristic of Kanban to assign explicit limits to how many items may be in process at each workflow state. This helps to identify bottlenecks and streamline the process.

Working agreement A set of rules that every person on the team agrees to follow. This is created and maintained by the team and can be brought up for discussion in the retrospective meeting.

Working software The goal in Agile is to deliver working software on a frequent basis. Working software has been designed, developed, and tested and is ready to go into production.

XP (Extreme Programming) An Agile methodology that promotes high customer involvement, rapid feedback loops, continuous testing, and close teamwork to deliver working software at very frequent intervals. Based on four simple values—simplicity, communication, feedback, courage—and 12 supporting practices.

XP planning game A form of backlog grooming used in Extreme Programming where the team considers priorities, levels of effort, and complexity to plan the work. The activity consists of the exploration, commitment, and steering phases.

Yesterday's weather A term used for a calculation of team velocity, considering only the most recent sprints and using the assumption that as a team's performance improves, only the most recent data is relevant for estimating future velocity.

Index

Note: Page numbers followed by *f* indicate figures; those followed by *n* indicate notes.

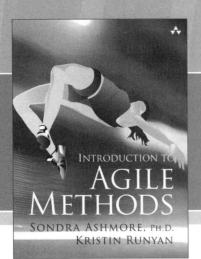